D1736420

TELEDEMOCRACY

RECENT VOLUMES IN . . .
SAGE LIBRARY OF SOCIAL RESEARCH

TELEDEMOCRACY
Can Technology Protect Democracy?

F. Christopher Arterton

Volume 165
SAGE LIBRARY OF
SOCIAL RESEARCH

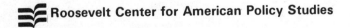 Roosevelt Center for American Policy Studies

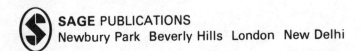 **SAGE** PUBLICATIONS
Newbury Park Beverly Hills London New Delhi

For information address:

SAGE Publications, Inc.
2111 West Hillcrest Drive
Newbury Park, California 91320

SAGE Publications Inc.  SAGE Publications Ltd.
275 South Beverly Drive   28 Banner Street
Beverly Hills   London EC1Y 8QE
California 90212   England

SAGE PUBLICATIONS India Pvt. Ltd.
M-32 Market
Greater Kailash I
New Delhi 110 048 India

Printed in the United States of America

Library of Congress Cataloging-in-Publication Data

Arterton, F. Christopher.

    Teledemocracy: can technology protect democracy?
    (Sage library of social research; v. 165)
    Includes index.
    1. Political participation—United States. 2. Communication in politics—United States. 3. Democracy. I. Title.
II. Series.
JK1764.A773   1986   323′.042′0973   86-17447
ISBN 0-8039-2872-6
ISBN 0-8039-2873-4 (pbk.)

The Roosevelt Center is a nonprofit, nonpartisan, public policy institute with offices in Washington, D.C., and Chicago, Illinois. Its goals are to clarify the policy choices before the nation and to encourage and facilitate the participation of citizens in the decisionmaking process at all levels of government. The Center's program develops a comprehensive range of reasoned options and strategies concerning critical policy issues facing the United States.

In all cases, the Center maintains a strictly nonpartisan and non-advocacy posture with respect to policy choices. This decision to forgo the more traditional institutional approach of advocating particular policy alternatives was carefully made. It stems from a bedrock belief that the genius of American society springs from a free market in ideas, and that policy decisionmaking should be no exception.

Founded in 1982, the Roosevelt Center takes its name and inspiration from three Roosevelts—Theodore, Eleanor, and Franklin—who courageously addressed our nation's future and brought clarity to America's vision of itself.

TO

ITHIEL de SOLA POOL

AND

ROBERT ALAN DAHL

CONTENTS

ACKNOWLEDGMENTS

In writing this book, I have incurred intellectual debts too numerous and too substantial to be repaid. My greatest appreciation goes to many who will, of necessity, remain nameless; literally hundreds of project organizers gave freely of their time, shared their recollections and opinions with us, and opened their files and libraries to our prying. To all our meddlesome investigations these public spirited individuals gave their complete and candid cooperation.

The research and writing that made this book possible grew as a team effort. The research staff, based at the Roosevelt Center in Washington, participated as coequals in investigating and reporting upon twenty projects in which technology had been employed to stimulate citizen participation. John Griffen wrote the original versions of the five field reports; I have borrowed liberally from his work. Edward Lazarus developed the institutional dimensions of participation that became so central to our evaluations of the projects investigated. Monica Andres completed the report on Alternatives for Washington found in Chapter 6. Even more valuable was her remarkable ability to ferret out and secure books and articles on technology and politics and the most bewildering collection of unpublished reports, studies, and documents. The efforts of these three friends and coworkers made this research possible; in relying upon their work, I hope that I have not distorted their thoughts and contributions.

Many other individuals at the Roosevelt Center contributed to this book. Originally, this research was conceived under the direction of Doug Bennet and Bobbie Kilberg. They had the foresight to believe that some intellectual progress could be made on the question of changing communication technologies and democracy. Roger Molander and Michael Higgins, who became the Center's president and executive vice president while this research was in progress, tolerated with an uncommon degree of good humor long delays in completing this manuscript and the research report that undergirds it. They remained strongly supportive throughout the project. Mark Rovner, who came to the Center to conduct its public engagement efforts, provided many helpful suggestions for this book and much good criticism. The most advantageous advice, however, came from Wendy Russell, who taught me what a neophyte I was in book publishing and in promotion. Finally, my gratitude and respect goes to Sue Leander, who cheerfully put up with not only innumerable substantive revisions, but one comma change after another after another, stretching into literally scores of versions of each chapter. Together we raised the profit margin of Kimberly-Clarke by at least a percentage point.

This research was supported by the John and Mary Markle Foundation. For Deborah Wadsworth, serving as a program manager meant much more than just providing the money and checking periodically on progress: She opened her files, she provided me with her contacts, and she involved me generally in all she knew was currently happening in this field.

I owe a large debt of tutelage to an advisory committee of academics and practitioners. Bob Dahl, Gene Eidenberg, Russ Neuman, Rick Neustadt, Ithiel Pool, and Bob Teeter sat through long meetings, plowed through awkward drafts, and willingly provided collective and individual guidance. I strongly hope this book does justice to their efforts, their prodding, and their confidence.

CHAPTER 1

THE DEBATE OVER
TECHNOLOGY AND DEMOCRACY

Two hundred years after the signing of the Constitution, American democracy is beset with problems that threaten its vitality. Among American citizens, voting rates have recently declined, while cynical attitudes expressed about political institutions and leadership have increased. Election politics have become media campaigns, dominated by personality, image, deception, and superficiality, rather than by considered public discussion of the policy issues facing the nation. A rapidly increasing torrent of campaign money pours out of the coffers of political action committees, advancing their narrow agendas and distorting the processes of representation and accountability to the public. Legislatures are surrounded and besieged by clusterings of special interest lobbyists and pleaders, dampening by their cacophony the ability of representatives to hear the voices of the people. And growing bureaucracies at all levels of government isolate elected leaders from the citizens they are supposed to serve.

At the same time, the United States is undergoing a rapid and sustained transformation in communication technologies. Developments in satellites, computers, cable television, videotex, cellular radio, videoconferencing, computer networking, and a host of other technologies raise many intriguing possibilities for new life-styles and economic benefits. For some contemporary observers, the arrival of all this new technology is a cause for concern as to its possible effects on our social and political institutions; others greet high technology with considerable enthusiasm, seeing in it potential cures to grave problems that now afflict our political processes.

The dominant stream of thought on this problem among scholars and practitioners of American politics is one of worry, worry that the social change spurred on by these "hi-tech" developments will create a whole cast of new problems for our political and governmental institutions. One need entertain only briefly the massive changes allegedly wrought by television in order to grasp the potential in yet another set of "unforeseen consequences" spilling out from communications media into politics.

Many forecasters and futurists, on the other hand, argue that the promise of democracy can be fulfilled through the political use of the new media. They foresee a day when technology will permit all citizens to become directly involved in public policy-making. They bandy about the term *teledemocracy* as a catchword for the establishment of direct democracy through the use of communications media. As they envision the democratic politics in our future, they believe the American people will consider the problems facing the nation and, from their living rooms, register their opinions as to how these matters should be resolved. Representative institutions will disappear; citizens will truly govern themselves.

Writings under the rubric of teledemocracy run a gamut from fanciful efforts to describe how such a system would work, to expansive predictions that such an evolution is inevitable, to experimentation with how adequately communications technology serves to give the people control over policy. Here I hope to give new meaning to the term: I use *teledemocracy* to refer, not to a politics that would undercut our established representative machinery, but to the use of communications technology to facilitate the transmission of political information and opinion between citizens and their public leaders.

The issue at stake is not merely a definitional question. While we fight about meaning, the new media will be changing the behavior of those active in politics. Through this door, technology is shaping our political institutions; it's a door we cannot close. The question is not *whether* the new media will influence our politics, but *how*. While we may not be able to predict, much less control, the development of new media, we can make choices about how they should be used politically. Before the potentials for change become fully manifest, we must consider what political institutions should be put in place in order to make use of these new ways of communicating.

If we cannot accurately predict the media's evolution, however, how can we conceive of addressing its effects? Despite the difficulties, the question's importance demands that we try. As a nation of democrats, we need to move onto center stage the discussion of the politics we want to emerge from the communications revolution. The question, as we shall see, is primarily one of collective values and ideals. We should initiate the discussion of technology and democractic values by examining the concrete results of trial-and-error experimentation that has already taken place. In fact, one can identify an impressive number of instances in which electronic media have been used to stimulate citizen participation. These I refer to as "teledemocracy projects." In the process of discussing their virtues and limitations, we will be able to consider the role of citizens in a democracy, a topic that may not embrace the entirety of democratic principles, but certainly does involve a core value. Citizen participation facilitated by technology is the central thread of the teledemocracy argument.

Political Change in a Technological Environment

The research conducted for this book was grounded in the assumption that the structure of communications available to a society will markedly influence the workings of its political institutions. The assertion is controversial. By no means should the reader accept this relationship casually, either when it is advanced as a general statement or when someone proposes a specific analysis such as, for example, the claim that television has contributed to the decline of political parties. Those scholars who have looked hard at this relationship disagree as to whether the media affect our politics or reflect them. Nevertheless, I will argue here that the communication structure is a major, but not a determinative, element shaping the conduct of politics.

Politics is a form of communication. Those who seek political power do so by organizing the behavior of others; organization implies communication. Leaders wish to convey their policies and their visions to citizens; active members of the public seek ways of expressing their support and their needs to those in authority. Many of the tasks usually accomplished by political institutions require communication between individuals and among groups: appeals for support, negotiations over competing objectives, articulation of policy alternatives, raising political money, building coalitions, registering demands or needs, and even issuing threats. Thus the capacities for communication are embedded in political processes. For example, whether or not national political leaders are able to transmit their messages directly to all citizens will shape the political apparatus needed to govern. Since the structure of telecommunications available to a society will determine the capacities of the politically active to communicate, moreover, those who are successful politically will, in the long run, shape politics, political institutions, and the superstructure of communications to their liking.

In every society, political messages can be exchanged in many ways. Custom and convenience will heavily influence which of those means are used for different kinds of messages. In admitting this possibility, I abandon the simple assertion that the causal connection between communication and political activity works only in one direction. Technology does not determine politics. Political values and social behavior certainly influence the structure of political communication. Yet in writing this book, I have paid more attention to the effects of communications on our politics simply because, in the last three decades, our means of communication have been evolving rapidly, driven by technological change.

If we had thought about it four decades ago, we might well have been optimistic about the potential improvements in politics that could be achieved by television. Citizens were mainly ignorant of the specific policies advanced by the two parties. In many cases, voters even pulled the lever for candidates *en masse* without recognizing their names. Party labels substituted for real political awareness. These, in turn, were tied to ethnic and group identifications that determined political loyalties. Rational and informative debate was sharply limited by the number of citizens and the inadequacies of communication to such a vast and differentiated electorate.

By contrast, the prospects for more direct communication between leaders and the led must have seemed attractive, especially viewed against the backdrop of a political system dominated by party bosses. Television promised a revolution of information for citizens; a freer, vital, robust political discourse. The idea of televised debates among candidates must, alone, have held forth great promise for educating voters as to the choices they faced. Further, communications would bring more understanding across social groups, lessening political tensions and cleavages.

Needless to say, television has not fulfilled this great promise. Instead of informed debate, we got campaign commercials. Rather than emphasizing their proposals or preferred policies, candidates now stage "media events" that project favorable images of their characters (Arterton, 1984). In the place of great diversity and vigor in the points of view available to citizens, television networks provide a bland and almost identical diet of news (Robinson & Sheehan, 1983). Where the electronic media might deepen and enrich our political lives, analysis of the response of broadcasters demonstrates reluctance to cover politics as news and begrudging compliance with requirements for public affairs programming (Leary, 1977; White, 1978). In spite of the direct link between politicians and voters, many citizens remain profoundly ignorant of even the most rudimentary political information. Rather than a marked jump in participatory politics, the last 20 years have witnessed a disturbing decline in voter participation.

In the United States, the broadcast media have developed as privately owned corporations, fulfilling the Constitutional values of a press relatively unrestrained by governmental power. Television has functioned reasonably well in achieving that result, but it has not delivered so successfully upon the affirmative requirements for an informed electorate and an active, vital citizenry (Wolfson, 1986). We may, in fact, be better off in many of these aspects than we were before television, but it is more certain that we still have a long way to go.

But the case lodged against television goes deeper than just nondelivery upon utopian promises. For many observers of American politics, the television age ushered in a series of changes in our politics that have been largely undesirable. Change was so gradual that much of the impact was not observed along the way. In retrospect, however, a series of profound effects are now laid at television's door (Polsby, 1983; Ranney, 1983). Political parties have deteriorated and candidates have developed considerable independence in fundraising and support building (Rubin, 1981). News exposure has given more prominence to presidential primaries, causing state party leaders to expand their numbers and, hence, their significance to the voters (Patterson, 1987; Robinson & McPherson, 1977). Whether in campaigning or policy-making, the visual coverage of television news highlights personality and events over issues and philosophy. Networks are alleged to give greater attention to organizations that claim to represent the public interest as opposed to traditional interest groups that mediate the self-interest of their members (Polsby, 1983). Instead of actively engaging in political discussions with other citizens, television viewers receive their political information passively and individually, isolated in their living rooms and without the capacity for talking back or questioning the source (Manheim, 1976; Pederson, 1984).

Now we face a second, and perhaps more radical, transformation in telecommunications media. The alleged "communication revolution" brings to the fore vague concerns as to political implications yet in store for us. This general problem has many facets, all of which demand attention, hopefully before they are upon us. The use of cable television by candidates for office, for example, could reformulate the nature of electoral appeals and coalition building (Arterton, 1983). Interest groups and political action committees might seize the new media as means for enhancing still further their influence on policy. The capacity to communicate more readily with other citizens who share the same interest might result in strong groups that transcend geographical boundaries, thereby straining even further political institutions that are rooted in geography.

While the potential consequences of technology extend to every sphere of our politics, this study concentrates upon a limited domain of these possible effects: whether hi-tech politics can encourage more frequent, intensive and effective citizen involvement in politics. I was led to this problem by several popular pieces that expansively claimed that a revolution in communications would nurture a profound transformation in our political institutions toward direct democracy. I was intrigued because citizen participation is so central to our notions of democracy. My interest in these new technologies was stimulated even more by the recognition that it would be better to foresee these disturbances before they occur than to adjust to them after the fact.

The Debate over Teledemocracy

What could the developments of cable television, satellites, computer networks, and videotex mean for our political life? Does it matter politically whether the television industry is dominated by three national networks or fragmented into a host of channels on the basis of specialized programming tastes? Can we envision possibilities for improving our political institutions by using emerging technologies to promote citizen participation in public policymaking? Can the communications revolution deliver on the unfulfilled promise of television by creating a vibrant citizenship in America? Can push-button democracy become a practical reality?

THE PROPONENTS

A few prominent forecasters and thinkers have begun to argue that we stand on the threshold of a major transformation of our political system. Not only will the emerging technologies of communication make possible new forms of association and political discourse, they will also unleash strong forces for political change. John Naisbitt (1982) and Alvin Toffler (1980), to cite two popular "futurists," take the view that a "communications revolution" will transform our politics. Electronics will enable a vast polity to function like a New England town meeting in which citizens can hear and contribute to the community discussion of issues. Electronic voting will both make possible and stimulate the holding of referenda or plebiscites. Citizens will be able to decide matters for themselves rather than surrendering decision-making power to representatives.

Toffler and Naisbitt write of this trend as inexorable. They are joined by Ted Becker (1981, p. 8) who predicts that "public opinion will become the law of the land." Becker and Scarce (1984), Barber (1982, 1984a, 1984b), Hollander (1985), Martin (1978), Tydeman, Lipinski, Alder, Nyhan, and Zwimpfer (1982, p. 265), Williams (1982), and Wolff (1976) are more cautious in their predictions of the inevitability of this transformation, but they are no less persuaded of the desirability of such a change.

The advocates of "teledemocracy"—as this evolution is being called—have, nevertheless, given little attention to the process by which such a transformation will come about. The evidence cited by Toffler and Naisbitt is largely anecdotal and nonsystematic. They gathered reports of many instances in which technology had underwritten participation, often accepting uncritically the claims of the project initiators. By reciting numerous examples, they appear to argue that accelerating experimentation will perfect ways of using the technology and will generate broad demand in society for replacing or modifying existing institutions so as to increase the power exercised directly by citizens.

Frederick Williams (1982, p. 199) appears to view these two processes of change as one:

> The political order of nations is being rapidly transformed from the written document and spoken word to an electronic communications network enveloping everyone. The new political order is the communications structure. . . .The new communication technologies offer the opportunity for citizen information and participation undreamed of by our Founding Fathers . . . we may have to adjust our democracy away from the constraints of the eighteenth century and toward the advantages of the twenty-first.

For some, like Williams (1982) and Hollander (1985), the engines of this political revolution are the technologies themselves. Recognizing that modern telecommunications can permit large numbers of citizens to register their preferences, some contend that direct legislation "by the people" is inevitable. For others, the argument is that a communications revolution will generate a new social class that will restructure politicial institutions to its liking. In unison they argue that our current political institutions—parties, representative legislatures, bureaucratic agencies—will prove increasingly incapable of dealing with the demands of a large and ever more complex society.

Valaskakis and Annopoulis (1982) are a little more specific; they believe the communications revolution will generate a class of information producers and transmitters. As this group increasingly occupies a dominant position in society, its members will develop an interest in and the power to reshape political institutions and processes. They will naturally seek to ensure that information exchange becomes the basis for the new polity, though the precise institutional form cannot be predicted now.

Becker and Scarce (1984) argue that through teledemocracy experiments in direct democracy, "the representative system itself can be substantially improved by augmenting it through imaginative and bold uses of telecommunications." But they also conclude that

> The participatory democracy movement . . . has advanced as present forms of government have weakened under the stress of size, increasing demands upon them, citizen dissatisfaction, and growing awareness that the people on the street are often as capable of making decisions as their "representative." (p. 29)

The most elaborate proposal for experimenting with institutional transformation has been advanced by Benjamin Barber in *Strong Democracy* (1984a). If new mechanisms—such as a lottery system of elections or a civic videotex service provided as a free channel by every cable company—were gradually put into place, citizens would learn the civic values of public responsibility and involvement. The result would be a stronger form of participatory democracy, though one in which many of the present representative institutions still functioned. Barber believes that the idea of true self-government would take root, producing "a campaign to win the substance of citizenship promised but never conferred by the victory of the vote." He offers ten proposals that, if adopted wholesale, would provide sufficient checks to safeguard democracy, whereas if adopted piecemeal they might be used to undermine democracy.

Thus even within the small community of those advocating the use of technology to strengthen democracy, one finds differences of emphasis and elaboration. They all agree, however, that the decline of participant behavior is a sign that our political institutions are not functioning adequately to meet today's needs. They tie the observed drop in voting to cynical and alienated attitudes produced by "an ever more meaningless and weak form of democracy" (Barber, 1984b). And they propose that the remedy lies in making citizen participation more abundant and more effective, aided by communications technologies.

Most of their speculation has revolved around the possibility of conducting votes or plebiscites electronically so that decisions could be made by all the people. Barber calls for both a national initiative and referendum process and experimentation with electronic balloting. Hollander (1985) believes that local experimentation with "video votes" will increase and gradually create a climate of legitimacy surrounding electronic plebiscites. Then, the stage will be set for national legislation that will create the legal authority for what he calls "video democracy." Wolff (1976) calls for a system of national voting through an unspecified electronic system linked to television. Becker's experiments with "teledemocracy" involve voting via telephone lines by a randomly selected sample of citizens who have been given detailed information and sufficient time to consider their choices.

But voting is only one form of citizen participation. With the exception of Barber, whose ideas go well beyond voting, less attention has been directed toward other ways in which technology might be used to promote participatory politics. The potentials are also significant for using modern hardware to forge closer bonds among individuals and groups (Laudon, 1984). The emerging telecommunication systems could be harnessed to make possible the exchange of large volumes of written and visual information (Blomquist, 1984) and to permit citizens to advocate their viewpoints to others either individually or in groups. By so doing, the role of citizen participation in the processes of agenda formation and policy determination might be expanded.

Using new telecommunication technology for electronic plebescites, though no mean feat, would be functionally equivalent to placing a polling booth in every person's home or workplace. Some hope this might reverse the downward trend in voter turnout. The state of Oregon, for example, has had considerable success in increasing turnout by allowing citizens to vote in local bond issues by mailed ballots. Even so, such uses do not come close to tapping the participatory potential of more rapid and convenient information exchange. Recall that interest group membership, campaign work, writing to elected officials, and engaging in political discussion are fuller, and often more effective, forms of participation in politics than mere voting. Therefore, why should electronic referenda be the ultimate goal for the political application of telecommunication technologies? Voting is a limited notion of participation, whether by means of a paper ballot, a voting machine, a computer punch card, or an electronic box. The new technologies certainly have important applications here, but they can also be used more ambitiously. They can be used to facilitate the means by which citizens communicate with each other and with their chosen leaders. Communication, dialogue and information exchange are, after all, the cornerstone of an informed body politic.

THE CRITICS

As in most topics relating to political processes, the advocacy of teledemocracy has not gone unchallenged. Critics such as Elstain (1982), Gitlin (1981), Malbin (1982), Pool (1973b), and Laudon (1977, 1984) argue that direct democracy would be unworkable even with instantaneous, universal communications. For example, Laudon argues that putting citizens into greater contact with leaders also provides those leaders with greater direct access to citizens. He fears that public accountability will be lessened by the great inequalities of power in such a relationship. Without an intermediating stratum of secondary leadership to provide alternative opinions and information, the result could be less democracy, in the sense of less power, initiative, volition, and alternative choices for citizens.

Jean Elstain (1982, p. 108) expands this argument by strongly rejecting the contention that voting can be equated with real democracy. She notes that authoritarian politics can be carried out ''under the guise of, or with the convenience of, majority opinion. That opinion can be registered by easily manipulated, ritualistic plebiscites.'' Beyond aggregated opinions that cannot constitute a civic culture, she points to our need for a deliberative process, involving discussion with other citizens, developing a shared sense of moral responsibilty for society, and enhancing individual action and identity through mutual involvement. She reserves a special ire for systems, such as Warner-Amex's Qube, through which citizens participate as autonomous individuals, systems that privatize what should be a social discourse.

Ithiel Pool (1973b) adds to our understanding by pointing out that teledemocracy will complicate the policy-making process considerably since public consultation will inevitably be time-consuming and costly and will raise the prospect for stymie. In the process, policy matters will become more visible and public concerns heightened. He then puts his finger on a critical dilemma for teledemocracy:

> The more intense and real the involvement that electronic feedback creates for the citizen in public affairs, the more crucial it is to limit the scope of its operation and what is affected. If citizens are brought, by effective personal participation, to the point of caring very deeply about political outcomes, then there had better not be too many important political decisions, for every time one is made there are losers as well as winners. (1973b, p. 244)

There are other arguments that can be raised against direct democracy, technologically induced or not. One results from the fact that citizens vary dramatically in the intensity with which they desire certain public outcomes. A majoritarian solution does not handle very adequately circumstances in which a majority is lukewarm in its support for one alternative and a minority ardently desires another. Another frequently voiced complaint is that many citizens do not care deeply about political matters and will refuse to become involved. Others argue that, even when they are interested, average citizens cannot possibly master all the details that go into policy decisions. Congressmen, for example, are full-time policy-makers yet even they have to specialize in a limited range of issues. Finally, there is the fear that the public will be irresponsible and fickle in its support of different policies; majorities will form and rapidly dissipate, policy will shift with ephemeral public opinion.

Proponents and opponents often talk past each other on different levels. The former, accepting without question the normative proposition that individuals and groups should decide for themselves, concentrate their attention on the fact that hardware may overcome the problems created by large numbers of citizens. In their view, the sole justification for representative institutions is that they constitute an expedient compromise necessary to make democracy feasible in large-scale societies. This rationale will be removed by the communications capabilities of emerging technologies.

Meanwhile, the critics of direct "teledemocracy," considering this problem on a theoretical and institutional level rather than as a normative assertion, argue that representative machinery is necessary to ameliorate divisive conflicts over political interest, to contain political ambition, to balance inequalities of participation and knowledge, and to safeguard minority rights.

The proponents and critics of direct, electronically induced democracy agree that declining rates of political participation—principally voting—and high levels of cynicism and civic distrust constitute severe threats to the health of the American political system. The question for both is whether modern communications can eliminate this cancer. While the answer of those advocating a transformation of our political institutions toward direct democracy is clear, their critics are less unified. After rehearsing the impact of changes brought by television, some of them feel that technological change cannot offer much of an improvement. Other critics of direct democracy wish to harness these new media to improve and strengthen existing representative institutions.

Here we encounter a different version of teledemocracy that has not received a great deal of attention. Even the most staunch defender of the status quo will admit that our political institutions do exhibit some problems that might be mitigated by technology. Low rates of citizen involvement is one such problem. A related concern results from the vast inequalities in participation across different social classes. Less well-off citizens simply are not as involved in political matters as are the more wealthy and better educated. Presumably, the outcomes of politics more closely reflect the preferences and wishes of those who are involved. Perhaps communications technologies can be used to redress this bias.

Consider another problem in the functioning of our political institutions that technology might help. Political figures often confront difficulties in surmounting the institutions that ostensibly they direct. Bureaucracies can become powerful filters of information, isolating elected leadership from the citizens they represent. Legislators frequently find themselves surrounded by staff, lobbyists, and interest groups who purportedly speak for the public. In these circumstances, communications media may be useful in putting representatives in direct contact with their constituents. Enhancing their capacity to respond to citizens will, however, potentially expand their capacity to influence the public; as Pool (1973) notes, electronic manipulation is the other side of the electronic democracy coin.

Technology and Democracy

Neither side of the debate over teledemocracy, however, has much systematic evidence to support its assumptions about the potential of telecommunications media for strengthening political participation. In large part, this results from the fact that academics whose work should be relevant to this question have been largely focused upon related, though essentially different, questions. The existing studies of political participation have, by and large, been psychologically or sociologically oriented (Milbrath, 1965; Nie, 1970; and Verba & Nie, 1972; Verba, Nie, & Kim, 1971). Since most of these studies are based on survey research, they discuss primarily what causes *individuals* to become involved. The institutional context within which participation occurs has been given very little attention.

Similarly, an abundant literature on media and politics, much of it framed in the electoral context, has endeavored to answer the questions of whether and how the media affect the political behavior of citizens.

The net results are surprising. Despite all the concern with the media's impact on politics, a long line of empirical research originating in the work of Paul Lazarsfeld and his associates (1944) has failed to demonstrate a direct affect of the content of television news directly upon the evaluations voters make of presidential candidates (Becker, McCombs, & McLeod, 1975; Comstock, 1980; Iyengar, Peters, & Kinder, 1983; O'Keefe, 1975; Patterson, 1980; Seymour-Ure, 1974; Shaw & McCombs, 1977). This "law of minimal consequences" has, however, been somewhat modified by more recent findings that television coverage can highlight some issues in the public's mind, raising their priority and placing them on the agenda of issues for government to resolve (Shaw & McComb, 1977).

Moreover, careful research indicates that exposure to television news may be strongly related to voter turnout (Blumler & McLeod, 1974; Glaser, 1965). But another group of researchers (Lemert, Mitzman, Seither, Cook & Hackett, 1977) argue that in many instances news reporting does not give citizens information that would stimulate their involvement in politics. Rarely are readers or audiences informed as to where they could go, how they could act, and whom they might contact in order to influence events that are reported in the news. Recently, Lewis Wolfson (1986), himself a former political reporter, has criticized news reporting for perpetuating this inadequacy and suggested ways in which reporters might give citizens more information about politics and, thereby, stimulate their involvement.

The arguments over teledemocracy thus stand at the juncture of two major bodies of research and scholarship, that concerned with participation and that devoted to the media's impact on behavior. In both cases, however, research has been primarily focused on the individual citizen, not on the environment, institution, or context in which he or she participates. As a result, the existing studies are less helpful when it comes to understanding how our political institutions of citizen participation might be changed by the application of new media.

This study was first conceived because the arguments over teledemocracy raised some very important issues for American democracy, and yet both sides of the debate lacked factual information. Rather than speculating broadly about the benefits or detriments of using technology to strengthen democracy, I set out to investigate systematically a number of teledemocracy projects, instances in which communications media have actually been used to encourage citizen involvement. I wanted to find out how the media have been used and what the consequences have been.

I must frankly admit that I began with a question in mind that proved to be naive: Which technologies of communication would prove most useful in facilitating political participation? To address this inquiry, I monitored the successes and failures of twenty demonstration projects and experiments in which different kinds of hardware had been enlisted to encourage citizen involvement in policy-making. I discovered, however, that the largest differences in the nature, the role, and the effectiveness of political participation were rooted not in technological capacity but in the models of participation that project initiators carried in their heads. Essentially, what I had taken to be an examination of the capabilities of different technologies proved to be an exercise in evaluating a number of institutional arrangements or contexts in which citizens participate politically.

Discussions about the usefulness of communications technology for democratic participation generally produce confusion because the nature of the causal connection between technology and political effects is so nebulous. On the one hand, despite an abundance of industry forecasts and projected patterns of growth for different technologies, we remain largely uncertain about the precise direction that the communications revolution will take in the near future. It makes a difference, for example, if we move toward a diverse set of video offerings carried to the vast majority of America over cable television systems versus a consumer-dominated market of videotapes. The extent to which our society is willing to invest in interactive services as part of cable or videotex systems will also have important consequences.

On the other hand, as Chapter Three will discuss in detail, neither can we be certain about the causes for low rates of citizen involvement. Alienation and cynicism may erode citizens' interest in political action; economic downturns may sap the resources needed for involvement; general satisfaction may alleviate the incentives to participate; or a lack of information, perceived stakes, or recognized opportunity may reduce the involvement of less well-off citizens.

Finally, the extent to which these causes may be affected by communications technology can be difficult to determine. Simple technological determinist arguments—that technological change causes social change—are frequently not spelled out clearly enough for detailed scrutiny or empirical examination. Alvin Toffler's *Third Wave* (1980) is a case in point. He catalogues numerous institutional and social problems, cites anecdotal evidence about changing patterns of communications, and asserts that the two are related to one another such that our society will emerge transformed from the present disarray. The mechanism of influence is nowhere made clear.

As vehicles for human communication, different technologies do have certain capabilities that determine the social use. We cannot be sure that humans will want to communicate in given modes, but if there exists a real need, then providing a capacity to facilitate that need will allow individuals and institutions to adapt their behavior. For example, in the 1940s, the idea that the great majority of American homes would tune in to essentially the same roster of entertainment programs was mere conjecture. Although they maneuvered to benefit from this change in behavior, the networks did not cause the change, rather their existence allowed it to take place.

Thus at each stage in the logic of this argument—what social scientists refer to as the independent variable, the dependent variable, and the causal link—we confront uncertainty that complicates our efforts to address this problem. Nor can we be very optimistic that prior knowledge of the likely consequences will allow us to intervene and shape that impact substantially. At the most, we may be marginally able to affect the process. Yet given the potential for change suggested by analyses of the impact of television, we cannot merely walk away from the effort to understand this relationship.

It is precisely at this point that our values come into play. While it may be possible to suspend normative judgments in the process of empirical research, using the knowledge gained through research implies making value judgments about political processes. Description, theory, and value assertions are thus intimately involved. To reiterate, the discussion of the use of technology to secure political values should give its primary emphasis to a consideration of values. We must decide first what we want to accomplish through technology. Then we can move on to assess the degree to which that is reasonably possible and to consider the most appropriate set of political institutions in which to harness technology to move toward our goals. Merely applying technology and observing its effects will not suffice; nor can we hope to strengthen or safeguard democracy by standing by and allowing technological change to continue apace, unexamined and unfiltered by the values we hold dear. To do so would be to surrender our future to directions we may not now understand and might not accept if we did.

CHAPTER 2

THE PROMISE OF TECHNOLOGY

When Alexander Graham Bell and Guglielmo Marconi first speculated as to how their inventions might be used commercially, each thought roughly in terms of the eventual application of the other's invention (Solomon, 1984). Bell dreamed of large numbers of people holding telephones to their ears and listening to a single speaker, while Marconi thought radio waves would carry messages between individuals. Even if largely apocryphal, the anecdote serves to sharpen our thinking about the potential evolution of a revolution in communications technology. For one thing, the story forces us to recognize in a concrete way that forecasting developments in the applications of new technologies can be extremely risky, even for those in the best position to know the developments on the forefront of invention. Mere knowledge of the hardware is not enough. A complicated relationship of social needs, cultural patterns, economic constraints, and technology capacities exists, implying that technologies alone are not highly determinative of their political application.

Furthermore, when we speak of emerging communication technologies, we mean more than simply the invention of new capacities. In order to be used for human communication, technologies must be supplemented by social engineering, what I refer to as the "institutional housing" that surrounds and makes available a physical capability. For example, speaking of television in our world connotes a great deal more than the simultaneous transmission of voice and moving pictures from one location to another; as it is "practiced" in the United States today, television means large corporations investing heavily in production, supported by advertising, and drawing large audiences. A simplistic interpretation of Marshall McLuhan's famous dictum, "The medium is the message," will not suffice. The medium means more than hardware.

However, we must also recognize that a given technology does have certain characteristics, properties, or capabilities that may well determine its social use. Transmission of voice alone may be perfectly sufficient for certain communication needs. The printed word, though slower, may be better suited to conveying logical, analytical thoughts than expressive content (Meyrowitz, 1985). Thus by satisfying different needs by providing new capacities for contact, the existence of a given technology may change human behavior. This position falls a good deal short of technological determinism. Here we follow the lead of Ithiel Pool (1983) who argued for a "soft" technological determinism in advancing the view that the newer technologies are more likely to stimulate pluralism since the emerging communications system will become much more competitive.

If one can demonstrate that any changes that occur to our social and political institutions will be a product of more than mere hardware, then political changes will not be inevitably forced upon the political system. They will come about as a product of political and cultural values combined with new capacities for communicating. Any consequences of these changes for our political institutions will result not just from technology, but from complex interactions among several streams of American life: developments in telecommunications hardware, patterns of corporate investment and marketing, changes in consumer acceptance and preferences, independent changes in our political institutions, and the public policy climate.

Analyzing the Communications "Revolution"

Even though prediction can be a hazardous undertaking, we cannot allow this topic to go unaddressed. If the example of television's impact is illustrative, the potential spillover into the political realm is too substantial to ignore. The most precarious forecasts involve prediction as to which medium will emerge to dominate communications behavior and the rate of change. To avoid these most tenuous assertions, I will discuss broad characteristics or directions that the emerging media may take while steering clear of the attempt to foresee their precise form. The following appears to be the important feature emerging in the structure of communications as a result of technological invention.[1]

The first of these fall into what might be called the Bernoulli principles of information flow: speed, volume, and cost. For many decades, the amount of information exchanged and the speed of communication have been increasing rapidly, while the cost of each unit communicated has been falling. These trends appear likely to continue in the near future, although the rate of change will probably not remain even.

By now, it is irrefutable that the costs of communicating information are dropping, even though the costs of producing it may remain unchanged. In any case, decreasing unit costs have clearly been a spur to increased volume. At the bottom of many of these shrinking costs lies the silicon chip, which is central to the computerization of information exchange. The price of computer chips has been falling faster than their size. The combination of computers and high-speed laser printers, for example, has reduced the cost of placing large numbers of personalized letters in the mail, resulting in a tremendous increase of what many Americans regard as "junk mail." Satellites, to cite another example, have made the transmission of voice and video nearly insensitive to the ground distance over which messages are transferred. As satellites have become more abundant, furthermore, the cost of renting an individual transponder, capable of transmitting a television show or thousands of telephone calls simultaneously, has declined sharply. It is now cheaper by far to distribute a program by satellite to many locations than to pay for and ship videotapes. In terms of wiring costs, to provide a final example, cable operators are almost indifferent to systems that carry 12, 36, or even 150 channels. The costs of producing content—providing programming for that number of channels—have served as the principal restraint on the numbers of channels, not the actual costs of delivery.

While costs are tumbling across the board in most of the newer forms of communication, the point at which most American consumers will decide to invest in these systems is less certain. The U.S. mail costs recipients either nothing or the small price of a mailbox. Evidently most Americans have been willing to pay the installation and monthly fees for telephone service. Radios are cheap and color television sets have become almost universal despite their price tags. But only half of the homes that could receive cable actually subscribe, and, despite all the promotion given to home computers, only a tiny fraction of American homes boast a computer which can do more than play electronic games. With few exceptions—the *Los Angeles Times's* Gateway and Knight-Ridder's Viewtron—videotex systems have not really been marketed commercially to American consumers, and both these exceptions appear to be running behind expectations in the number of subscribers (Arlen, 1984a, 1984b). As a result, much of the promise of these newer systems for citizen participation remains just that. Until costs fall further to the point at which American consumers decide that the attainable benefits justify the price tags, these mechanisms will not be available as instruments for widespread political participation.

The rapid increases in the amount of information exchanged and in the speed of communication have been so widely noted in most arenas of human activity that observations about information overload have become commonplace (Toffler, 1980). Whether or not we are enjoying all this accelerated and more extensive communication lies beyond the scope of this argument, but it does seem clear that increasing amounts of information about politics and public policy will be exchanged. Since we will also be communicating more about the whole gamut of human concerns, one can question whether these trends portend any real change for political discourse and for political participation. Just because more information about our politics is available does not mean that many people will be interested in receiving that information.

Consider a second trend. Technological invention and recent regulatory decisions have combined to ensure that the emerging telecommunications structure will be characterized by a vastly greater number of channels for the exchange of messages. This trend has also been under way for a number of years, as can be seen in the growth of television and radio stations since the 1950s. As the newer technologies become available, they will not replace the existing means of communication but take their place alongside them. Thus the potential number of conduits will expand dramatically. The cable television industry, which now appears to be emerging from severe financial troubles, poses the best example. Home delivery of video programming will be available to subscribers through cable over a larger number of channels. Both broadcast television and cable delivery will enjoy competition from a variety of other means such as multipoint distribution service (MDS), subscription television (STV), satellite master antenna television (SMTV), low-power television (LTV), and direct broadcast satellites (DBS) (see *Channels*, 1983). The market in videotapes for home use is now exploding into a further avenue of competition; videopublishing may become a significant conduit of information exchange. Of course, not all of these media will survive as viable forms of delivery, but in any case, we will not return to the days of three national networks.

This trend reaches well beyond the television industry. Computer networks, videotex systems, video teleconferencing, teleconferencing, cellular radio, and telephone marketing systems are joining the more established vehicles of broadcast, closed circuit television, movies, broadcast radio, shortwave radio, CB radio, telephones, magazines, newspapers, mail, leaflets, bulletin boards, posters, and face-to-face speech. Some of these new vehicles will be useful primarily for private communication between individuals; others will serve more public forms of interchange. Though much of the discussion of media in politics centers upon mass communications, those wishing to establish private interchange between individuals will also have available a vastly expanded array of conduits that will carry more information, more rapidly.

This observation warrants a brief digression: The history of cable television demonstrates how human needs and economic conditions must be added to technical capabilities in order to understand change in the communication structure. Cable television was first developed back in 1948 in Mahanoy City, Pennsylvania, as a means of providing better reception for communities blocked by mountains or distance. Gradually, in other locations where reception was not necessarily poor, companies marketed their service as offering subscribers greater choice among signals "imported" from distant markets. Despite the existence of technical capacity, the cable industry did not really take off until after the formation of Home Box Office (HBO) in 1976, which offered paying subscribers movies uninterrupted by advertising. Only by providing something new that fulfilled a social need, did the cable industry start to grow dramatically. The anecdote does, however, include a role for technological advance as well: HBO was not really economically feasible until communication satellites made possible nationwide distribution of programs.

Let us take up a third of these broad trends in the communications industries: Some observers predict, while the more cautious hope, that, given the expansion in number of channels available, diversity will increase in the array of speakers addressing mass audiences. Democratic theorists argue that a robust political discourse requires diversity in the viewpoints expressed, and some worry that recent trends in the communications structure have curtailed this level of pluralism. Their worry stems from the decline in the number of cities with more than one newspaper, the increased concentration of ownership of the remaining dailies, the fact that the three television networks offer nearly identical programming, the tendency toward greater concentration in book publishing, and the pattern of cross-ownership in which movie studios, for example, become involved in cable television (Warner Communications, HBO, Disney). More channels offer the hope of greater diversity in content.

Two related points are involved here: A long-standing body of regulatory law and policy has been directed toward ensuring diversity in ownership and control over the means of communication, while other observers have focused primarily upon the content of communication. Ownership diversity, a means of encouraging content diversity, has been a major tenet of broadcast regulation since the 1930s. Even though diverse ownership cannot guarantee content diversity, it may provide a check against the political abuses that could occur in a monopoly situation. Despite the proliferation of outlets, therefore, this general policy will probably endure since there appears to be no inevitable tendency for ownership to become diversified.

Whether or not the new technologies will generate increased diversity in the content of messages is more debatable and more serious. Some hope that it will, based upon the following logic. Commercial television, which is financially dependent upon the size of its audience, will not be able to maintain the same profit margins under the competitive conditions predicted by the opening of so many new conduits. The existing advertiser-based financial structure will have difficulty supporting a multitude of channels each earning the present high levels of profitablity. Competition that leads to a decline in network audiences, should serve in the long run to undercut the prices charged to advertisers. Subscription services provide a major alternative, but there are others possible. If new conduits adopt an advertiser-supported financial pattern, a different financial structure could be found in the emergence of a market based upon more complicated calculations than mere audience size or "gross rating points." Research is already well underway to document patterns of life-style and demographic characteristics exhibited by audiences for different forms of entertainment and information (Neuman, in press). A crude version of the possibilities has long dictated the placement of, for example, beer ads in sports programming and soap commercials during daytime television. If enough advertisers become convinced that they can be more cost-effective by directing messages to particular audiences than by reaching mass audiences, then the conditions will be right for revising the financial structure of the industry. Some outlets would maintain large audiences that would sell to advertisers whose products have a universal appeal (toothpaste, soft drinks); other channels would attempt to build audiences with special interests (backpacking or business) or given characteristics such as income level, gender, or ethnic groups (computers, pregnancy services, books in Spanish). Content diversity would come about as those who control the means of communication attempt to derive a secure financial structure for the industry given a plethora of outlets.

The scenario of diverse content moving through many channels depends, however, upon the assumption that different groups have different tastes in entertainment and are interested in different kinds of information. A greater array of conduits will offer recipients more choice among competing vehicles. If these channels provide different types of information and entertainment, then the possibilty exists for the development, alongside the vehicles of mass communications, of audiences that are specialized through the choice exercised by recipients.

This trend is clearly interrelated with the last. Without diversity of messages, there can be no specialization of audiences. On the other hand, unless different audiences can be constructed around content, there will be no incentives for those who control the content to provide a tremendous array of alternative programming.

Undoubtedly this will happen to some degree because it already exists today. Newsletters and magazines, for example, survive by reaching a specialized audience that is willing to pay for their information. We cannot, however, be more precise about the degree to which this trend will take hold because the argument is really one about human characteristics rather than technical capacity. To what extent are we similar in our interests and tastes? To what extent are we different individuals? How strong and extensive are our bonds of community? And how divided are our political interests? Technologically, the opportunities for satisfying individual differences are now expanding. In the not too distant future, we may discover whether the uniformity of mass audiences for the three networks has been forced upon us by a lack of choice, or whether the networks' broad appeal lies in similarities of human, or at least national, interests and tastes.

Another characteristic of emerging telecommunication technologies will facilitate the emergence of specialized audiences. Through invention, recipients are acquiring greater control over incoming communications. Beyond expanded choice, technical developments such as video recorders, for example, allow television viewers to determine the time at which they will watch different programs. No longer must they passively accept the choice offered at any particular time by the broadcasters. Similarly, videotex systems are engineered so as to allow subscribers to request some information while ignoring other material. Just as different readers of the same newspaper may read an entirely different set of articles, so subscribers to the same information service may "access" very different material.

Those who predict that this trend will lead to a sharp decline in the dominance of the television networks speak of the fragmentation of the audience, which may come about as a result of greater choices exercised by recipients. This development, which is by no means certain, is often discussed with some concern. Observers like Richard Reeves (1983) and Jeff Greenfield (1982) argue that the pool of common political information shared by Americans may be eroded. Others disagree, pointing out that there have always been great diversities in the information possessed by American citizens. Many newspaper readers, for example, skip quickly to the sports pages or the living section with scarcely a glance at the front page news. As Ithiel Pool (1983) has argued, the national sharing of political information is a creation of the twentieth century. Before radio and television networks, the nation functioned quite well with, presumably, great regional differences in the information known by different citizens.

There is, however, an important difference between the circumstances of the past and the direction of the present trend. Our political system is rooted in geography: We assume that political interests will become manifested primarily through representation of geographically based constituencies. The creation of strong political interests that transcend geography may not be so easily accommodated by the present institutional structures.

The traditional analysis of communications media has differentiated between point-to-point communications and point-to-mass, a distinction based on a one-versus-many dichotomy. Even though there have always been vehicles between these extremes, we have usually thought in terms of the mass media versus the private media. The telephone, for example, has been considered the essence of a point-to-point medium, providing private communications between individuals. However, combined with computers and tape recorders, the telephone can now be used to reach large numbers of people with the same message; that is, it can become a point-to-mass medium. At the other extreme, mass vehicles may become more focused; as noted above, television audiences might be honed to more precise audiences. In other words, the emerging technologies are filling in the midpoints of the traditional dichotomy.

In this development, we may begin to appreciate that a more fundamental concept than mere numbers lies behind the distinctions we make in the capabilities of different communication vehicles. A relationship exists between the message to be delivered and the nature of the audience. At one end of a continuum—no longer a dichotomy—communicators need to deliver messages to specific individuals about whom they know a great deal of information relevant to the communication. Friends talk on the phone or write letters about last summer's vacation. They use point-to-point communications; in the future, they may make widespread use of conference calls or computer conferencing. As we move down the range, away from this end point, several things happen simultaneously: the audience size increases, the information known about the receivers diminishes, and the messages to be delivered become increasingly general. Another way of thinking about these changes is to observe that increasingly the recipients become substitutable one for another. At the broadest level, the other end of the continuum, we arrive at the point at which advertisers and politicians become concerned mostly with audience size, not with the characteristics that make up the

audience. As discussed above, the archetypal point-to-mass communications, television, has been used by most advertisers based on a strategy
of purchasing the largest audience possible in "gross rating points" per
week.

These communication patterns will undoubtedly continue. Through
newer vehicles and more precise market research, however, the message
can be tailored to the information known about the recipients. But for a
good deal of the way along the continuum, the receivers of messages are
treated as a class of persons, rather than as individuals in their own
right. In the latest jargon, politicians refer to this capacity as "targeting"
while commercial marketing is abuzz with talk of "segmentation."
Direct mail marketing and magazine advertising are probably the most
developed media for achieving this middle-range pattern of communication. As a result of these developments, mass communications are
becoming less massive, while some forms of personal contact may become less individualized.

Instead of mass media, which carry messages from one point to
nearly everyone, or private conduits through which individuals
communicate in pairs, the expanding array of options appears to be in
media that might be called *semiprivate* or *semipublic* vehicles.

Semipublic media are those available to a large mass of receivers but
used by only a small percentage of them out of habit or preference.
Politically, the Cable Satellite Public Affairs Network (C-SPAN), which
carries the U.S. House of Representatives debates to over 2,000 cable
systems is an ideal example. The number of homes that receive C-SPAN
(20 million) is far higher than the actual audience; the difference results
from choices made by the potential audience. Media of this type are
useful politically when the sender is willing to allow the receivers a high
degree of self-initiative. In other words, one can stimulate participation
through semipublic media only by giving up the goal of universal
involvement.

Semiprivate electronic media, on the other hand, are those in which
the reach is controlled by the senders, that is, they can determine who
will receive the communication. A major development in the so-called
communications revolution is that these conduits may be capable of
reaching very large numbers of people simultaneously. Direct mail,
videoconferencing, and computer conferencing come to mind as
examples of these media. They can be used by one speaker to send a
private message to 10,000 of his closest friends. In the area of interest
here, they can be used to encourage broad-scale citizen participation
only when accompanied by a massive outreach effort to contact
individuals and groups and bring them into the communications loop.

The proliferation of these conduits in the intermediate band between mass communications and private channels may confound yet another neat distinction in our thinking about communications media. As Ithiel Pool (1983) describes, the media providing private communications have been generally regulated as common carriers, while the mass media have either been subjected to content regulation (as in broadcasting) or provided the First Amendment protections of a free press. But the development of media that share characteristics with both private communications and mass channels raises major ambiguities for communications laws that seek to regulate access for political speech. It is very uncertain which of these principles apply or which constitute appropriate policy (Homet, 1985).

The degree of control exercised by subscribers to videotex systems highlights a final property of the new media; they will increase the prospects for interactive communications. This characteristic is especially important from the viewpoint of political participation, which inherently demands an interactive form of communication. In the past, most mass media have been primarily one-way vehicles. As we shall see, these media are often combined to permit "pseudointeractivity" using "feedback" processes such as letters to the editor, op-ed pages, editorials, replies, public opinion polls, call-in formats, or mail back ballots. Given that these combinations have been constructed from instruments that are essentially one-way, they have been less open to a level of receiver influence and control than promised by truly interactive media.

A number of different media are currently being developed that place scattered participants in direct contact with each other, allowing them to exchange their ideas or actions quickly and yet extensively. These include cable television systems equipped with push-button equipment for feedback, videotex systems that link terminals to a main frame computer, computer conferencing that functions much like citizen band radio by connecting many smaller computers, electronic mail that can deliver messages instantaneously to a single individual or hundreds of computer users, and videoconferencing or teleconferencing through which group meetings can be held without regard for geography.

Each of these means opens up new possibilities for stimulating politically relevant communications. But the lessons of citizen band radios should not be ignored. The capacity allows individuals to talk about what they have in common: in this case, driving conditions, cars or trucks, road emergencies, and citizen band radio equipment. Political communication is virtually nonexistent because the citizenry banded together by these radio waves has little common political interest. The new media will not change this fact.

Combined, these five characteristics of the new media—greater volume at increased speed and reduced costs, a substantially larger number of channels, the possibilities for greater diversity of speakers through mass media, the prospect of specialization in the audiences, and enhanced interactivity through telecommunications—add up to a significant amount of change in the patterns of communicated information. Whether or not these changes will be revolutionary depends less on technological imperative than on how we choose to use these means and the institutions we develop to contain these communications.

Participation Technologies

Stepping down from these visions of our "high tech" future to the empirical present can be a bit jarring. In the next section, I discuss the technologies that I found in actual use mediating political participation. One fact is immediately apparent: Since the interactive media discussed above are not yet widely available, most of the project organizers innovated by combining two of the existing channels of communication.

TELEVISED CALL-IN FORMATS

When I actually looked at instances in which media were used to stimulate participation, I found that the most widely used arrangements combined point-to-mass broadcasting with mass-to-point telephone "feedback." Within this general pattern of communication, some variation was evident in both links of the interactive processes. For example, the "outgoing" messages or televised portions were transmitted by broadcast stations, over cable systems, or through closed circuit delivery systems. The program itself was just as likely to be a live show as a prerecorded production. Then, on the other side of this interactive communication, participants were enlisted in several different ways: They were sometimes permitted to ask questions or make comments on the air, their opinions were solicited to a closed series of questions posed by either an operator or a tape recording machine, or, in some cases, citizens found that merely by dialing a number their opinions were registered as a vote for one of several alternatives (through AT&T's 900 service).

Most frequently, however, call-in formats resemble radio talk shows: A moderator or guest—often an elected public official—will respond to questions posed by viewers. The outgoing communication, which in this case must be a "live" show, can be carried by broadcast TV or over a cable system. In other instances, viewers are encouraged to call in to express their views, but are not able to interact directly with a personality "on the air." In these cases, the citizen responses are usually recorded and a summary tally is reported back to the viewers.

The second format can handle responses from many more viewers. From our observations in a variety of settings, it appears that when viewers' questions or comments become part of the outgoing program, only about 20 such calls can be handled in an hour. In contrast, a half-hour broadcast on a controversial topic may elicit hundreds of calls to a phone bank operation, and a computer that merely records how many calls are made to a particular number may log in thousands of "votes" (Sanoff, 1984). The most widely publicized of these demonstrations, for example, was a "900 number" call-in organized in 1980 by ABC after the Carter-Reagan debate. Over 700,000 voted their opinion as to who had won the debate. Naturally enough, there is a simple proposition at work here: The more extensive the interaction between participants and initiator, the smaller the number of citizens that become involved.

MAIL BACK BALLOTS

A large number of projects have encouraged citizens to voice their views by mailing in specially printed ballots. Most frequently, initiators distribute the ballots by having them printed in local newspapers, often as a special supplement. On other occasions, they have been placed in public buildings and banks for passersby to pick up and return. Less frequently, the project will send ballots to a randomly selected sample of citizens who may fill them out at their own volition.

In most of these cases, the effort to stimulate citizens into returning the ballots—that is, the outgoing communication—is conducted over several weeks and through a variety of media. Those who want citizens to express their views run public service spot advertisements on radio and television, arrange for community leaders and spokespersons of various points of view to appear on public affairs programming, draft and distribute explanatory pamphlets, and put up eye-catching billboards and posters on public transportation vehicles. The wider the net of citizen participation sought, the more extensive these efforts.

These projects are normally single-shot efforts to solicit citizen views and preferences in one policy area, usually of major importance. Examples might be regional growth issues, school financing strategies, or proposals for mass transit expansion. Experience has proven that large numbers will respond to a well orchestrated campaign. Fortunately, a systematic study of such efforts has been conducted by Barry Orton (1980).

INTERACTIVE CABLE TELEVISION

There are a few cable systems that offer, for an additional charge, interactive technology in which viewers are able to respond to questions by pushing buttons on a hand-held device connected through the cable. In most cases, a central computer "sweeps" each household to determine whether one of the available buttons has been pressed. The computer records the vote of each household and can quickly give the system operator a tally of the total number of "votes" for each option. Assumedly, consumers do not sign up for this interactive technology in order to become more involved in politics. These companies offer additional services such as the ability to order merchandise or to tie in home security and fire alarm systems. But with the technology installed, those at the "head end" can use the system to conduct instantaneous polls in which viewers respond to questions posed on one channel.

While the political uses of this technology have been decidedly secondary to its entertainment or commercial applications, there have been a variety of instances in which citizens have been asked to respond on political matters. Unfortunately from the viewpoint of assessing their potential contribution to democracy, the companies that offer these services—notably Warner-Amex and Cox cable—believe that more detailed information beyond the percentage of respondents pushing each button should be guarded both as proprietary information and in order to protect the privacy of subscribers. In most cases, one cannot even find out how many viewers responded to a given question. This severely limits the usefulness of these instances as demonstration projects in citizen participation; we may learn that 75% prefer option A, but we also need to know whether this means three of the four viewers bothered to respond, or 8,113 out of an audience of 32,464.

TELECONFERENCING AND VIDEOCONFERENCING

Limited numbers of participants, scattered in many locations over large distances, can hold political discussions using audio or video channels. These media have been available for some time; until recently they have been quite expensive. Satellite distribution of the required electromagnetic signals has been one factor reducing these costs to a point at which their use appears to be increasing rapidly. Several commercial services are now available that can arrange videoconferences with a minimum lead time, either from studios or through portable equipment brought to the various sites.

Politically, a few experiments have been conducted in which a modest number of citizens have been able to participate in electronically mediated policy discussions. Most frequently, public officials at one site converse with citizens in remote locations—a congressman in Washington holds office hours with constituents in California, a legislative hearing in Juneau, Alaska, enables citizens on the North Slope to testify without leaving their villages.

These systems resemble most closely the normal conduct of face-to-face contact. They are electronic extensions of well-established means for citizens to press their concerns and for politicians to build public support. By eliminating travel, however, technology can be used to lower the costs of participation for citizens. In the process, more groups and individuals can be incorporated into the political process than would otherwise become involved.

COMPUTER CONFERENCING

Through computer software now available on a growing number of mainframe computers, owners of small home computers can be linked together through telephone lines. Essentially, multiple users share common computer files in which they can send messages to each other and read the contributions of others. Though its advocates like to bill this medium as a mass-to-mass mechanism, practical limits on the number of people that can be involved in a conversation really make this a "few-to-few" instrument. A major benefit of computer conferencing is that messages can be exchanged at times convenient for both senders and receivers. Participants can read the comments of others that may have been written days or minutes before, then add their own thoughts for others to read when they "log on" to the system.

This vehicle holds forth some promising political uses for groups of citizens who share a particular interest. In most systems, the software permits any member of a conference to ask the other participants to vote in response to one or a series of questions. However, conferencing by computers will probably never be a vehicle of mass democracy as in voting because its strengths lie as an instrument of discussion, and discussion implies some limits on the number of participants who can conveniently add their thoughts. Instead, the voting option can help groups organize their discussion collectively. Voting can, for example, establish whether the group wants to discuss one aspect of an issue more than other dimensions or whether most participants want to move on to another subject. Thus it appears that the instrument will more likely serve other purposes than registering votes: either for discussion of policy ideas and strategy among a modest size group of individuals who are already heavy participants in political processes or as a vehicle linking citizens with their public officials.

ELECTRONIC MAIL AND VIDEOTEX

In the course of this research, several other forms of computer-aided communications turned up. Electronic mail, for example, resembles the U.S. postal system, except that messages are delivered to the recipient almost instantaneously. A few congressmen do engage in computer messaging with constituents and Alaska legislators have established a number of sites around their state from which citizens can send electronic mail to Juneau.

As in letter mail, messages can be directed to a specific individual or can be simultaneously sent to whole classes of recipients (all members of the legislature, all Republican legislators, all state senators from Anchorage). Evidently, legislators respond to electronic mail much like postal mail; if the message is personally directed to them by a constituent, they treat it more seriously than a message delivered in bulk to all legislators.

Videotex systems resemble computer conferencing in that small computers or terminals of limited capacity are connected to a large computer. The principal difference is that in most cases videotex systems do not put the participants in direct contact with each other. Instead, the system operator provides an abundance of information that subscribers "retrieve." These systems tend to be hierarchically arranged, rather like the point-to-mass character of broadcast television. As such they can enable a large number of subscribers to register their opinions and preferences (Blomquist, 1984; Carey, 1982). While there has been some messaging and polling related to politics in the few field trials of videotex in this country, I did not find this experimentation significant enough (or accessible enough) to warrant investigation.

Conclusion

Having discussed the technology side of the teledemocracy question, we should turn to the political aspects. What do we need to know about citizen involvement in politics? There are two answers to this question. First, we need to establish some basic understanding of why some citizens turn to political activity and others avoid it. In particular, we would like to know whether American democracy has been weakened by a sharp decline in citizen participation. What are the causes of this decline and can they be reversed by a dose of technology? Second, I need to introduce those instances in which communications media have been used to facilitate participation.

The next chapter serves these purposes. I will briefly describe what we know about the declining political participation of individual citizens and then move on to describe the teledemocracy projects and begin the discussion of their differences in terms of institutional aspects of political participation. Two conceptual dimensions appear to be particularly important in differentiating among these efforts. When put together in combinations, these dimensions delineate four types of projects. Each of the four subsequent chapters discusses one of these types in detail. Thus as indicated in the introductory chapter, the basic division among efforts to encourage citizen participation is based upon the goals of the project initiators, not on technical differences in the communications hardware employed.

Note

1. An original version of this section was revised after a discussion of these characteristics with Professor Gary Orren and Steven Bates of Harvard University. I have profited greatly from their thoughts and comments.

CHAPTER 3

THE INSTITUTIONAL CONTEXT
OF POLITICAL PARTICIPATION

The promotion of citizenship is hardly a new phenomenon in American politics. From the Jeffersonian democrats to the most recent election campaign, examples abound of political elites who have sought to extend the base of participants in political life. Most of these cases possess a self-serving quality: leaders and statesmen seeking to reinforce their own power by stimulating citizen participation. In the main, therefore, broadened participation has been purposively promoted in order to accomplish certain desired policies or to secure political power.

In a smaller number of instances, those who would encourage greater involvement in political processes have done so without regard to substantive policy results. They have sought instead to improve the quality and quantity of participation as goals in their own right. In most of these projects, the instigators or initiators maintain a posture of disinterested democrats: They merely provide greater opportunities for citizens to exert influence, while they try to avoid influencing the outcomes of the process they set in motion. These initiators assume that the involvement of citizens in public life is a social benefit in and of itself. While they convey political messages and bring a wider array of individuals into politics, they impose upon themselves rather high standards of ensuring that the information they provide is objective and balanced and that the new groups incorporated do not represent a limited range of interests.

These experiments have been going on for some time. It appears, however, that projects of this nature have become more frequent in recent decades (Langton, 1978; Orton, 1980; Perlman, 1978). If this assumption is correct, at least two possible reasons could explain the increased interest in experimentation with means of promoting citizen participation. First, one could cite the general backdrop of declining rates of voting participation and escalating instances of cynicism about political institutions. Alarm about the voting decline and the development of civic distrust have spread to many in the politically conscious community. These projects appear to be ad hoc responses, efforts to see if other avenues can be developed that will repair some of the damage.

I also discovered a belief—or perhaps only a hope—that the evolving communication technologies could be harnessed to mitigate this problem. The degree of enthusiasm for a "technological fix" varied considerably, but most of these teledemocracy projects were conceived with the idea of using greater technology to lower the burden of involvement for average citizens. Thus the fact that this experimentation takes place shortly after the spread of cable television and computers is probably no accident.

Of course, similar experimentation is certainly taking place among those who seek to mobilize political power to accomplish specific policy outcomes. The electronic ministers of the New Right, the Republican National Committee's computer, the satellite network of the Chamber of Commerce, Senator Bradley's weekly cable show, and the expanding use of teleconferencing by labor unions are all examples (Arterton, 1983).

I chose, however to evaluate policy-neutral projects for a pair of reasons. First, they are less susceptible to the uniqueness of the policy matter involved and other surrounding political circumstances. Second, the outcome-oriented efforts are more likely to stimulate political opposition that, in turn, will certainly influence the participant behavior evoked by the original undertaking. To some degree, I avoided these problems by focusing on projects that merely sought to elicit participation without any preconception of a desired policy outcome.

Before describing the teledemocracy projects, however, I need to return to the discussion of declining participation in American elections. As noted, this trend provides a background for many of these efforts to expand involvement; many of the organizers explicitly justified their efforts by referring to this drop as a crisis of legitimacy in the American political system.

Participation in Decline?

Most political observers would readily agree with the proposition that recently participation has been declining in the United States. The evidence most often cited to support this claim is the steady drop in voter turnout in U.S. elections since 1960. Yet joining interest groups, contributing money, phoning public officials, writing letters, knocking on doors, and a myriad of other activities ought to be included in our definition of active citizenship in a democracy. The fabric of democratic politics is woven more reliably by these strands than upon the ability to cast ballots. Because it is the most observable and measurable form of involvement, however, most attention has been paid to the decline in voting.

The Kennedy/Nixon contest drew 62.8% of all voting-age citizens.[1] By contrast, only 52.6% of voting-age residents of the United States cast a ballot in the 1980 presidential election (and 53.3% in 1984). The same trend has occurred in midterm congressional elections. In 1962, 45.4% of the voting-age population turned out as compared to 35.5% in 1982, a slight increase over the 34.9% who voted in 1978.

How can we explain this decline in voting? The largest single drop in turnout for presidential elections occurred between 1968 and 1972 (from 55.1 to 50.7). For congressional elections, the largest drop was between 1970 and 1974 (from 43.5 to 35.8). For this reason, the Watergate events and the inclusion of 18- to 20-year-olds receive most of the blame for decreased turnout. Watergate, so the argument goes, caused massive voter disaffection, increased feelings of voter inefficacy, and raised levels of skepticism toward politics in general. These attitudinal changes continue to manifest themselves in lower turnout rates. Extending the vote to 18- to 20-year-olds reduced turnout rates because 18- to 20-year-olds have the lowest turnout levels of any age group.

Notice that conceptually these are two very different accounts of the same phenomenon. The first is a psychological explanation: Voter confidence in the political system has been eroded. We know from surveys that those disenchanted with the political system are the least likely to vote, so the explanation appears to fit with our understanding of who votes and who does not. The second account relies on demographic changes: The group with the lowest rate of voting has become a larger share of the electorate. In other words, this explanation suggests that contextual elements account for the decline in voting. By this telling, the drop in turnout is a natural by-product of public policy and not a matter of great concern about the legitimacy of the American system.

While these two arguments have some validity, they cannot fully explain the rates of decline seen over the past twenty years. First, neither could have had anything to do with the decline between 1960 and 1970. Watergate was only a minor issue in 1972; it became a visible influence on elections only in 1974. Moreover, if Watergate did have a depressing effect on turnout, that effect should have started to dissipate in 1980 as increasing numbers of younger citizens without memory or knowledge of those events have entered the electorate.

What of the younger voters? Perhaps they constitute an important factor in the explanation quite apart from the psychological effects of events in the early 1970s. Examining turnout as a function of contextual patterns since 1952, Hansen and Rosenstone (1984) found that every 10% increase in the proportion of the electorate under 25 caused a 3.3% drop in voting participation. They argued that nearly all of the decline between 1960 and 1968 and about one-half of the precipitous drop over the next four years was due to the electorate growing younger. While this is certainly a major factor, we must seek alternative explanations: Either other forces are keeping these young voters from voting as they grow older, or something is keeping older voters from voting as much as they used to, or both. Since franchise was extended to 18- to 20-year-olds in 1972, the proportion of the eligible electorate in the 18- to 20-year-old category has been steadily declining. As a result, turnout should be increasing.

Among the many possible alternative or complementary arguments that could possibly explain the decline in turnout, several seem plausible after careful examination. The first alternative is by far the easiest to demonstrate: The decline is not as much the result of a decrease in voter interest since 1960 as it is an artifact of artificially high levels of voter participation in the years leading up to 1960. The trend in voting before 1960 was upward at nearly an identical (but opposite) rate of change for midterm congressional elections, and close to the same change for presidential races. The current decline may be merely the reversal of a trend that peaked during the heated campaign between Kennedy and Nixon, and the early Kennedy years. This explanation, however, leaves much to be desired; it fails to answer the question of why political interest increased so rapidly between 1940 and 1960, as well as why participation dropped so rapidly after 1962. And it fails to explain why the rates of voting in the United States are usually well below those of most European democracies.

A second possibility, similar to the 18-year-old argument, is that the recent decline in turnout is the result of other baseline shifts in the demographic composition of the electorate. According to this argument, different population subgroups have continued to vote at the same rates, but the composition of the electorate has changed in such a way that subgroups with traditionally low turnout are growing, and those with high rates of turnout are shrinking. We know, for example, that rates of participation are related to economic well-being, the better off are more likely to participate. Since 1970, the long-term trend in the national economy has been downward; it is possible that this trend is responsible for a portion of the decline in turnout. Hansen and Rosenstone (1984) found that one-third of the drop in presidential voting over this period could be related to the percentage of citizens who identified the economy as the nation's most pressing problem. While they also found that direct measures of the economy could be related to the decline in voting, their perceptual indicator—those citing economic problems as most pressing—turned out to be a better predictor.

A major stumbling block for the general argument that low turnout subgroups have been expanding, however, can be located in the finding that education is the single largest factor affecting turnout (Wolfinger & Rosenstone, 1980). Since levels of education have been rising over this period, it seems unlikely that growth in lower SES groups would have such a large impact on turnout, especially given that the fastest and largest rise in levels of education is among the lowest SES groups.

Yet another line of argument suggests that the news media have been covering politics in such a way that voters have developed increased feelings of inefficacy or disinterest. While it is beyond the scope of this project to determine the direct impact of the media on voter attitudes, I do feel compelled to make a few observations about media coverage of elections. First, whereas media coverage of presidential elections used to begin in earnest only after Labor Day, the post-1968 party reforms to increase participation in the nomination phase have fostered an expansion of media coverage more than a year before the general election. The presidential contest now becomes a top news story during the fall preceding the presidential election years. Sixteen months of extensive and nearly continuous coverage may exhaust the interest of most citizens. Furthermore, the abundant polls released by news organizations may serve to make the presidential races even less exciting. If there is no secret about who is ahead of whom, some voters may feel that there is no point to their expending the energy to go to the voting booth. Worse still, election night forecasts in 1980 and 1984 told many Western voters the contest was completely over before they had a chance to vote. As the use of exit polls increases, we can expect more and more voters will hear predicted outcomes broadcast before they have even had a chance to cast their ballots. While the evidence is murky and disputed, these predictions may depress turnout.

The increased use of polls and the more saturated media coverage of elections may well lead to the furthering of citizens' feelings of inefficacy. Just as Watergate increased cynicism, media coverage and projections that cast an election as over before it begins make voters feel their participation is meaningless. We should note that the news media are not the sole (or even major) contributors to decreased efficacy, for certainly the actual political events covered by media have an impact.

Washington is far away from most people, and elected representatives are kept far too busy for many voters to feel their input is sought, heard, or acted upon. In short, the complexity and size of late twentieth-century government may have led to reduced feelings of citizen efficacy, which in turn results in reduced turnout.

We should also consider the fact that not only has government become very complex, but life in general is growing more hurried and complicated. Voters' lives are getting even more busy, leaving less time to perform the duty of a "good citizen." The workplace itself has become more specialized, requiring better command of technical skills. But more important, perhaps, is the tremendous growth of distractions available during the little leisure time citizens have left. In the days of smoke-filled back rooms, politics was a hobby. Today, there are many more hobbies to compete with politics. For the vast majority of citizens, politics has always been a leisure time concern. Now this interest may be giving way to many newer, perhaps more engaging, leisure activities.

A perplexing aspect to this problem is illuminated by comparisons to other industrial democracies. In recent elections, the United States has ranked near the bottom (twentieth out of twenty-one) in turnout as a percentage of voting-age population (Glass, Squire, & Wolfinger, 1984). While Glass and his coauthors point out that the United States does not do nearly as badly when turnout among registered voters is compared, their analysis is less persuasive on the point of why so few Americans register to vote. Granted our registration laws may be somewhat stiffer, but the burdens of going through the registration process do not seem that great. Moreover, many of the changes in political context we have discussed here—the demographic changes, the increased importance of media, the complexity of contemporary life-styles—are also being felt in most European democracies. We do not have an adequate account of why the United States is different, and until we do, the decline of participation will remain a troublesome problem.

We should recall, at this point, an observation made earlier: Voting is not the only form of political activity available to citizens. Reduced voter turnout may not mean a net reduction in political participation. In fact, many other forms of political participation may well be far more valuable both instrumentally and as a form of citizen duty. Working in a neighborhood association, donating money to a candidate, volunteering for a campaign, joining an interest group, going to political meetings, signing petitions, attending lawful demonstrations, or writing to elected officials are all more complete forms of political participation than is mere voting. These alternative forms of participation may have increased regardless of whatever apparent trend exists in voting turnout.

In the 1960s, political scientists Sidney Verba and Norman Nie (1972) conducted a major study of the instance of many forms of participation by the American people. They documented that citizens engage in these other political behaviors, such as campaigning, contributing money, writing letters, holding office, lobbying, and so forth, much less frequently than they vote. For example, around 40% reported trying to persuade others to vote a certain way, 25% said that they had recently written to a national or state official, and 20% remembered attending a meeting or political rally. They were able to classify only 11% of the population as "complete" activists; twice as many citizens fell into the "inactive" category. Despite these low rates, the comparative picture may be somewhat brighter for the United States; a study from the mid-1970s found that Americans exhibit higher rates of participation of these varieties than do citizens in Austria, the Netherlands, West Germany, and Great Britain (Barnes & Kaase, 1979).

Earlier, Lester Milbrath (1965) proposed that different behaviors could be ranked as a hierarchy, such that those who take part in higher forms of participation constitute an increasingly rarified group. While some individuals reach a plateau by, for example, limiting their involvement to voting, those at the top engage in the full range of "lower" participant behaviors.

Verba and Nie's data disproved the proposition of a strict hierarchy in these acts of participation. Some individuals engaged in letter writing and other forms of contacting officials, even though they had failed to vote. Milbrath's ranking is, nevertheless, intriguing as a statement of the degree of difficulty citizens encounter in engaging in these different behaviors. Voting is the easiest type of participation: it occurs at regular intervals; takes only a few minutes; is subsidized by the state; is well publicized by candidates, journalists, and voting officials; and is actively encouraged by society. Other forms of involvement cost the individual more, either in terms of time, skills, information, or money. In general, as these burdens increase across different forms of participation, the instance of involvement decreases. The most frequent behaviors are the least costly; the most costly are engaged in by the fewest citizens. It appears, in addition, that increased burdens can be associated with a stronger relationship between participation and indicators of social class (Keeter & Zukin, 1983, p. 184). The inequalities of involvement observed in measures such as education or income appear to become greater when we examine the more difficult forms of citizen involvement.

The notion of burdens or costs entailed by participant acts is close to the heart of this study, for if technology offers anything, it is an opportunity to reduce these burdens for citizens. By making participation easier for all, communication technologies may be able to reduce the inequalities that now severely grip different avenues for citizen involvement in policy-making.

In addition to investigating the instance of electoral involvement, Hansen and Rosenstone (1984) have used a data set compiled for other purposes by the Roper Poll to examine the declining instance of four nonelectoral forms of participation over the past decade. They found that interest in current events, letter writing to public officials, attending local meetings on town or school affairs, and signing petitions had all declined from 1974 to 1982. In each instance, they trace the decline to either changing demography or economic hardship.

> Interest in current events has declined over the 1970s because the demographic group that has little interest in politics has grown to comprise a larger proportion of the voting age population....Meeting attendance is 1.5 percentage points lower for every 10 point rise in the percentage who are worse off financially. Participation in local governance declines when people need the money, time, and energy to tend to their immediate financial needs. (pp. 31–32)

Hansen and Rosenstone conclude by disagreeing with those who contend that these declines are due to attitudinal changes such as the increase in the level of cynicism or a decline of trust in government or the sense of citizen duty. While these feelings accompany the failure to participate, they do not explain the decline once the characteristics of the political, economic, and social environment have been taken into account. Instead, these authors argue that citizens participate

> because they have the opportunity, because they have something at stake, because they have been stimulated, because they can afford it, or because someone else has mobilized them to act. (p. 39)

Their principal finding leads directly to the question posed by this research: Can communication technologies be used to stimulate political participation? Can we construct political institutions that use modern technology to increase the opportunities to participate, to communicate to citizens their stakes in politics, to reduce the costs and burdens associated with involvement, and to act as an agent mobilizing and catalyzing citizen involvement?

Perhaps we should first take up a more fundamental concern: Why should we be interested in encouraging political participation? The declining rates of participation constitute a more aggrevated public policy problem if they can be directly traced to the attitudinal problems discussed above. Rising cynicism, declining trust in government, and so forth paint a picture of a polity in trouble, a crisis of legitimacy in a system of government supposedly based upon the consent of the governed. Hansen and Rosenstone reject this argument based upon some persuasive evidence. If these attitudes and the rate of citizen participation are derived from different political and economic situations, then the problems are less deep-seated and may, in fact, be only temporary. Changing demography (i.e., a decline in the size of the youngest group of citizens) and a return of economic prosperity may lead to expanded participation.

Concern over the low rates of citizen participation would still be genuine for those who do not accept the legitimacy crisis argument, but the perceived nature of the problem would be different, based instead upon political inequality. Different social and economic interests have differential access to the information and resources that make participation possible. In fact, the general decline in citizen involvement may well have increased the level of inequality among social groups in their ability to put pressure on the governmental system. Presumably, this shift has resulted in greater responsiveness of the political system to the interests and benefits of those active, for example, those better off economically and organizationally.

In other words, the temptation may be strong to phrase the quest for expanded political participation in broad terms of a general crisis in the legitimacy of the American political system. This is the principal argument of the proponents of teledemocracy. However, a more empirically valid and, therefore, more responsible rationale should be staked upon the age-old pursuit of political equality. The political vitality of the American system is not in severe jeopardy, but it still has fallen well short of the ideal of government by the people.

This alternative approach highlights the importance of reducing the burdens and costs of citizen participation. Such improvements in the political circumstance within which American citizens act should provide the most promising way of reducing the existing inequities across social groups. If it is true that the more demanding the form of political participation, the steeper is the relationship to social and economic indicators, then the prospect of using communication technology to reduce these inequalities seems promising indeed.

The Participation Projects

For this book, I will analyze thirteen different projects in which elites set out to encourage political activity by citizens. Analytically, these projects constitute a degree of tinkering or experimenting with various institutional arrangements for containing political participation. As such, they take a different approach than that employed by most academic writings on participation that gives attention to explanations of the ways individuals behave. By examining the institutional context within which participation occurs, we may gain insights beyond the numerical instance of participation, moving on to investigate the quality and effectiveness of citizen involvement.

Many of the projects studied were demonstration or pilot projects deliberately conceived to research the possibilities offered by new technology. About half of them, however, were serious attempts to establish new mechanisms that would involve the public more extensively in public policy formation. Detailed evaluations of the teledemocracy projects can be found in Chapters Four through Seven.[2]

Alaska's Legislative Teleconferencing Network. State legislative committees can take testimony from citizens scattered all over our largest state. The system is supplemented by a computer network containing information about pending legislation and amendments and the timing of floor and committee action. Electronic mail messages may be sent via the computer network to legislators in Juneau.

Alternatives for Washington. From 1974 to 1976, then Governor Daniel Evans of Washington organized a planning project to consider future directions across a range of state policy issues. A group of citizens, nominated by political leaders and interest groups, were brought together to discuss future directions in detail. Their work was subsequently submitted to broad public choice in the form of mailed back newspaper ballots. The project also solicited citizen participation in the form of numerous community meetings, questionnaires, and telephone polls.

Berks Community Television (BCTV). Located in Reading, Pennsylvania, BCTV provides city and county officials with regular opportunities to discuss via a cable channel their policies and actions with citizens who telephone questions and complaints to the studio. In addition to "electronic office hours," Reading public officials frequently hold official hearings to discuss and solicit citizen input in their planning processes.

Choices for '76. Designed in 1973 to facilitate planning in the New York metropolitan region, Choices for '76 consisted of five films aired on 18 stations in the New York area. Citizens returned ballots printed in local newspapers covering five different regional issues.

Computer Conferences on The Source and EIES. Computer conferences are just beginning to emerge as a communications vehicle open to a growing number of owners of personal and minicomputers. The Electronic Information Exchange System (EIES) and The Source Telecomputing Corporation (STC) provide to the public the most extensively used computer conferencing systems open to their subscribers. I examined both the political content of open conferences and the pattern of participation within discussions of public policy issues.

Des Moines Health Vote '82. Sponsored by the Public Agenda Forum in December 1982, Health Vote '82 involved a substantial proportion of the Des Moines, Iowa, community in a sophisticated campaign combining public relations skills with a detailed presentation of the significant trade-offs in health care service delivery. Citizens returned ballots printed in the Des Moines Register.

Domestic Policy Association: National Issues Forum. The Domestic Policy Association (DPA), a joint project of the Kettering Foundation and the Public Agenda Foundation, stages each fall a nationwide series of community meetings or issue forums to discuss and debate three selected policy matters each year. After the local meetings have concluded, the DPA holds a large, national meeting in which representatives from around the country can discuss these same matters with "decision makers" linked through a satellite distributed videoconference to an increasingly large number of sites around the country.

Hawaii Televote. Actually the Televote project is a series of discrete efforts undertaken by Professor Ted Becker at the University of Hawaii. First, a random sample of citizens are telephoned and asked if they are willing to participate in the vote. The project staff sends those who agree ballots and information describing all aspects of the selected policy question. They are given a certain interval to read about the topic and to consider and discuss it with others. Finally, the participants either call in to cast their votes or are called back by the project's initiators.

Honolulu Electronic Town Meetings. The electronic town meetings in Hawaii combine television shows on the pro's and con's of a particular issue with two forms of voting. Citizens who wish to express an opinion are able to participate by mailing back the ballots from the newspapers or by calling in to register their opinions during and after the broadcast.

Markey's "Electure." From December 1983 to February 1984, subscribers to The Source Telecomputing Network could participate in an "electure" lead by Congressman Edward Markey (D-Mass). By entering his position papers into a computer conference, Markey initiated a series of discussions on different aspects of American nuclear arms policy. Those who joined the conference could react to his thoughts and those of other contributors.

MINERVA Electronic Town Meeting. Designed by a sociologist (Amitai Etzioni) and an engineer, MINERVA was an attempt to broaden participation in the regular meetings of a community group without diminishing the quality of participation. Panelists discussed the various aspects of an issue over a cable access channel serving the apartment complex, and residents could walk to a convenient room in order to videotape their response to the presentation or the comments of others. At the end of this electronically mediated discussion, viewers were asked to fill out a questionnaire in which they stated their response to the show, their opinions as to how the matter should be handled, and their satisfaction with the experiment.

North Carolina's OPEN/net. North Carolina's OPEN/net is a continuing project of the state's Agency for Public Telecommunications. Weekly three-hour shows are produced on matters under consideration by various legislative and executive agencies and are distributed by satellites to over 50 cable systems around the state. During the first half, viewers watch an unedited, videotaped meeting or hearing in which state government officials deal with a pending policy matter. Then, citizens from around the state have an opportunity to telephone comments, complaints or questions to studio guests who are usually the key decision makers in the areas under consideration.

Upper Arlington Town Meeting over Qube. Installed by Warner-Amex in Columbus, Ohio, as part of its franchise agreements, the Qube interactive system gave the paying subscriber a box of push buttons with which to signal a response to questions posed during a cablecast. A central computer quickly processed the results, allowing viewers and interested others to learn the outcome of such a poll instantaneously. One of the most dramatic uses of Qube involved a four-hour planning meeting held in the Columbus suburb of Upper Arlington. A presentation by the Planning Board on traffic and zoning problems evoked considerable discussion and a high level of "voting" over Qube by the town's residents.

Institutional Characteristics
of Participation

Let us take a look at these projects analytically. We need to examine the nature of citizen involvement that each project attempted to stimulate and the institutional constraints imposed upon that participation.

Political participation is a concept for which nearly everybody has a rough, general understanding. On the one hand, most people can look at another person's actions and agree as to whether or not those actions are "political." And we all carry around a rudimentary notion of participation as interactive behavior through which citizens are involved in influencing policy-making. However, in evaluating the successes or strengths of different institutional frameworks for democratic participation (or to establish such systems for that matter), one must employ a more specific definition of political participation than these intuitive understandings provide.

The first step is to consider precisely what is meant by participation. Immediately a host of disputes crop up. One could argue, for example, that watching the six o'clock news constitutes participation in the U.S. political system, even though that behavior is essentially passive. Similarly, one might propose that for each individual citizen voting in an election is not truly participation since, after all, the impact of a single vote is effectively meaningless. But rather than getting snarled hopelessly in numerous definitional problems of a theoretical nature, I think, for the purposes of this study, it is better to take an operational approach. That is, I will allow a conception of participation to emerge from the projects that billed themselves as endeavors to encourage political participation. By noting the distinctions among the projects in the goals and objectives of those who organized them, we are led to a number of subtle nuances in the nature of political participation. For example, who should be eligible to participate in the first place, and what are the grounds on which those not eligible to participate should be excluded? Who decides how issues are ultimately framed? Who determines the order in which issues arise? What if these decisions affect the outcome of participation?

Let us look at this from the viewpoint of the project initiators. Essentially, they face a series of decisions as to the desirable characteristics of a participatory process and the institutions designed to structure that process. Ultimately it is the manner in which these problems of management, administration, and incorporation of participants are solved that determines the success or failure of the experiment. Their decisions about how to manage the participatory elements of a project are the direct results of the trade-offs in the priorities they are willing to establish among conflicting values. In order to evaluate the strengths of the various projects, we must first decipher the operational characteristics of the participatory process the initiators established. Thus our evaluation of the extent to which these projects facilitated political involvement becomes an examination of how each project's initiators dealt with various problematic characteristics of participatory systems in general.

We wish to analyze systems and to describe the institutions through which participant behavior is channeled. With the exception of recent work undertaken by Mark Hansen (1985) or the earlier studies of Janice Perlman and the other authors in Langton's collection (1978), few studies have examined the institutional context in which participation occurs. The following discussion[3] falls well short of a comprehensive treatment of all the elements of democratic participation that one might consider in designing or evaluating a participatory process in the abstract. Rather, the points to be discussed emerged from a study of the various teledemocracy projects, and they provide the best means of distinguishing among these efforts. A complete discussion could have considered other institutional elements, such as, for example, the distinction between legitimate and nonlegitimate forms of participation. Since all of the projects studied here set out to encourage legitimate forms of activity, however, I have omitted this dimension from the list that follows. As a result, while the inventory here is not all inclusive, it is comprehensive enough to evaluate the structural advantages of uses of new technology in facilitating political participation.

Given that we are interested in extending democratic participation, a natural beginning to this discussion can be found by asking whether a participant system allows equal *access* by all members of the community. Conversely, there might be restrictions upon who can participate and under what conditions? The cable system in Reading, for example, allows something close to universal access. Because television reception in the city is very poor, cable penetration is high. Those without a telephone or television can drop into the studio whenever a BCTV takes to the air. To cite a counter example, the political use of the Qube system in Columbus offers access only to those served by the Warner cable franchise who pay the extra charge for interactive service. Meanwhile, participants in telephone surveys conducted in Hawaii televotes or by the Alternatives for Washington project could take part only if they were selected by those conducting the poll.

The way in which a participatory system handles matters of access says a great deal about how open or widespread the organizers truly desire participation to be. At some point, designing a participatory system that allows access to only a very few is obviously not an effort to increase democratic participation.

The second dimension integrally linked to access, is the notion of access *reach*; it is a measurement of how many of those who could participate actually do take part. Using this terminology in the electorial context, one might note that while the right to vote (access) is constitutionally guaranteed to almost all adult citizens, the actual number that turn out (reach) is significantly smaller. Many prospective participants are not reached by the normal electoral process.

Among the teledemocracy projects, I observed several different reasons for low levels of reach. In some cases, the institution established to channel participation became overloaded; for example, in some cases more people wanted to call in than the phone systems could handle. Most televised call-in programs can take only about 20 calls per hour. In other cases, citizens prove to be largely indifferent to the participatory system. From what one can observe of forums conducted over the Qube systems, for example, it appears that only a small number of the potential participants actually watch these shows and respond to the questions.

Ideally, a participatory system, assuming it is to fulfill democratic principles, should be designed and implemented in such a way as to maximize both access and reach. The media employed in any given effort can effectively limit both. More troublesome for those who hope that technology will spark, or at least facilitate, near universal participation, is the observation that frequently the gap between access and reach can become uncomfortably large.

These projects also differed as to whether citizen participation had an actual impact on policy or was a simple exercise in process. I will refer to this third dimension as the *effectiveness* of participation. Practically speaking, if participation is absolutely incapable of having any effect on the final policy outcome, citizens may consider their effort to be largely a waste of time. In this regard, many of the teledemocracy projects are open to serious question. As we shall see in Chapter Four, projects in which formal political leaders are not directly involved usually perform poorly on this dimension of participation.

A fourth dimension raises the so-called *agenda-setting* question. Determination of who controls the agenda of a political system can be one of the most crucial aspects of organizing citizen participation. What issues will or will not come before the participants? In what order will the issues be decided? How will the questions and discussions be framed? What information will be provided? Who will provide this information? Who will decide these questions? The answers to these questions may have more to do with the final outcomes than any other characteristic of the system.

The Qube system, for example, allows the viewers at home virtually no flexibility in which questions are put to a vote, how they are worded, when they will be discussed, and when they will be decided upon by participants. Participants can only respond to choices framed by someone else. This situation is not unknown in traditional politics; it is rather like that faced by a voter deciding on a ballot issue. In other cases, technology can provide participants with significantly more latitude in influencing the agenda. Electronic office hours, for example, allow constituents to talk about whatever is on their minds, while interest groups and lobbyists can try to use the opportunity technology provides to reformulate a legislative issue to their benefit.

Project organizers face a difficult trade-off here: giving more latitude for participants to control the agenda also requires more from them in the way of involvement. When participants can influence the agenda, they must exercise more initiative and, to be effective, they must be better informed. A higher level of demand, however, may restrict the reach of a project. But if one decides to leave agenda setting to the project initiators, then one immediately establishes an elite that can exercise disproportionate power by virtue of its ability to control the timing and framing of decisions. Unduly tight control over the agenda may stifle the interactive aspects of participation and thereby effectively diminish the project's reach.

In general, there exists an inverse relationship between citizen control over the agenda and the reach of a project. The larger the number of participants sought, the more project initiators engineer the system and, thereby, reduce the latitude allowed citizens. While there is obviously a certain logic to this relationship, the process involved is more complicated than a simple cause-and-effect chain.

A separate point is whether political institutions permit citizens alternative strategies for exerting influence. I refer to this rather complex notion as the *diversity of access paths*. In evaluating an institutional design for citizen participation, we must ask whether diversity exists in the information sources and the avenues of participation such that people at all levels of the socioeconomic and education ladders can learn and participate according to their abilities, interests, and needs. Many of the teledemocracy projects under consideration here designed into their plans multiple mechanisms whereby citizens could acquire knowledge of the system, learn the substantive material being considered, and actually participate. For example, in Alternatives for Washington, the organizers communicated through many different media so that whether a citizen was a newspaper reader or a television news watcher or simply received information from billboards, he or she still had a way of learning about the project. Then they organized local and regional meetings, mailed back ballot campaigns, and conducted telephone and questionnaire surveys so that citizens had a variety of ways of expressing their opinions.

Assumedly, the greater the diversity of a system the more readily it can reach a broader number of participants in ways that will not intimidate or bore them. A broader range of participation paths also allows citizens with different capacities and skills to choose the means of involvement with which they feel most comfortable. Accordingly, these systems may enhance their effectiveness and extend their reach.

The length of time and number of iterations over which a participatory system is intended to operate, or *duration*, can have major consequences. The rate of partipation, the legitimacy conferred upon a system, and the system's ability to achieve its goals, can all be affected. Projects that are planned to last only for a short time or as a one-time experiment deny citizens the possibility of benefiting from actual political experience in trial-and-error adjustments. They are, moreover, less likely to be taken seriously by potential participants. Prospective participants are asked to take time from their lives to become involved in something that may not be around for much longer and that has not yet demonstrated an ability to deliver on its promise.

Naturally, the duration of the project will have much to do with its initial goals. Most often single iteration time projects will have short-term goals suited to shorter durations; they tend, for example, to be confined to one policy area rather than providing an instrument in which a broad range of public policy can be addressed.

Teledemocracy projects that attempt to determine how new technologies can be used in a one-time experiment suffer the additional handicap that their findings may be differcnt from what would be learned in a long-term application of the same technology. The novelty of a new "gimmick" will draw attention, yet the knowledge that the gimmick is only a trial or a passing fad will discourage potential participants or, at the very least, alter their behavior.

Consider yet another dimension: It is pertinent to ask whether participants took part in the devised system as individuals or whether they acted as members or representatives of interest groups. Does the system promote *group-based or individual* participation? As we know from observing the normal conduct of American politics, there is a tremendous difference between a democratic system in which the relevant actors are interest groups rather than individuals. In such a case, participants have to base their claims and arguments on the impact of an outcome on their societal group, and individuals without a relevant group affiliation may be denied a voice. On the other hand, if the only legitimate claims that can be made are those by individuals, then participants may lose the important benefit of participation organized and backed by large groups.

Whether the project organizers perceived appropriate political behavior as the involvement of autonomous individuals rather than interest-group members, produced important differences in the technology they utilized and the role they assigned to participation. Group involvement was associated with longer-term institutions and with efforts to exchange information and negotiate differences. These requirements lead to technology in which citizens could converse with each other or with political leaders. If citizen participation was viewed, on the other hand, as requiring the involvement of a large mass of individuals, then the broadcast media were seen as perfect for this communication.

Another important distinguishing feature among these projects can be derived from observing the level of *initiative* required of citizen participants. Did a given system foster self-starters, or did participants have to be contacted, encouraged, and perhaps mildly coerced by elites? For example, in some projects, the organizers make numerous calls to encourage participants to do their part. In other cases, citizens become involved entirely as self-motivated volunteers. These latter institutions require participants to exercise a much higher level of initiative; the former may impose a mild degree of coercion to stimulate involvement.

All other things being equal, the ideal system would be one where participant behavior is free of inducement and coercion, relying instead on the interest and dedication of those taking part. But this dimension also appears to be inversely associated with reach: the higher the level of initiative required, the lower the practical reach of the project. In general, the politically active seek to mobilize the inactive by lowering the initiative required of them.

To some degree, participation involves inconvenience or lost opportunities for engaging in other activities. The dimension of *costs* attempts to assess these burdens. To what degree do participants have to inconvenience themselves in order to take part? Costs of this sort can be either monetary or nonmonetary. For example, taking part in a computer conferencing experiment requires not only that one buy the appropriate machinery, but that the user also subscribe to the computer network that will carry the conference. Participating in a mail back ballot campaign may not require large monetary outlays, but in order to do it correctly, citizens must spend a substantial amount of time learning about the issue in question.

At some level, individuals should have to bear only minimal costs for their participation. However, costs cannot be eliminated for if participants are to learn enough about the issues before them to make choices for themselves or their communities, they will have to invest some of their time in the process. This investment will no doubt discourage many potential participants. The amount of effort, energy, or monetary resources that a system requires from its participants will, therefore, be a telling characteristic as to how the organizers chose to handle the trade-off between broad inclusion and informed participation. Of course, the whole idea of using communication technologies to encourage participation is directly related to the possibilities of lowering the costs that must be borne by participants.

In many cases, participants come away from the process better informed over a range of policy issues under consideration. We should not ignore the *educative value* of participation. Other things being equal, we would prefer that participants learn something as a result of their taking part in the project. Certainly, one of the by-products of participation ought to be educating the public. While this dimension is one to which organizers can easily pay attention, yet it is not always the case that the projects operate in a way as to educate the public on the issues being considered.

Finally, related to the educational aspects, a separate question concerns whether or not a project fostered the development of citizen skills necessary for responsible participation in a democracy. I refer to this as *political competence* building. Did participants develop leadership skills, a sense of self-confidence, and competence in dialogues and discussion? Did they acquire knowledge of the functioning of the political institution? Some projects neglected this aspect; others made it their *raison d'être*. These eleven dimensions are summarized in Table 3-1.

I should recall for the reader that this exercise is largely one of brute empiricism; these dimensions were defined inductively on the basis of how the projects differed. Often the differences were only in matters of degree. This inductive approach was forced upon us by the inadequacies in the existing writings about participation, material that largely ignores the contextual elements—primarily the institutional structure—within which participation occurs. Here we need this conceptualization to get on with the work at hand; one hopes that this effort to poke a little way down this path will stimulate others to explore these structural dimensions in greater detail.

TABLE 3.1
Dimensions of Institutions for Citizen Participation

(1) access—the range of citizens able to participate in a teledemocracy project.

(2) reach—the percentage of those citizens able to participate who actually do become involved.

(3) effectiveness—whether or not citizen participation can have a direct influence upon public policy.

(4) agenda setting—the level of control citizens are able to exercise over the issues to be decided, the alternatives to be considered, the timing of and order of participation, and so forth.

(5) diversity of access paths—the number of ways through which citizens can learn about and participate in a project.

(6) duration—the length of time and number of iterations over which an institution for citizen participation lasts.

(7) individual or group based—whether citizens can participate as individuals or as members of organized interest groups.

(8) initiative—the degree to which citizens must discover and generate for themselves opportunities to become involved and the information upon which that involvement is based.

(9) costs—the burdens, financial and otherwise, imposed on citizens in connection with their participation.

(10) educative value—the degree to which participants learn about the subject matter or policy area under consideration.

(11) political competence—through their participation in a teledemocracy project, the skills and confidence to become more generally politically active.

Conceptions of Political Participation

While these distinctions prove fruitful in assessing the strengths and weaknesses of the projects studied, their number naturally raises the question as to whether any of them are more important than the others. In analyzing these efforts at teledemocracy, I found that two broad, theoretical questions provided the most powerful vantage point for understanding the major differences among projects. That is, the basic architecture of citizen participation was shaped by definitional choices as to (1) whether or not political participation should have direct impact on public policy and (2) whether the project was intended to stimulate community consensus or to foster an exchange and accommodation of differing interests. Both of those questions are broadly theoretical in nature, and they reach into disputes that have plagued students of government since Aristotle. Not surprisingly, therefore, I will be unable to settle these issues definitively in this study. Rather, by highlighting them I hope to serve notice that those who set out to encourage participation will have to answer these questions for themselves either explicitly or implicitly. Their answers will affect the design choices they make in establishing an institutional context within which citizens will be asked to participate.

The first question revolves around whether or not the definition of participation should refer only to citizen efforts to influence directly the selection of political officials or their official actions. Some scholars, observers, and project organizers prefer to include the efforts of citizens to discuss and debate policy matters whether or not these actions are intended to achieve a direct political impact. Through such activities, citizens may gain the competence, knowledge, and propensity necessary to influence public policy in the future.

Regardless of which side of this dispute one prefers, the distinction reveals a great deal about the goals of the initiators, reflecting in part their normative views of the relationship between citizens and the state. On one side, we find instrumentalists who believe that government is the creation of society to provide collective and individual benefits. People enter into politics in order to improve their well-being. On the other side, the state has an expressive function that is viewed as just as important as the self-serving aspect. Government exists both as a manifestation of a sense of community among citizens and in order to create and nurture the community. Participation in politics should, therefore, include activities in which people both learn and express their collective bonds in symbols and joint behavior.

The second theoretical distinction or choice that project initiators must make is derived from their conception of the citizenry. Some may believe that there exists a general will of the citizenry as an organic whole; others conceive of the citizenry as a composite of individual and particular interests, such that a general consensus, desire, or purpose either does not exist or is decidedly secondary as a motive for political activity.

In either case, participation is key. If the objective of democratic politics is to nurture the general will of the citizenry, participation provides a means by which citizens share their needs and desires so that a consensus can emerge. Thus educative processes of citizen participation should be encouraged, for they constitute the best means of making the general will manifest. On the other hand, those who view the citizenry as composed of separate and particular interests believe that participation is the best way to register those interests in concrete form. In this view, the objective of political processes must be to negotiate and compromise differing interests in order to achieve workable policies.

By interviewing many of those who had established participation projects or by reading their reports and articles, I discovered that often projects are instituted to faciliate the emergence of a general will among the citizenry as a whole. For these organizers, the promise of participation was to provide a means to identify public policies that enjoy near consensus. They use technology to allow "the people" to decide matters for themselves; they assume that a broad set of interests unites the public. That is, these projects adopted a "populist" conception of the appropriate role of citizen participation.

In contrast, other project directors argued that political interests are diverse and in conflict, a conception that has been called the "pluralist" perspective on politics. For those who hold this view, politics is marked by the struggle for advantage among conflicting goals and aspirations, rather than the pursuit of a common good. By this telling, it is not meaningful to speak of "The People," for the citizens are conceptualized as broken up into groups with different interests and different resources. Politics is the interplay of the forces unleashed by differing interests and intensities of concern. The law of the jungle is kept in check by the fact that every individual belongs, of course, to many groups simultaneously. Thus pluralists believe that politics is not necessarily warfare; instead they look upon political institutions as mechanisms for negotiating, bargaining, and compromising these interests. Democracy is viewed almost as the absence of total domination of this bargaining by one group or coalition.

The lines of these two arguments can be traced in the highest-level theorizing of political philosophers. But, I also found them deeply embedded in the thinking of those who set out to encourage participation; that is, these theoretical debates were reflected in decisions that project initiators made in trying to encourage participation. First, an important divergence among participation projects could be discerned in whether or not political officials were directly involved in the project. Many of these projects were structured so that citizens could interact directly with political leaders, the authoritative decision makers who would actually establish public policy. These projects constituted operational expression of the effectiveness test for participation: a belief that citizen involvement must be intended to influence directly the recruitment or behavior of public authorities. On the other hand, in many other projects, the political authorities were not involved, and in these instances, the project initiators placed a greater value on the educative aspects of citizen involvement. As they saw it, participation in their projects would exert a longer-run or less immediate impact on policy. Through their involvement, citizens would learn about specific policy matters and acquire civic skills for the future.

A second projection from theoretical disputes down to empirical distinction occurred among these projects: Whether the initiators sought to encourage a dialogue or to conduct a vote of citizen preferences reflected their assumptions about the existence of a common will. For those populists who conceived of the citizenry as an organic whole, the natural outcome of participation was to register that general will through some voting mechanism. A plebiscite would allow the "voice of the people" to be heard loud and clear. On the other hand, those who saw the citizenry as composed of particular interests searched for ways in which participation could promote mutual understanding, bargaining, and compromise. Rather than channel citizen involvement into a plebiscite, these initiators sought to encourage a continuous dialogue among citizens and groups of citizens, hoping that public policies could be adjusted to competing vested interests and readjusted to satisfy emerging demands and aggrieved parties. They wished to promote and expand the influence of individual citizens and groups in politics, rather than to have the citizenry as a whole reach a decision.

These two dimensions are arrayed in Table 3.2. In this fourfold distinction, "focus of participant activity" directs our attention toward whether or not citizens are able to express their wants and needs directly to governmental actors or agencies. The projects investigated either attempted to engage citizens directly in the ongoing processes of government decision making or they were somewhat more tangential endeavors. The "nature of participation" dimension refers to whether the project initiators wished primarily to stage a plebiscite of sorts or whether they sought to promote discussion and dialogue.

Upon first impression, the involvement of government officials (or lack thereof) appears fairly straightforward. In assigning projects to one category or another, however, I had to distinguish between whether political leaders were engaged in their official capacities as governmental authorities or were merely acting symbolically. For example, a governor might appear on a television show in connection with an effort to involve citizens in policy discussions but not intend that, by so doing, he or she would be opening a new formal avenue for citizen influence on policy. The distinction here only makes sense if we confine the notion of governmental projects to those instances in which formal authorities act in their official capacities and intend to pay due regard to citizen input.

TABLE 3.2
Major Distinctions Among the Teledemocracy Projects

Nature of Participation	Focus of Participation	
	Governmental	Private
Dialogues	Berks Community TV Alaska LTN North Carolina OPEN/net Markey's "Electure"	Computer conferences Domestic Policy Assoc.

Plebiscites	Alternatives for Wash.
	Upper Arlington Town
	  Meeting by QUBE
	Health Vote '82
		Hawaii Televote
		Honolulu Electronic
		  Town Meeting
		Choices for '76
		MINERVA

We do not require that citizen participation definitively determine their policies, only that they are susceptible to influence.

Those projects in which government officials were not involved emphasized instead the personal development of civic competence and consensus rather than a direct impact on public policy outcomes. In the course of this study, I investigated examples of projects conducted by a variety of private or nongovernmental actors, such as academics (Hawaii Televote, *Minerva* project), groups of planners or futurists (the futures or goals projects), nonpartisan foundations (the Domestic Policy Association, Health Vote '82), and even private corporations (Warner-Amex's Qube, "Participate" on The Source).

Whether they were staged by government officials or someone else, strictly speaking, none of the projects investigated held a true plebiscite. That is, while they all involved a voting mechanism and thus deserve the label, in no case did the expressed citizen preferences actually determine public policies.

I should warn the reader that the number of projects investigated by this research in each grouping does not reflect the distribution of all participation projects that have been attempted in the last decade and a half. If I had chosen a random sample of all projects, the goals or futures projects—which fall mainly in the upper right quadrient—would have been much more abundant. Instead, I purposively selected projects to represent the many ways in which communication technologies have been used to promote participation. Where projects were similar in terms of how participation was encouraged and structured, however, I chose to investigate only a few of them, reportedly the most well run.

The next four chapters follow the lines of this basic architecture. In the next, we will take up the plebiscitory projects organized without the direct involvement of government officials. Here we find those efforts organized in the spirit of teledemocracy; most of the initiators see their efforts as experimentation with a transformation of our political institutions. Subsequent chapters will take up each of the other major types of teledemocracy projects.

Notes

1. These turnout data are taken from *The Statistical Abstract of the United States,* U.S. Department of Commerce, Bureau of the Census, 1986, (Washington: Government Printing Office, 1985) p. 255.

2. Research reported elsewhere (Arterton, Lazarus, Griffen, & Andres, 1984) discusses twenty different projects, some of which were dropped from this book because they were duplicative of other projects or did not really fit the selection criterion of using telecommunication technologies.

3. I owe a considerable debt to my research assistant Edward Lazarus for his help in thinking through these dimensions and in drafting an initial version of this section.

CHAPTER 4

BRINGING "THE PEOPLE"
INTO POLITICS

Throughout our history, many Americans have remained suspicious of organized politics. The belief that technology may provide a needed antidote to the problems created by a representative system is the latest manifestation of a long tradition of American political thought that deplores the usurpation by political elites of power justly residing among the citizenry. The Declaration of Independence was, after all, a flamboyant rejection of unaccountable political power, and the Constitution devised a unique and elaborate architecture to contain the abuses of sovereign power derived from the consent of the governed.

Austin Ranney's (1975) prominent study of changes in the presidential selection process is one of many arguments that a gradual erosion has occurred in institutions that were designed to mediate between the governed and those who govern. This scholarship highlights a political chronology from initial domination by a landed aristocracy through expansion of the franchise, collapse of the congressional caucus, the institution of primary elections and direct elections for senator, and presidential nomination reforms.

Political change in this direction, while episodic, may not have been exhausted: when asked, the American public registers huge majorities in favor of further modifications such as the creation of a national primary or elimination of the electoral college. Intellectually, the call for direct democracy, for allowing the people themselves to decide policies and priorities, may reach a substantial and sympathetic audience.

The discussion in Chapter One summarized the theoretical arguments for citizen participation in political decision making which might occur through emerging technology. These predictions and normative proposals have stimulated various experiments and demonstrations in which citizens are induced to become more active in politics. Given the numbers involved, these efforts have usually confined citizen involvement to voting, although frequently discussion does precede the plebiscite.

The Private Plebiscites

Among the teledemocracy projects introduced briefly in Chapter Three, four were plebiscitarian efforts that did not involve government officials. I will describe each of these privately sponsored plebiscites in detail, and then turn to discussion of their comparative strengths and weaknesses.

CHOICES FOR '76

In 1973, the Regional Plan Association (RPA) of New York conducted the most ambitious project studied in this research, "Choices for '76." The Association had been actively trying to engage citizens in discussion of regional planning issues for more than ten years prior to their more extensive effort in CHOICES. RPA had established a pattern of public engagement combining television productions with small, locally arranged, face-to-face meetings in which citizens discussed the issues raised in the documentary and completed questionnaires expressing their opinions.

The project director for CHOICES, Michael McManus, felt that this established process of public engagement, which involved contacts through dozens of governments and organizations, needed to be improved by a large dose of direct citizen participation. He wanted to give citizens from Trenton to New Haven "information on issues effecting their lives and the opportunity to be heard on what they felt ought to be done to solve various problems" (Shore, Anderson, McManus, Goldbeck, & Hack, 1974, p. 9). In the process, RPA hoped to enlarge the number and type of persons who took part "by stimulating the passive majority to express their viewpoints on issues now decided under pressure from a vocal minority" (p. 10).

In conducting CHOICES, the RPA enlisted the cooperation of 18 New York area television stations that agreed to broadcast a series of five programs presenting major issues facing the region (housing, transportation, environments, poverty, and relations between cities and suburbs). Fifteen daily newspapers printed ballots for all five "Town Meetings" so that citizens could mail back their views to the RPA. These papers had a total circulation of 2 1/4 million. Thirty-one weeklies also published the ballots and another 11 dailies printed four of the five ballots. In addition, these publications ran news articles on the meetings, editorials, and advertisements (which were paid by corporate contributions). The RPA also prepared a background book discussing the 51 critical policy choices facing the region. Inexpensive copies were sold at newsstands and bookstores in the area and distributed by many social science teachers.

The RPA made a detailed effort to assess participation in CHOICES: They conducted an analysis of their television audience, prepared careful tabulations of the returned ballots, and asked a random sample survey to assess the impact of the shows on citizen opinion. By their figures, a very large number of citizens watched these broadcasts—an average of 500,000 residents watched each show. In the process the residents presumably learned something about regional issues. The RPA arranged small group meetings wherever possible to discuss these matters. They estimate that between 20,000 and 30,000 people attended these meetings. An average of 26,500 citizens returned ballots on each of the five issues.

These figures demonstrate a measure of success; large numbers of citizens participated in the project through one of its five means (watching TV, reading newspaper articles, returning the ballots, reading the book, or attending a meeting). In the process, CHOICES expanded awareness of regional planning issues among the affected population: pre- and postsurveys conducted by the Gallup Organization demonstrated that CHOICES did measurably affect opinions held on some issues by the regional populace at large.

These accomplishments are demonstrably better than politics as usual or than normally accomplished through traditional political institutions such as lobbying or attending hearings. There is, however, another side to this picture. Given that the project organizers justified such a massive effort by stressing the need to let the citizens or the people participate in policy-making, we think it fair to compare participation in CHOICES against the standard of universal involvement or even against turnout in elections. In these comparisons, the rates of involvement in the RPA project do not stand up very well.

There are, to be sure, some problems computing the number of people involved in CHOICES. Estimates of the TV audience are roughly drawn, and we cannot be certain how many read the book, read newspaper articles, or attended the meetings. One also encounters problems in deciding the appropriate denominators to use when calculating the participation rates. For example, in figuring the rate of involvement in the plebiscites should one use the total number of adult citizens in the region or the number of ballots printed? Similarly, in figuring out the percentage that viewed the CHOICES broadcasts, one could use either estimates of the total number watching television during the broadcasts or the number of citizens in the adult population. Even if we adopt the most advantageous numbers, however, turnout was disappointingly low.

While 500,000 is a lot of viewers for public affairs programming, the number of potential participants is vast: There are 6 million households in the region. If one considers only those households that were actually watching television at the time of a CHOICES program, the result is still well below expectations: Only one broadcast (at 1 p.m. on WCBS on Sunday) drew more than 10% of the audience. Since each program was aired repeatedly throughout a three-day period on different stations in the region (as many as 23 broadcasts), the overall audience is undoubtedly larger (although one cannot simply add up the percentage from each broadcast). A Gallup survey estimated that 14% of the region's adults had seen at least one of the films.

The rate of ballot returns was particularly disappointing. A conservative estimate suggests that more than 2 1/4 million were distributed in each of the five waves. An average of 26,500 were returned to the RPA, which translates to a rate of 1%.

Finally, the number of citizens participating in discussion groups was also infinitesimal: By the most expansive calculation, only around 25,000 took part in the first and most successful town meeting. (Gallup put the number at 20,000.) We do not mean to underrate the difficulty and amount of work necessary to involve that number of citizens to community meetings, but in terms of the pretentious goals of the undertaking, the actual delivery was modest.

Because of its scope and length, and due, in no small part, to the integrity of the reports issued by the CHOICES staff, this project allows us to study a marked decline in citizen participation over the life of the project. Nearly every rate of involvement in CHOICES fell from the first to the fifth wave. By the last program, the total estimated television audience for CHOICES had dropped to 64% of those that watched the first production (from 700,000 to 450,000). Much of this decline, but not all, can be attributed to a general decrease in television viewing, which fell to 71% over the period as the spring prime season turned into summer reruns.

Watching programs such as those produced by CHOICES is, moreover, a fairly passive form of involvement. The more active forms suffered even sharper declines. The returned ballots dropped from 41,000 to 14,500 (one half of a percent of the ballots distributed), which means that the last return was only 35% of the first. Similarly, the estimated audience at discussion meetings declined continually, so that by the end the number attending these meetings was only half of those who turned out for the first set (25,500 down to 13,000).

One reason for this decline may be related to our test of the effectiveness of participation. The RPA is a private association that sought to involve the citizens in a discussion of public policy. They did not, however, make any systematic attempts to involve government officials in the project (as in placing them on the receiving end of all this participation), although McManus hoped that "if many people got involved, the politicians would have to listen to what people said ought to be done" (Shore et al., p. 9). The final report states, "We were going to ask the public for a great deal of their time and promise to try to lever their opinions into political action" (p. 36), but the project did not develop an institutional structure that would allow this to happen. A small sample of public officials in the region conducted by the Gallup Organization found that only a third of those contacted had themselves even watched one or more of the CHOICES broadcasts. In short, public officials simply were not brought into the project in a way that would encourage responsiveness to the citizen participation stimulated.

As a result, while the self-enhancing dimensions of education and political competence building are clearly satisfied in CHOICES, citizens may have wondered what the purposes of their participation were. This argument is especially true of mail back ballots, which suffered the most marked drop in involvement. Watching television and attending discussions have their own rewards. The CHOICES staff may have aggrevated this problem in the difficulties they encountered in disseminating the ballot results. The ballots came in sporadically and processing them proved burdensome, though they kept to a promise of holding a press conference ten days after the ballots appeared in the newspapers. Even so, interest may have dropped by this time. Despite their willingness to print the ballots, newspapers proved reluctant to disseminate the voting results: only six did so, out of the 15 that had carried the ballots. Even though the CHOICES staff used the results in public addresses, the general public is unlikely to have heard the ballot outcome. This lack of reinforcement undoubtedly contributed to the decline in subsequent ballots.

The data gathered by CHOICES provides a rich source of information about the effects of different forms of involvement on citizen opinion. Part of the ballots asked participants to check off whether they had been exposed to other parts of the whole project (the TV shows, the newspaper articles, the book, or the discussion meetings). Only 12% of those who returned ballots said they took part in all the other activities. Of those who mailed in ballots, 75% had seen some of the CHOICES films on TV; 40% said they had read newspaper articles about the issues; 12% claimed to have read the book; and 39% said they had discussed the issues with others. (Note that the last activity appears to refer generally to discussion than to the meetings arranged by RPA.) These answers can be compared to the 16% of the returned ballots from those who said that mailing in the ballot was all they did.

If, as the RPA staff argued, willingness to accept new solutions to regional problems is the criteria of evaluation, the combination of watching the films and reading the book produced the greatest amount of attitude change across the five issues. It appears that these two means of communicating information had about equal effect on ballot results. Some self-selection is evident: Book readers had greater education than TV viewers. Since those who had more education were also more likely to give stronger support to the RPA proposals, the effects of book reading are probably overstated. The project staff concluded that TV was the most powerful medium for developing support for proposed changes.

Strikingly, involvement in group discussions appears to have diminished support for new policies below that predicted by the other means of contact in which they took part (Shore et al., p. 46). The RPA analysis offers (but partially disputes) the explanation that if the audience was unduly swayed by the broadcast, subsequent discussion allowed the effects of television to cool off. We might note that the issues at stake probably demand a more complicated thought process than is possible during a television presentation. Discussion brings out the complications and puts the issue into a broader, social context. Here we encounter some empirical support for the notion that submitting issues to the public via television may result in citizens more likely to accept the solution proposed by political elites, because they are participating as autonomous individuals. Dialogue in a social context restrains this effect, as citizens learn the perspectives of their peers.

CHOICES allowed virtually no citizen involvement in establishing the agenda of issues considered or the proposals advanced. The project was undertaken after RPA had conducted a detailed assessment of the region's needs and problems. They had, in the process, developed a series of proposals in each policy area and they wanted to stimulate citizen attention and reaction to their ideas. For this reason, much of the analysis of the ballot returns was conducted from the viewpoint of which methods produced the greatest support for new proposals.

The RPA did establish a 137-member Citizen Advisory Committee to ensure the clarity and objectivity of their material. That group did not, however, exercise any influence over the agenda because, in negotiating with the television stations for access even before the group was assembled, the RPA had committed itself to films on the five chosen topics. So, although the matter was discussed at the first meeting of the

Advisory Committee, there was no real capacity for it to shape the agenda. Far less was offered the citizens; their influence over the agenda was limited to decisions as to whether to become involved, to watch or not, to read or not, to discuss or not, to vote or not.

The detailed observations made by the RPA staff about the audiences for their television productions also provide some valuable insights into the political use of television. In only 2 out of 30 broadcasts for which there are data, did the audience remain stable over the entire show produced by CHOICES. In five shows, the audience for one 15-minute segment (Nielsen's unit of measurement) fell to less than half of the average audience for the whole hour. The RPA report notes that this degree of flux is not unusual for television audiences of entertainment programs. In any case, in comparison to audience flux in face-to-face meetings we may have uncovered an important limitation on the political use of the medium: In exchange for greater reach, one acquires greater fickleness of those citizens engaged through television than through many other forms.

The CHOICES project well illustrates the weaknesses of using the currently available media for citizen engagement. In the first place, projects such as this must rely upon the public spirit of privately owned, commercial media. The organizers start off in a supplicant position; they have little leverage and must accept what they are given. This relationship pervades many aspects of the CHOICES experience.

For one thing, the broadcast stations demanded high (and expensive) production quality, insisting on an escape clause under which they could refuse to broadcast any film that did not meet their standards. The entire project became oriented by a mindset of competition with mass entertainment. Professionalism also required a "top-down" approach, which dovetailed nicely with RPA tendency to view CHOICES as a means to expanding awareness of the issues and the policy changes they had identified. In short, RPA's interest in maintaining control over the agenda was reinforced by the normal functioning of the medium employed for outreach.

The CHOICES staff was able to arrange over 100 hours of free television time in the New York area (including some VHF stations in New Jersey and Connecticut). Most of these broadcasts, however, were made during nonprime time. In their evaluation, the RPA staff noted that their best ratings occurred near noon on Sunday, around the time when the network interviews usually occur. They theorize that the competition from popular entertainment shows in prime time would overwhelm attention to their presentations of serious issue discussions. That is exactly the point. This project was executed competently and had at its disposal ample funds, yet it drew the attention of only 14% of the target population.

Even though the surveys taken before and after the CHOICES campaign indicate some small public opinion shifts, the reach of this project fell way short of its goals of incorporating "the people" into the policy process.

Finally, a note as to cost. Most observers have not rated CHOICES as a success because, given the potential and the resources expended, the number of citizens involved was small. In the 6 months of public engagement, CHOICES spent nearly $2 million in money and donated services, a substantial sum for a disappointing return.

HAWAII TELEVOTES AND
HONOLULU ELECTRONIC TOWN MEETINGS[1]

The Hawaii Televote and Electronic Town Meetings (ETMs) are almost entirely the creations of two political scientists, Professors Theodore Becker and James Dator of the University of Hawaii. These are separate projects, constituting two different methods for increasing participation, although conceptually they are interwoven and the two organizers helped each other and coordinated their efforts.

Becker and his associates have conducted eight Televotes in Hawaii, one in New Zealand, and one in Los Angeles. In devising the Televote system, Becker and Christa Daryl Slaton adapted a design originated in California by Vincent Campbell (1974) under an NSF grant. Televotes are actually a special type of public opinion poll. Volunteers call a random list of telephone numbers, explain the nature of the Televote to whomever answers the telephone and ask if they would be willing to participate in the Televote. Evidently, about one-half of those contacted agree (Valaskakis & Arnopoulis, 1982, p. 60). A brochure presenting different perspectives on the Televote topic is forwarded to the homes of those who agree to participate, and an appointment is made for a return call during which the participant's opinions will be recorded. Becker allows these participants a period in which to consider their opinions before the second set of calls. Ideally, participants will discuss the topic with other family members, work associates, and friends; ideally they will study the materials with some care and reflection. For their convenience, participants are allowed to initiate the opinion-tallying calls after the agreed upon interval. Evidently, as many as 85% miss their appointments and have to be called by the volunteers often several times before they can be reached and tallied.

Televotes do respond to two major problems with survey research. First, in answering normal polls, respondents may manufacture opinions simply to satisfy the requirements of the interview situation. The thoughts thus expressed may not be politically relevant; the real truth is that citizens have not thought much about an issue and do not care very much about it. A more serious problem is that survey research asks citizens to respond as autonomous individuals. Politically relevant opinion is social opinion, developed through contact and discussion with others and with relevant groups of others. The Televotes permit and even encourage respondents to reflect on a matter in social context. It is hoped that the preferences expressed at the end of this period of consideration will be shaped by social influences as well as autonomous evaluations by the individual. This achievement is a major virtue of the Televote mechanisms, but may not be a major advance down the path of a plebiscitory, direct democracy (Becker & Scarce, 1984).

Becker has released the results to the major Honolulu paper, which often prints an explanation of the Televote and a description of its results. In his writings, Becker (1981, 1984) proposes that Televotes are one step along the path toward teledemocracy in which citizen participation will exercise a major, perhaps determinative, role in policy-making.

In contrast to the televotes, the Honolulu Electronic Town Meetings (ETMs) do not start by drawing a sample of the population for study. Instead anyone and everyone is encouraged to voice their opinions through self-selection. Though the many iterations of ETMs differ dramatically, the intent of their founder, Professor James Dator, has remained the same: He wants to spark interest and debate among Hawaiians on public policies affecting their welfare. The first ETM was an outgrowth of Hawaii's constitutional convention in 1978. Through the ETM, the issues facing the convention delegates, especially the feasibility of initiative petitions, were brought to the attention of the citizens of Honolulu. The second and third focused on the nuclear arms race and how Reaganomics was likely to affect the state and what changes in state government should be undertaken to compensate for those changes. The first Electronic Town Meeting took place over a month-long period and allowed for considerable advance participation, while the second ETM was staged in a four-hour period. Whereas the first required participants to voice opinions on the details of proposed constitutional changes, the second solicited only the most general reactions from participants about the nuclear arms race.

To help stage an ETM, Dator has enlisted the cooperation of the major newspaper, the *Honolulu Advertiser*, which has agreed to print a description of the project, an explanation of the pros and cons of the issue under consideration, and a ballot that can be filled out and sent in to the University. Perhaps more importantly, Dator has successfully arranged broadcast television time to air a show of his own production that presents the opposing viewpoints and solicits participation over the telephone. In one iteration, a network affiliate donated broadcast time; in another instance they used the public broadcasting station. Viewers of these shows call in to a phone bank of volunteers at the University who record their "votes."

One of Dator's most creative ideas has been the use of theater to dramatize issues and capture the citizens' attention. For one ETM, a local improvisational acting company staged several scenes depicting the advantages and disadvantages of using state funds to shore up traditional industries such as sugar and pineapple versus underwriting investment in new, high-technology industries.

In carrying out their ideas for citizen participation, Becker and Dator are careful to use technologies that are available to most citizens. Both professors wanted their system to be easily transferable to other locales should it prove successful in Hawaii. As a result, the processes they created are rather uncomplicated, and citizens do not have to learn how to use a new technology.

Becker and Dator clearly intended the ETMs and Televotes both to broaden the base of participation in politics and to raise the quality of that participation above simply voting for representatives. Quantitatively, it is difficult to assess how successful the two different experiments have been in attracting additional people into the political process, though it is somewhat more possible to assess involvement in the Televotes. As previously noted, Hawaiians who participated in the Televotes first agreed to become involved. Though their commitment to participate was voluntary, the method for recruiting them and obtaining a commitment did not require a large amount of initiative on their part. Moreover, since participants were drawn from a preselected sample designed to be representative of the population, not everyone had the opportunity to join in the process. That is, access was severely restricted to the sample of randomly selected citizens.

In one respect, this design is an improvement over the self-selected samples derived in the Electronic Town Meetings: Becker at least knows that he has reached a demographically representative group at the initial stage. Most of our normal processes of citizen participation, however, involve a high degree of self-selection and initiative that citizens must exercise.

The representativeness of those involved in Televotes may deteriorate as the project proceeds. According to Valaskakis and Arnopoulous

(1982), the percentage of the randomly selected sample that agreed to take part in each Televote is about 50%. Among those who did agree to participate in the Televote, only an average of 70% ended up responding to the questionnaire. For example, 405 persons responded to the Televote questionnaire on public education out of a total of 565 that were distributed. In another iteration, after sending out questionnaires to 588 persons soliciting their views on how to handle crime and criminal matters, Becker received 419 responses. Reporting on the results of the Televote, the *Honolulu Advertiser* (March 21, 1978) reminded its readers of the fact that the nearly 30% non-response rate tends to increase the potential margin of error in this survey.

Putting these two rates of completion together indicates that approximately 35% of the original sample actually participated in the recorded Televote. While this figure may seem disappointing to those familiar with completion rates in public opinion surveys, it is pretty much in line with other participatory projects studied such as the MINERVA town meeting (35%) or the Des Moines Health Vote (24%). A major difference is that these other efforts were reaching for the adult population of their respective communities, whereas Becker's efforts are directed toward a sample.

Becker's accomplishment might aptly be labeled "representative participation." Those participating in the plebiscite are viewed as representing the citizenry as a whole. Presumably, the argument would be that if the entire population had an opportunity to study and discuss the pros and cons of a given issue, their resulting opinions would not differ substantially from those expressed by the Televote sample. Becker mobilizes demographic data to demonstrate that the sample of participants in Televotes is not very dissimilar from the full population (Becker & Scarce, 1983, 1984). He cites sex, age, ethnicity, party affiliation, education, and income to make his case. But even though the resulting sample may be demographically close to the population, there is no guarantee of political representativeness. Those who volunteer to become involved in politics are more likely to be joiners and already active. Their opinions may differ from those who resemble them in other ways. One indication that this may be the case is the fact that the percentage of Televote samples with a college education or more tends to run about 10 points higher than the figures for Hawaii. This discrepency is the largest gap between the demographics of the sample and those of the population, but it is a revealing one.

The representativeness of participants appears to us to be partly a mechanical problem, but it has a conceptual level as well. Even granting that Televote projects could produce representative samples, one could still point out that "representative participation" constitutes a major retreat from the plebiscitory, direct democracy principle of universal involvement.

Ascertaining the numbers of people involved in Electronic Town Meetings and the consequent rates of participation can be even more difficult. For one thing, the available evidence indicates that more citizens wanted to participate than could be handled by the system established at the University of Hawaii. Four incoming telephone lines were manned during the broadcast to receive and tally citizen opinion; they were not enough. The lines were jammed for most of the time, only 140 calls were taken, and Dator heard from many afterward that they had tried to get through but could not.

This experience underlines a persistent finding in our investigations; stimulating citizen involvement is not cheap. While technology can be used to reduce the costs of involvement for citizens, it usually does so by shifting them to the project organizers.

Unlike his colleague Becker, Dator does not gather demographic data from his participants. He does not attempt to demonstrate that the results of the ETMs are representative of the opinions of all Hawaiians or residents of Honolulu. Instead his purpose is to provoke public discussion by giving visibility to issues that are generally ignored in the speeches of politicians or news coverage. If an ETM generates a sufficient number of calls and ballots, then Dator believes the endeavor has been successful because at least a number of citizens paused to think about an issue long enough to cast a vote.

Given the inadequacies of the system for recording citizen votes, we cannot know how large that number is. Nevertheless, it is undoubtedly subject to the same sort of interpretation as other participation rates we encountered: far, far less than universal, but probably more than the number of citizens involved normally in policy discussions. Whether any citizens participated in more than one ETM is also unknown, although this measure can be a crucial calculation in our consideration of whether participation mechanisms will work on a continuing basis.

Notice that because they reserve agenda-setting powers exclusively for the originators, both of these projects place rather heavy burdens upon the organizers to maintain standards of fairness and access. Becker and Dator decide when and on what subjects citizen opinion will be stimulated; these decisions are not subject to citizen influence, except through their option of refusing to participate. Moreover, given that Becker and Dator choose issues in which they feel public attention has been inadequate, the citizens are likely to be heavily dependent upon the information provided them in the context of the project. The televised shows produced for the ETMs or the material sent to Televote participants must fairly and accurately present both sides of the issue. No one can accuse either of these professors with trying to "stack the deck" on one side of an issue; they are aware of their responsibilities and obligations. The point is, however, that the design of these projects lessens their applicability to many political situations, for they posit politics without advocacy, politics without strong self-interest, politics without leadership.

In most circumstances confronted in American politics, advocacy and support building are necessary and inherent. Normally we solve the problem of regulating advocacy through the market place. Political speech now takes place primarily through media that must be purchased, resulting in grave and deplorable inequalities of access. Becker and Dator evidently yearn for something different. By providing equal weight to both sides of an argument, they hope citizens will be persuaded by the merits of the case rather than by inequitable capacity to communicate political information.

An attempt has been made in broadcast law to solve this problem: Television licensees are subject to regulations mandating fairness, equal time, and equal access. Candidates for federal office are given reasonable access to equivalent time as their opponents at the same lowest rate charged. The experience, however, has not always been successful. Many observers feel the net effect of these provisions is to decrease the level of political information carried over the airwaves (Pool, 1983). Whether that is so or not, the problems encountered in making that law work would be trivial in comparison to those of a system through which citizen opinion was to be actively solicited for public policy formulation.

Both Becker and Dator see their work as early experimentation with procedures for a political transformation to more direct forms of citizen democracy (Becker & Scarce, 1984; Dator, 1983). They are able to show that many citizens will become involved in policy discussions given the opportunity; but, they have yet to demonstrate these critical links to their argument: (1) that those who participate are politically representative of the population, (2) that citizens will continue to participate after their initial involvement, (3) that their project designs can embrace robust political conflict, and (4) that these designs can reasonably approach anything like universal involvement.

In our interviews, Becker and Dator were somewhat disdainful of politicians and the current political processes. In some respects, their separation from active politics hurts their own case: In other projects the involvement of public officials serves to boost participation rates. If a

mayor or a governor staged a Televote to help decide some matter, rates
of involvement might be a great deal higher. But Dator and Becker are
not interested in direct impact upon policy, instead their efforts are to
facilitate the development of consensus about certain policy issues. They
set for themselves an educative task; to tap citizen opinion and allow it
to better inform citizens' policy discussions. Accepting their definition
of objectives to be pursued through citizen participation, however, leads
one to recognize two limitations of their work. The first is that a whole
category of political disputes cannot become the subject of a Televote
Town Meeting. These are issues in which there exist pronounced and
aggravated differences of opinion, often undergirded by self-interest. A
Televote on income maintenance might worsen a political dispute, as
would a town meeting on abortion policies. These issues are better left
for dialogue and negotiation, rather than public plebiscites.

A second limitation of these efforts at consensus building occurs at
the point of communicating back to citizens the results of their participation. Tallies from the Televotes are usually published as news items by
the local papers. While the *Honolulu Advertiser* has been willing to print
the ballots for Electronic Town Meetings, the news desk has refused to
carry the results on the grounds that they are an unscientific sampling of
opinion. But whether or not the data appear in the newspapers, it seems
to us that an endeavor at consensus building should not take the form of
a single effort at opinion measurement followed by a press release. In
other projects, studies such as Alternatives for Washington, opinion
measured at one time lead to subsequent steps of engagement and participation. The Hawaii projects miss this dimension.

While Dator and Becker have each undertaken several iterations of
their respective projects, each instance is essentially a one-shot endeav-
or, lacking the cumulative presence or follow-through that would be
necessary to document the continued attractiveness of this form of
participation or to experiment fully with their consensus-building conception of participation.

MINERVA ELECTRONIC TOWN MEETING[2]

During the early 1970s, when the potential uses of communications
technology for enhancing citizen participation were first coming to light,
a team of engineers and social scientists centered in New York City
began work on Project MINERVA. Simply stated, MINERVA attempted
to explore the range of participatory mechanisms that might be used in
activating groups of citizens too large to conduct face-to-face town
meetings. At the same time, the project's designers wanted to make sure

that the technology employed was widely available so that, if MINERVA proved successful in facilitating citizen participation, the project could be duplicated in other settings. Unlike a number of other projects examined here, MINERVA was not designed to meet the needs of a community or to solve a problem. Rather the team headed by Columbia Professor Amatai Etzioni wanted to test a series of hypotheses concerning citizen participation.

In the spring of 1973, members of the Project MINERVA team conducted electronic town meetings at two different apartment complexes in the New York City area: "Triple Towers" consisted of 1,300 apartments, while "High Rise Village" held over 2,300 apartments. The inhabitants of the two complexes shared similar demographic profiles— most occupants of the apartments were white and middle class. The project's engineers adapted the telephone lines and cable television capacity of the two complexes to enable participants to become involved in group discussions even while remaining in their own apartments.

Both meetings began with a panel of tenants, representing different sides of the issue under discussion, broadcast to the apartment residents. At Triple Towers, the segment was televised, while at High Rise Village this part of the meeting reached participants over the radio. If home viewers wished to comment on the proceedings at this stage, they could go to a ministudio inside their building, stand in front of a remote camera, and record their views. These were aired after the panel was finished presenting the issue. After all of the prerecorded comments of those participating at home had been shown over cable, the tenants' panel reappeared to reflect on viewer comments before the issue finally came to a vote.

Voting occurred through use of a system called Telepoller that enabled participants to dial one number on their telephone to vote for the first option, a second number to vote for the second option, and so on for as many different responses as was desired for the question.

Because the MINERVA Project took place over ten years ago and involved a limited number of people, this report necessarily relies on written reports of the original researchers. I did not observe first-hand the quality of discussion initiated by the tenants' panel or the taped responses of homeviewers presented over cable TV. I also lack a sense of the participants' political history and the larger political environment within which this experiment took place. I could examine, however, the format used to encourage participation, the advantage and disadvantage of the way it was executed, and the impact, if any, MINERVA had on the political issues it confronted.

A guiding philosophy for the architects of the MINERVA Project was that the ideal participatory framework includes room for both dialogue and polling. In his working paper entitled "MINERVA: A Study in Participatory Technology," Professor Etzioni describes an optimal version of MINERVA that embraces the "capacity to address a group," the ability to conduct a "real-time group dialogue of a geographically dispersed membership," "the injection of expert information," and other such requisites of a political environment in which informed participation is the result. Etzioni was equally concerned that the result of the project not just be intelligent discussion but that the dialogue result in an expression of opinion that had a noticeable political impact. Participants debated solutions to issues that had personal as well as political impact on their lives. At High Rise Village for instance, the tenants' association solicited ideas on how to combat the rising number of crimes in the complex in the hopes that discussion and voting might reveal several solutions acceptable to a majority of apartment owners. At Triple Towers, the discussion involved the rapidly escalating cost of food.

Although each iteration of MINERVA was a one-shot effort, the project appended itself to an ongoing tenants' association. Unlike some other projects in which citizens were asked to take part in an entirely new process, those participating in MINERVA had dealt with the tenants' association leadership before and were, assumedly, less susceptible to being manipulated by a new form of participation. The technology served to expand participation well beyond the number that would normally attend a face-to-face meeting of the association. Quite a few of the citizens were elderly who might be expected to participate more frequently in a meeting they could attend in their own apartment. Especially in a discussion of building security, the addition of senior citizens, who are most often the victims of crime, was an important step in making the meeting useful to the residents.

Whether for ease of participation, comfort of anonymity, or some other reason, postinterviews revealed that residents of both complexes preferred the electronic meeting to the face-to-face meeting. While many of those polled may have only participated in the electronic meeting and, consequently, may not have had very solid grounds for comparison, 52% of High Tower residents and fully 62% of Triple Towers occupants favored the electronic town meeting. Only 17% of Triple Tower residents, on the other hand, liked the face-to-face format better.

Faithful to Etzioni's belief that rules of access must be established for any participatory mechanism, MINERVA set down two rules governing access, one termed "representation by viewpoint" and the other "open access." The first principle ensures that different points of view were advanced by someone. The MINERVA team hoped to anticipate a number of participant comments defining the alternate views and thereby encouraging discussion on the relative merits of each position. Rather than allowing the meeting to waste valuable time as a disparate group groped towards several distinct security problems, the tenants' panel at High Rise Towers presented a number of clear choices that could then be debated from the participants' individual perspectives.

The second rule, "open access," ensured that in practice everyone who wished to, could participate in the dialogue. As previously mentioned, residents could tape their reactions to the discussion so that their comments could be broadcast at a later date along with the panel's reaction to comments made on the tape.

Since the MINERVA team hoped to create and test a participatory mechanism that could be adopted to other situations with a minimum of time and expense, they did not undertake to install technology that would permit instantaneous audio and visual link-ups among large numbers of people. Their concern with allowing everyone to see as well as hear the individuals speaking emanated from their belief that elements of a face-to-face meeting, such as gestures and physical presence, are important both to the political identity of the individual talking and to the proper functioning of the collective group.

While televising taped commentary over cable may alleviate some problems in widening the scope of tenants meetings, it may create others. When participants at Triple Towers were asked how important was the lack of true face-to-face contact, around two-thirds (67%) responded that it was somewhat important (or more). At High Rise Village, where all segments of the meeting received cable coverage, 40% felt it was at least somewhat important, a lower but nevertheless significant group.

At High Rise Village, close to fifty people appeared in the studios to register their views. Since at this juncture in the experiment, people could talk for as long as they cared to, the tenants' panel eliminated some people's views and severely edited the remarks of others. This action infuriated many residents who understandably felt they had been manipulated. The solution to this problem, that participants could only take five minutes for their presentation, further limited the role of citizens to commenting on previously offered solutions to the problem at hand.

Another drawback associated with the participatory scheme provided by MINERVA lies in the presentation of opinion after opinion during the taped section. In a summary article, Robert Zussman and Nancy Castleman (1973) indicate that a number of original or provocative thoughts arose during this segment, but that lumped one right after another without any clear logic to their order, they did not seem to help those watching decide between competing solutions. A particular line of argument could not gain momentum as more individual comments amplify and explicate those expressed by one individual. If, for instance, a new method for preventing entryways from being left open were broached by someone on the taped segment, it would not be fully debated and would only be explored if the tenants' panel picked up the idea during the commentary period. Certainly, this new idea would not receive the same attention as that given the preselected viewpoints.

Zussman and Castleman do not credit this part of the experiment with much significant impact on the final outcomes. In fact, the citizen input portion of the MINERVA system could have caused a number of people to drop out of the experiment. Since the process itself was so disparate and the chance for effective citizen impact so minimal, there is a strong possibility that interest in participation dwindled considerably after the first few comments.

MINERVA can claim the advantage of attracting more people into the apartment complex's political forum than was true without the technology. Electronic participation in meetings ran higher than actual attendance in person. As noted above, moreover, the tenants expressed general satisfaction with this new means of involvement. At High Rise Village, where one would expect the issue of building security to be of concern to many inhabitants, the electronic town meeting polled more than 35% of the complex's households on alternative solutions to the security problem. Castleman (1974) compared these figures to a questionnaire survey, taken a year earlier, that sparked interest in only 325 of the 2,300 households (14%).

Far fewer people participated in the Triple Towers meeting as only 160 households returned the questionnaire, 12.6% of the total number of households. The researchers ascribed this low participation rate to the absence of as strong a tenants' association as existed in High Rise Village. Another reason may lie in the fact that the issue debated at Triple Towers was rising food prices. Since tenants have greater control over building security than over food prices, the effectiveness and relevance of participation may have induced a comparatively higher rate of involvement in the first trial. In any event, it should be mentioned that in the latter case, an average of 35% of the questionnaire respondents indicated they "had attended all or part of the electronic meeting." That means that quite a few people who voted did so on the basis of little exposure to the information supplied by the project.

A strong disadvantage with MINERVA lies in the burdens associated with participation for those at home. In order to comment, residents had to leave their apartments and travel to a location (usually in the same building) where cameras had been placed. Participants, therefore, missed large parts of the meeting while they were recording their opinion. In addition, they could not know whether other tenants expressed a similar viewpoint in another taped segment. In short, interaction could not occur among the residents but only between the residents and members of the preselected tenants' panel.

Thus political elites figure prominently in the MINERVA experiment, while residents had very limited opportunities to influence the agenda of politics. By opening the town meeting with a comprehensive review of the alternatives, the tenants' panel set the tone for the ensuing meeting. Moreover, the panel remained responsible for determining which ideas or opinions merited further attention.

Given this structure, it is less surprising that no significant political activity surfaced during the course of the meeting to push a particular proposal. While Zussman and Castleman reported that over half (56%) of the tenants discussed the issues with others in the complex, there is no indication that these discussions sparked further political activity on this issue.

These advantages bestowed on the tenants' panel would decrease over time only if the participatory mechanism provided incentives for participants to immerse themselves fully in the discussion of community issues including the electronic town meeting process. Since MINERVA functioned only for two meetings, it is difficult to know if it would have increasingly engaged tenants.

Because the intention of MINERVA was to test the system itself, not to measure its effect on the outcome of a problem, some important questions remain unanswered. On a practical level, for example, was building security improved as a result of the MINERVA meeting? Did occupants pay more attention to how their actions affected the security of others? If the MINERVA designers hoped that their system would receive widespread use in future issues, they had to demonstrate an ability to solve citizen concerns. While the hardware did appear to boost tenant involvement and satisfaction on a one-time basis, it is not clear that those beneficial effects would continue in subsequent iterations in the same population. Once the novelty effect wears off, higher rates of participation might be maintained only where the effectiveness of such involvement was visible.

On the other hand, there were some tenants who were initially suspicious of the enterprise who might be persuaded by a continual process that the technology afforded a real opportunity for involvement. One tenant, for example, returned a questionnaire with a blunt observation that the project was certainly a trick of the cable company to sell something. One hopes that such attitudes would mitigate if the project were continued and proved effective. Even so, we would expect that the effectiveness of one trial would sharply influence rates of participation in subsequent iterations.

Despite the intentions of its creators to provide diversity in the means of citizen involvement, MINERVA is best classified as a plebiscitory exercise. The most important aspect of participation fostered was not the dialogue but polling of citizens as to their preferences as to what should be done about a given issue. Even though Etzioni and his colleagues set out to encourage participation both in a dialogue and in electronic voting, the particular arrangements forced attention onto the plebiscitory aspects. In part, this result is an inadvertent consequence of their decision to rely as much as possible upon technology widely available at the time. Specifically, the arrangements for citizen dialogue were so rudimentary in the ways I have pointed out, that emphasis naturally flowed to the voting aspects. Moreover, in the more successful trial involving building security, tenant participation was treated as the final arbitrator of how the problem should be improved, not as a resource upon which the tenants' panel should draw in reaching a decision.

As the MINERVA reports make clear, the rate of participation was increased by technological means. Satisfaction with the involvement also appeared to have been enhanced. But there remain some very real questions. One cannot, for example, judge the effect of preexisting organizations. The more successful field trial in High Rise Village was achieved in a setting with an ongoing tenants' organization. The addition of telecommunications to reduce the burdens of involvement did boost participation over face-to-face meetings; that is clear. But, we cannot be sure of the degree to which the difference between the 35% rate of involvement in this trial and the disappointing 13% in Triple Towers was due to the lack of a strong tenants' organization in the latter case, the difference in issues under consideration, or the technology employed for the initial panel presentation.

Discussion

As efforts to encourage citizen activity, all of the teledemocracy projects need to be evaluated along the institutional dimensions offered in Chapter Three. We want to consider explicitly, for example, how well these populist plebiscitarian endeavors perform in providing citizens with an ability to participate (access) and in actually enlisting their involvement (reach). In this and the following three chapters, I will examine the projects within each category. The discussion in Chapter Eight will contrast and compare the four different types of tele-democracy projects.

Project initiators who advocate the populist plebiscitarian logic generally chose not to involve government officials directly in their projects. In this category we are more likely to encounter the advocates of participatory democracy, those who foresee and desire a fundamental transformation of our political processes. Many of those who initiated these projects have done so to discover whether or not technology can accomplish a workable direct democracy. As we shall see, this logic pervades most institutional aspects of the projects in this group.

ACCESS AND REACH

In general, these projects were successful in attracting larger numbers of individuals into political activity than normally become involved in traditional institutions of politics other than voting in elections. Upon the access standard, these projects differ, however, in that two of them sought to involve finite subsectors of the general population. Televote and MINERVA limited their target citizens sharply, in one case to a manageable number of residences, in the other to a representative sample. Meanwhile, the Honolulu Electronic Town Meetings and Choices for '76 reached out for the general citizenry within a geographical area. The Televote project stands out from the others in that, at the outset, the general population was to be represented by a random sample, that is, access was deliberately restricted. In the other set of projects conducted in Hawaii, approximately 150 individuals success-fully participated in each of the Electronic Town Meetings, a number significantly greater than can be accommodated in live call-in shows. But obviously this number is minuscule in comparison to an ideal plebi-scite among Hawaiian citizens. Likewise, the Choices for '76 and the MINERVA projects all had disappointing rates of reach or turnout.

Given these different targets, we should not be surprised to learn that the effective reach of the Televotes and MINERVA was substantially greater than for the other two efforts to involve everyone. For one thing, in Televote and MINERVA, the communications technology employed was more likely to be adequate to the task of capturing citizen attention. The project staff could, in effect, maintain a list of all potential par-ticipants and, through repeated contacts, make sure that each one was aware of the opportunity for involvement. By contrast, the ETMs and CHOICES could not be sure that the intended recipients were reached through newspapers and television.

In other words, the projects directed toward general audiences have trouble coping with competition from other aspects of social life and with the entertainment habits of many Americans. Even broadcast television with its high audiences and significant economizing of the resources of the communicator proved inadequate to the task of involving the citizenry as a whole.

The most appropriate analogy for deciding whether these projects were successful in attracting citizens into politics is the debate over whether a glass is one-third full or two-thirds empty. Conceived in a plebiscitory spirit, these efforts have demonstrated a very real capacity to get citizens to react to policy matters; communications technology can be used to bring policy questions to citizens, to lower the burdens of participation, and thereby to facilitate citizen involvement. But there are limits. All these projects fell far short of their goal of universal participation. In the most successful of these projects, fully 65% of those eligible did not become involved. This figure is far below that which should be considered necessary by those who advocate a political transformation to direct participatory democracy.

None of these projects, however, involved a true plebiscite in the sense that citizen votes provided the decisive word in policy formulation, a conceptually important limitation. Defenders of plebiscites will argue that participation was not universal because it was not definitive. Only when the public begins to recognize that its actions will actually decide matters, they argue, will citizens overcome their lethargy and participate in large numbers (Wolff, 1976). These projects deserve the label "plebiscitary" nonetheless. While the voting results did not determine public policy, the involved citizenry did express its preferences in a single vote that, at least within the context of the project, was intended to yield a decisive and final outcome.

Comparatively, the Choices for '76 experience was least successful of these projects. A great deal of money (almost $2 million) was spent encouraging a small number of voters to return their ballots. Whereas an estimated 700,000 viewers saw the first film, both the audiences for subsequent shows and the number of ballots returned fell off sharply.

DIVERSE PATHS OF ACCESS

Choices for '76 and MINERVA both provided multiple and diverse means of access so that citizens with different skills, interests, and resources could participate. In addition to the plebiscite, citizens could also attend meetings to debate and discuss the topic with others. In MINERVA, those who wanted to be intensively involved had available the "open access" opportunity to state their views over the closed circuit channel. This diversity was lacking in the design of the Hawaii projects, although in the ETM's citizens were offered the opportunity to vote by mail or by telephone.

Despite the existence of alternative avenues for participation, however, the nature of a plebiscite fairly well constrains the active role for citizens to the casting of ballots. All the attention and effort of those seeking to mobilize participation is directed into the vote. The alternative paths are decidedly secondary.

EFFECTIVENESS

Among this sampling of projects, actual impact on public policy is almost nonexistent. Based on interviews with key participants, Orton (1980, p. 198) characterized the policy impact of Choices for '76 as "questionable," a rating only slightly better than the "none" some projects received. Regarding the Hawaii projects, the chief political aide of Hawaii's governor and his press secretary stated they had not heard the results from any of the Televotes or the Electronic Town Meetings. In evaluating the MINERVA project, we can safely assume that the voting on food prices in the New York area had little actual impact. On the other hand, while we do not have observations as to the policy effectiveness of the discussion and voting in the other MINERVA iteration, 60% of those who participated more heavily in the project reported that they were "very much more interested" in doing something about the building security problem (Zussman & Castleman, 1973, p. 87). Finally, the poor turnout on ballot questions raised by the Regional Planning Association in CHOICES meant that the results did not become a serious part of the policy-making process surrounding those issues.

AGENDA SETTING

All of these projects suffer grave deficiencies from the agenda-setting aspects of participation. In every case, the policy topic of concern, the timing of the plebiscite, the information available to participants, and even the construction of options or proposed policies were tightly controlled by the project initiators.

It appears that this control is part and parcel of the desire to enlist vast numbers of citizens. In order to expand the projects' reach, the

requirements of citizen involvement are reduced to registering one's
preferences among alternatives supplied by the project team. In brief,
plebiscites resolve a trade-off between quantity of participation and
quality of participation in favor of the former. That makes their lack of
achievement—again the two-thirds empty glass—all the more serious.

GROUP VERSUS INDIVIDUAL PARTICIPATION

Most of the participation encouraged in these projects was on an individual basis. Although all of them made allowances for some formation
of opinion in a social context, the project designs worked to handicap
the operation of interest groups. In some cases, this handicapping was
deliberate. In the Hawaii projects, the efforts to record citizen opinion
was conducted too rapidly for groups to mobilize in order to affect the
outcome. The project design can serve to hinder or facilitate lateral contact among citizens, which makes it possible for groups to coalesce. In
the MINERVA project, for example, the apartment residents could
engage in a discussion with a panel of tenants, but the design did not
allow residents to debate options among themselves conveniently.

The data from Choices For '76 gives us an ideal opportunity to
examine the differences that this factor makes. The different patterns of
preferences shown by participants in CHOICES revealed that individual
involvement produces different results than discussion in a social context. Those who watched only the TV productions were more likely to
support the RPA's view of needed change, a finding that will confirm
the suspicions of those who worry about the quality of participation
from mass audiences composed of autonomous individuals viewing at
home. By contrast, those who had participated in community discussion
groups were far less likely to support dramatic changes in regional
policy. Perhaps they had learned from dialogue and debate the complexity of the issues and more about the reasons why existing policy was
formulated as it was; perhaps they were already more involved in the discussion of these issues before CHOICES came along.

To some extent, the tendency toward individual participation is a function of the technology employed. Television and telephone reach people
in their home and thus convey information to them as individuals. To
the extent that this conduit was the only means of receiving information
about the policy matter, the participants were driven to respond as individuals. Even the Televote project, which specifically allows citizens the
time needed to discuss the issue with others, does not really permit the
mobilization of group opinion. Since only Becker knows the names of
those constituting his electorate, those participating are unlikely to influ-

ence each other. Accordingly, his design would not reassure critics like Elstain (1982) who argue that public opinion must be forged from debate among conflicting groups.

EDUCATION

In most cases, the initiators of populist, plebiscitarian projects place a higher value on the educational aspects of their efforts. Here again the design of the project appears to be more important than the technology employed. Through their involvement, citizens are expected to learn more about the policy matter at hand and acquire participation skills that may be put to use later. Three of the projects relied upon video productions to pass along substantive information, while the Televote used mailed printed material. Certainly both these can be used to educate citizens, but since I was not able to document their effectiveness, only general comments are possible here.

None of these initiators thought to establish a preproject base line from which they could measure change. As we shall see in later chapters, the use of random sample opinion surveys can document the educational components of a participation project. We can hardly blame Ted Becker for this shortcoming since these measurements would fall victim to the inadequacies in polling that stimulated his experimentation in the first place. While Choices for '76 was interested in discovering whether the mailed back ballot was representative of the general populace, they did not think of conducting a survey before their shows were broadcast.

The MINERVA project staff attempted some postproject analysis of educational effects. Participants were asked to complete a questionnaire that asked, among other things, whether they felt they had learned more through this means as opposed to the usual face-to-face tenants' meetings. Approximately 50% stated they had learned "more or much more," compared to around 15% who said "less or much less." Television slightly outperformed radio in the opinion of these respondents—those who had watched the show were a little more likely to be positive than those who had listened to the radio version. In any case, the reliability of these perceptual reports is open to question.

INITIATIVE AND COSTS

Of these projects, MINERVA and the Hawaii Televote involved the highest levels of direct encouragement in the form of individual contact. Hawaiian residents were called and urged to participate; those who agreed but failed to call in their responses were telephoned again.

MINERVA staff members roamed the apartment complexes knocking on doors and leaving material hanging on doorknobs. In both instances, these encouragements were effective, as these projects exhibited the highest rates of turnout among the plebiscitory projects. In one MINERVA trial, almost one-third of the population participated (but, in the second, where the tenants' organization was less effective, the rate was a disappointing 10%). The Televote project appears to have an ultimate completion rate of 35%. Note, however, that both of these efforts involve a finite electorate, such that contacting individual citizens is a practical strategy for the initiators. As Orton's (1980) research makes clear, projects that attempt to capture the attention of a large geographical area exhibit rates of involvement not much higher than the CHOICES campaign.

Because it was undertaken by social scientists interested in gathering data on their quasi-experiment, the MINERVA project offers the best demonstration of how technology can be used to reduce the costs of participation. In the apartment complex that exhibited the higher rate of involvement, comparisons with the group normally active in tenants' meetings demonstrate that technology served to extend the set of participants to more than four times as many participants than the number usually involved in the process. Of their sample, 61% had never attended a tenants' meeting, yet they voted as part of the electronic meeting. The reasons most newcomers gave for their participation related to the ease of involvement from one's apartment in contrast to attending a meeting. Questionnaire responses amply documented their perceptions that the electronic town meeting was not significantly less comprehensible and workable than a face-to-face meeting.

This experience provides a clear demonstration that technology can expand the level of participation by lowering the costs of involvement. This finding, however, needs to be circumscribed by two caveats. As mentioned above, in the MINERVA and Televote cases the initiators of participation targeted limited subsets of the general population and invested substantial resources in contacting their electorate. Whether this conclusion is applicable to a political setting much larger than, for example, MINERVA's apartment complex may well depend on whether resources are available to contact citizens as extensively. The results from the electronic town meetings and the CHOICES project do not give much ground for optimism.

Conclusions

These four experiments in teledemocracy differ primarily in their definition of the target population they attempted to involve in policy matters. MINERVA and the Televotes, which more narrowly circumscribed their outreach to manageable numbers, achieved vastly higher rates of participation. Meanwhile, the involvement of citizens in electronic town meetings in Honolulu or in CHOICES occurred at disappointing rates, even though we should acknowledge that more citizens became activated than normally take part in policy discussions.

The push for larger numbers brings with it a major consequence in terms of the capacity of citizens to affect the policy matter under consideration. In these efforts, the agenda of policy matters under public scrutiny was tightly controlled by the initiators. This is not necessarily a heinous crime, especially since these projects evinced a policy-neutral cast and the initiators were interested in boosting participation without regard for the policy outcomes that might result. As a consequence, however, the gap between these plebiscitory experiments and the requirements of a functioning, ongoing political system yawns wide. The burdens assumed by these organizers are higher; the restraints upon them are weaker; and the reliance upon their goodwill to preserve democratic values of fairness and impartiality is all the more demanding.

At this point, my criticism of the plebiscitory endeavors is based on two limited grounds: First, participation falls far short of the promise and, second, the necessary assumptions about the behavior of political elites are tenuous. In short, from this research, it has become clearer that the real barriers to a workable plebiscitarian democracy are political, not technical. These projects give us no assurance that modern communication technology mechanisms can bridge the pronounced chasm between normative theory and the practical problems of unequal participation and managing political ambition and interest.

Notes

1. The original version of this section was written by my research assistant John Griffen.

2. The original version of this section was drafted by my research assistant John Griffin.

CHAPTER 5

BRINGING GOVERNMENT TO CITIZENS

A second group of teledemocracy projects employed a sharply contrasting view of citizen participation. In these efforts, the originators sought to expand the direct role that citizens can play in public policy-making by using communications technology to put them in to closer contact with public officials. In many cases, elected political leaders themselves initiated these projects as a means of overcoming inadequacies they perceived in the traditional channels for citizens. Where participation has been disappointing because of geographical barriers or lack of initiative on the part of citizens, these experiments have employed technology to reach out to citizens and to reduce the costs and burdens associated with their involvement in politics. In most cases, these projects were grafted on to existing political institutions; they were attempts to improve the functioning of established and legitimate processes. In contrast, the set of projects just described—the nongovernmental, plebiscitory efforts— tended to be created in a vacuum without institutional moorings.

Another important difference between these and the last group of projects can be found in the conception of participation employed by these projects. For those involved in government, the well-known social inequities that characterize rates of citizen involvement of all forms are part of the daily experience. As a result, most of these initiators harbor no illusions that they will be able to generate universal involvement of citizens. They are, nonetheless, willing to use technology to improve rates of participation marginally and to mitigate these inequalities in the process. Instead of trying to involve all the citizens, the initiators of these projects recognize the pluralistic structure of American politics. They acknowledge that varying levels of interest in different policy areas will inevitably produce a "lumpy" quality to citizen participation. To them, the perceived value of these projects lies not in allowing "the people" a political voice, but in increasing the number of individual participants and in incorporating a more diverse set of group interests in policy decisions.

In other words, public officials tend to be associated with incremental improvements upon ongoing processes rather than the pursuit of transformational and utopian goals. As a result, the number of citizens engaged by these projects tends to be much smaller than the numbers achieved in the plebiscitory projects. Moreover, since the incentives that bring people into these mechanisms are based largely upon the self-interest of the participants, those who participate are usually not demographically and politically representative of the entire population.

These projects also employ a different range of communication technologies. Because they do not attempt to secure universal participation, they are able to make use of newer communication vehicles that fall short of mass media. In Chapter Two we referred to these as either semipublic and semiprivate media, depending upon how their effective reach was restricted. In Alaska, for example, citizens participate in legislative hearings via a teleconferencing system. In Reading, Pennsylvania, and across North Carolina, citizens are able to question public officials on a regular basis, using telephone lines to reach a cable studio. In an "electure" staged over a computer network, citizens were able to engage Congressman Markey in a month-long discourse on nuclear arms policy.

The Government Dialogue Projects

With this brief introduction, let us turn to an examination of the four different teledemocracy projects that fit this mold.

BERKS COMMUNITY TELEVISION[1]

Located in central Pennsylvania, Reading provides the setting for a successful experiment in electronic dialogues. A city dominated by communities of Italian, Polish, Irish, and Jewish residents who maintain strong ethnic identities, Reading has witnessed a succession of mayors either supported by the Democratic machine or by reform groups in the city. An analysis of Reading's politics during the 1960s was entitled *The Politics of Corruption* (Gardner, 1970).

Berks Community Television (BCTV) began in Reading in the mid-1970s as an experiment in community programming for the senior citizen population. Sponsored by the National Science Foundation (NSF) through New York University's Alternate Media Center, BCTV originally consisted of several studio sites located in senior citizen centers from which the elderly could present programs to one another. Originally, BCTV looked more like a videoconferencing system in which general viewers at home were included. One important feature of the system was the use of a split screen so that the two sides to an electronic conversation could see and hear each other. After the NSF funds were exhausted, however, budgetary pressures have forced BCTV to eliminate most of its split-screen programming. In this sense, the system is now less interactive than it used to be.

BCTV's uniqueness stems, however, not from the technology employed, but from the use of a citizen participation model in the production of community shows rather than a broadcast mentality (Dutton et al., 1984). BCTV conscientiously adheres to a homegrown image, capitalizing upon a simple, casual, even homey format. The BCTV staff steadfastly refuse to professionalize their programming, believing that to do so would drive away their "participants" watching at home. For example, the same studio set, consisting of several potted plants, fold-up chairs, and a plain blue background is used for all shows broadcast from the studio. If the camera jiggles a bit, nobody becomes disturbed; in fact, the person "on camera" may even comment on the inexperience of the new volunteer cameramen.

Other precautions are taken to preserve the participatory aspects of the programming. To reduce the psychological distance between the viewer and those in the studio, moderators refer to "participants" instead of "audience" and they prefer the word "program" to "show." Those appearing on BCTV productions face the camera directly so that two speakers do not give the appearance of a dialogue between themselves. Viewers who call in are given first priority in posing questions or comments. Quite frequently, the moderator will interrupt the discussion in the studio in order to field a question from a viewer. In theory, all these steps signal to the viewer an expanded notion of the meeting: The participants at home are not watching an event, they are part of it. Perfection in programming would eliminate this inclusive style and would allow production values to overtake those of the events themselves. At BCTV, they believe the medium should be as transparent as possible.

BCTV broadcasts on an access channel provided by The Berks Cable Television Company, which serves not only the Reading franchise but an additional 21 communities throughout the county. There are approximately 50,000 subscribers in the Reading area. Systemwide, Berks Cable has a penetration rate of about 60%. From surveys of cable subscribers, the BCTV staff variously estimates that between 50% and 78% view some of their programming and that around 30% watch more than one show per week. During one year (1982), BCTV produced 1,144 live programs that involved a total of 7,600 participants. About half of these participations (3,723) came in the form of call-ins from home viewers. Not all of these programs and calls concerned political matters, but government and politics are consistently among the most stimulating programs produced by BCTV. These figures overstate somewhat the numbers of individuals involved, since the same people may call in more than once.

BCTV produces a number of regular political shows and sporadic specials on political matters. For example, *Inside City Hall* airs every Thursday evening and features one of the five city council members talking about subjects of communitywide interest. An open phone line allows viewers to ask the city councilman questions. BCTV covers both city budget hearings and community planning meetings on a regular basis. Since June 1983, most public hearings on city business have been conducted over BCTV. In these formats, the comments of citizens who telephone in are treated as testimony in the same way as those of people who participate in person.

Judged in comparison with other BCTV shows, political programming is one of the more popular offerings. Of those responding to BCTV's Viewership Survey, 65% "watch some form of government at least once a month," and 29% report themselves as frequent viewers. Of those who have watched government programming, 81% felt that the "helpfulness of the information" was either good, very good, or excellent. (These numbers should be treated with some caution, however, since the data were collected from a self-selected sample in a mail back questionnaire.)

From our point of view, the most important series is *Inside City Hall*. Each show features one of the council members and any city employees he or she may wish to bring along. In Reading, the mayor does not preside over all administrative departments of the city; instead they are divided among the five council members (one of whom is the mayor) who are elected citywide and serve in full-time, paid positions. Each council member is assigned jurisdiction over specific departments, such as highway maintenance or police. If the councilman who oversees the welfare department is on BCTV in a given week, the discussion usually centers upon the activities of that department or the long-term outlook for welfare programs in the area.

The nature of BCTV offerings and the response by citizens can be illustrated by an examination of programming designed to engage viewers in politics over three months in 1984. On the programming side, BCTV produced a rich and steady diet of political topics. In addition to three regular weekly programs—*Inside City Hall, What's County Government All About*, and *Borough Government News*—during the months studied, the local chapter of the League of Women Voters produced a continuing series on the election, the Reading School Board staged two shows, the Neighborhood Housing Service was on twice, a special set of panel presentations entitled *Cities in Crisis* also met twice, and there were two discussions of social security, one on food stamps, two on local municipal problems, and one on cancer.

The response of citizens to these different offerings varied dramatically, depending upon the type of show and the featured guest. By this measure, *Inside City Hall* clearly evoked the greatest amount of participation. However, since the equivalent show for the county generated the poorest response, we cannot conclude that direct access to government officials alone stimulates participation. The attitude of the receiving official may account for some of the differences—in our interview, county official Donald Bagenstose was noticeably less enthusiastic about BCTV than were the Reading officials.

Average Calls per Hour for Types of Shows
(Aug.-Oct., 1984)

Inside City Hall	10.4
Cities in Crisis	10.0
League of Women Voters	5.6
Reading School Board	5.0
What's City Government All About	2.8
Other Specials	3.5

Added to this may be the fact that the cable system does not line up completely with county lines and that BCTV as an institution is more heavily focused on the city and its problems.

Different officials from Reading's City Hall also generated different rates of questions, as can be seen below.

Average Calls per Hour to City Hall Guests
(Aug.-Oct., 1984)

Councilman Edward Leonardziak	21.0
Mayor Karen Miller	16.0
Chief of Police Steffy	10.0
Councilman Ronald Bibenedetto	9.4
Councilman Thomas Loeper	6.0
Councilman Thomas Gajewski	6.0

Some of these differences are related to the types of municipal services under each councilman's authority; for example, Leonardziak received numerous questions about trash removal, while Loeper's discussion of the fire department provoked fewer questions.

When residents of Reading participate by calling the main studio, BCTV personnel do screen callers, but only to judge the probability of obscene or clearly indecent remarks. Otherwise, callers can say anything they wish. Jean Toucci, the regular moderator, refrains from rephrasing questions or otherwise tampering with viewer participation. To an extraordinary degree, the viewers control the agenda, asking as many follow-up questions as they want, offering their own opinions, or raising new subjects. One drawback observed in most call-in formats is true of Reading: When the discussion really sparks viewer interest, the number of incoming calls almost guarantees disruption of the flow of conversation. Questions formulated earlier in response to the discussion, are asked later at an inappropriate time. The resulting conversation has a spasmotic, disconnected quality to it.

Comparing the earliest political programming produced by BCTV with recent shows, one notes a marked rise in the quality of questions asked by viewers. When *Inside City Hall* first aired, many questions exhibited a fundamental misunderstanding of how city government operated. For example, callers often asked council members about funding for education, an area over which the city has no jurisdiction. In separate interviews, both Mayor Karen Miller and Toucci underscored the fact that now viewers seldom confuse roles and responsibilities, illustrating a net gain in the level of political information among BCTV callers. Callers more frequently ask follow-up questions or seek clarification of answers given by guests in the more recent programs. Toucci added that she sensed a more analytical, less informational tone among more recent callers. Participants listen to the questions posed by others and think about responses, both in terms of whether they make sense and how they fit into the general discussion of public issues in the Reading community and over BCTV.

The number of budget and planning hearings held by the city of Reading has increased significantly over the past several years. BCTV has clearly sparked more community interest in these matters. Whereas in the past few people attended such sessions at city hall, now the BCTV studio fills up with people, and many more tune in at home. In general, interest in local government programming appears to surpass that directed toward political shows that have a national focus such as a discussion of the nuclear arms race.

The questions asked in both hearings and *Inside City Hall* often have a direct effect on the governmental action. For example, questions centered on specific problems with government services (such as poor trash removal) often put the politicians in the position of pleading ignorance to the specific concern but promising to remedy the problem.

In the process, these politicians acquire another source of information about the performance of their departments. Moreover, on the basis of some tentative evidence, one can presume that very often these specific complaints are accommodated and citizens are better off. In the long run, a more realistic portrayal of government results. Mayor Miller suggests that as citizens become better acquainted with how local government works and what it can accomplish, they have also become less cynical about local politics.

In a way, the evolution in the sophisticated questions has made life more difficult for the politicians. Formerly, council members could benefit politically by responding quickly to a viewer who called to ask why a particular pothole had not been filled. All they had to do was follow through with the proper city department and then point to the tangible improvements they had achieved. Mayor Miller once filmed the changing of a street sign that bothered a viewer and had it shown on a subsequent show. While elected officials still receive many of these detail-oriented questions, now they must also cope with more exacting inquiries that test their ability to present their policies in broad terms.

Karen Miller's successful plunge into local politics demonstrates the political potential of public access cable programs and BCTV. A recent arrival (1971) in a tight-knit town, Miller first ran for city council in 1975. In winning her seat she defeated better known city politicians with strong ties to the city's different ethnic communities. Her campaign featured a series of commercials run on the community access channel of the Berks Cable system. Miller became the first woman to serve on the city council. She immediately emerged as one of several advocates of the further development of cable access programming through BCTV. In her successful 1979 mayoral campaign, Miller benefited greatly from her exposure on *Inside City Hall.*

While governing the city, however, Mayor Miller has not differed outwardly from the other councilmen. Like the others, she rotates her appearances on *Inside City Hall,* appearing on the air only once every five weeks. But Miller exudes a charm on camera unequalled by peers. Her personality adapts well to the screen. Sporting a friendly smile and a concerned look, Miller quietly demonstrates an understanding of the Reading community.

This raises the question of whether the move of Reading politics onto the airwaves presages the development of a new type of city politician. The "homegrown" style of BCTV may produce a tolerance for awkwardness in front of the camera, but officials in positions of authority may fare better the more they appear to be at ease before the viewers. The transformation of councilman Edward Leonardziak on the screen provides an example of BCTV's effect on the style of Reading politics. On early editions of *Inside City Hall*, Leonardziak appeared to be an unpolished politician who responded to viewers' questions in terse, mechanistic phrases. For example, in one early show, he responded to almost all questions with a standard phrase, "I don't know, but if you'll call my office in the morning I'll have my staff get you an answer." Leonardziak's appearance has changed markedly in four years as he has become more comfortable and aggressive in the studio. In recent programs, he is competent, interesting, and responsive to viewer concerns.

Reading, with its ethnic neighborhoods, history of machine politics, and working-class traditions, would seem ideally suited to resist change. Nevertheless, Mayor Miller's career demonstrates that something new is clearly going on in Reading. As an outsider, a newcomer, and a woman, Karen Miller is not politics as usual. In 1983, she was reelected to a second consecutive term, becoming the first mayor to do so in over 100 years.

Yet, in the final analysis, it is impossible to determine whether BCTV has revolutionized Reading politics or whether the technology merely dramatized changes in Reading politics that were happening anyway. Miller, for example, is a fiscally conservative Democrat; her election can be explained as a response to Reading's changing economic situation. Nevertheless, it appears to us that the cause-and-effect argument—with the development of BCTV as the cause—is at least plausible.

In the fall of 1982, BCTV conducted a "Viewership Survey" in order to obtain a "demographic profile of BCTV viewers among Berks Cable subscribers" and to allow viewers to "respond and characterize their level of participation in BCTV programming." The response rate was only 15.7%, probably the 15% who are the most interested in BCTV. Despite this drawback, the survey did indicate that quite a few people watch BCTV on an informal basis, confirming the mayor's opinion that the station attracts quite a few casual viewers who watch every once in a while.

In part, BCTV's success may stem from the fact that Berks Cable currently carries only 12 channels of programming. A renegotiated franchise will probably call for 36 channels that would present Reading viewers with a larger choice of programming. For BCTV, this competition could well mean losing those individuals who watch every now and then when they encounter something interesting while flipping through the channels.

While the staff looks after the daily affairs of BCTV, the Board of Directors, which includes some prominent Reading citizens, most notably the former mayor, Gene Shirk, is responsible for planning its future. The board's primary substantive deliberations lie in fund-raising. A separate Programming Committee allocates the available time among competing requests where they arise. The committee seems to be genuinely solicitous of ideas from all members of the Reading community and only rejects programming if it violates very basic rules of decency, or if it is clearly intended for a particular individual's financial or political gain. Time slots are assigned by lottery and, to date, the requests for programming have not become so numerous that BCTV has to choose among competitors.

In sum, BCTV has improved the accountability of local officials to those whom they serve. Even when council members only learn of this pothole or that broken street light, BCTV has exposed city government to the real concerns of people. Conscious that their work will be open for scrutiny on BCTV, public officials have to ensure that their work is consistent with the law and is understandable by all. Those who are to receive blame or praise for the activities of government can be more easily identified so that a more accountable system has emerged.

In conclusion, Reading is not a case of new technology influencing the politics of a city. The technology is far less important than the spirit of community cooperation: In terms of hardware, BCTV broadcasts with ancient equipment. Political values married to new technology-based institutions may be the difference: an informal, supportive environment in which viewers can move beyond an armchair approach to politics and become involved themselves. True, politics may not be the most entertaining fare on the screen, but that is precisely because amateurs are participating together in an undefined endeavor. When citizens join in, they may be more willing to excuse the shortcomings of BCTV programming, realizing that BCTV's faults are the result of ordinary people like themselves trying to communicate to others what they feel is important.

ALASKA'S LEGISLATIVE
TELECONFERENCING NETWORK[2]

The state of Alaska has some unique geographical features that isolate part of its population from the bulk concentrated in major cities. A vast expanse of land covering more area than the eastern half of the United States, Alaska is home to fewer residents than Albuquerque, New Mexico. Most of the population lives in either Anchorage, Fairbanks, or Juneau; the rest inhabit more than 200 smaller villages, separated from one another by vast stretches of open land. The difficulty of traveling establishes the need for a communications system that will collapse the large distances. In addition, very different ethnic cultures live side by side in both places. Special efforts must be made to overcome these impediments to political participation lest government become the spokesperson for the dominant culture concentrated in Anchorage and Juneau and not the voice of all the people.

Alaska has been the scene of many innovative experiments in involving citizens in public life, including the project discussed here that consists of two communication vehicles, the Legislative Telecommunications Network (LTN) and the Legislative Information Network (LIN). Formed in 1979 as a result of a report prepared by the Legislative Teleconferencing Network Task Force, originally five sites were linked by a dedicated four-wire circuit for audio teleconferences.

The LTN centers serve legislators in three ways: receiving legislative testimony from citizens, holding meetings with constituents, and arranging special meetings with aides or others helping legislators with their daily work. Legislative hearings are the most common use. Comments provided by citizens over the system are taken as formal testimony and legislators can listen and cross-examine witnesses just as though they were in the hearing room.

As one might expect, many legislators approached the concept of the LTN and LIN with initial skepticism. Larry Golden, the consultant who wrote the final report for the task force, was instrumental in alleviating the concerns of legislators worried about control over the process, the productive use of their time, and access to the network. Anticipating the political implications of such a system, Golden's idea was to graft the LTN onto the existing political structure with as little disruption as possible. The LTN was only intended to be an extension of the legislative process, not a method of securing direct democracy or altering the system in other ways.

Arranging for a teleconference follows a fairly routine scheduling process on a first come, first serve basis within the priorities noted above (hearings, constituent meetings, other business). The LTN staff asks for at least two weeks notice so they can notify their workers in the field who will then alert the community to an upcoming event. Although there are still a few holdouts, most legislators use the system, quite a few on a frequent basis.

When the legislature is in session, the LTN averages around three teleconferences per day. Most hearings are arranged by the chairman and the ranking minority member of the appropriate committees. However, if a legislator or a group of legislators feels that public sentiment on a particular issue demands a public airing, a teleconference often results. At times, special interest groups that are in touch with legislative activity in Juneau may be able to muster enough support to launch a teleconference. If the legislators are flexible enough and if considerable interest focuses upon one issue, a series of teleconferences can be held. This was true, for example, when the state was deciding whether to award a dividend to citizens from the extra money collected from Prudhoe Bay or to use these funds for new projects.

Charity Kedow, executive director, and Kathy Baltes, manager of LTN, reported that network usage reached saturation levels during the 1984 legislative session; from then on it became necessary to choose between competing users. When prioritizing teleconferences, the LTN will follow seniority rules established for the Alaskan legislature.

The legislators also decide which parts of the state should be included in a teleconference. Since each member has an interest in appealing to a particular district or to particular groups in the state, tension over which sites should be included in the teleconference can occur, especially if the number of sites requesting time stretches beyond the practical limit for conducting an effective meeting. This situation rarely arises: Most teleconferences do not evoke a huge outpouring of citizen interest.

Anyone at a growing number of sites is free to listen to any teleconference, regardless of whether they are scheduled to speak or not. If the subject matter provokes unscheduled listeners to add their thoughts, they can call up the LTN center in Anchorage or use a "back channel" computer network to request permission to speak. According to Kathy Baltes, the staff member principally responsible for the teleconferences, it is very rare for such a request to be denied. So while LTN staff put the practical limit of participation at six sites and legislators often choose the sites they think will be most important to receive feedback from, no one is excluded from talking simply because legislators or the LTN staff overlooked them.

Both Larry Golden and Dave Hammock, a consultant to the LTN, maintained that allowing every site to listen in on every teleconference was vital to establishing the system's integrity. Secret meetings, behind-closed-doors politics, are not possible on the LTV, so that, in theory, universal access will keep elected officials accountable to Alaskan citizens.

There are two other uses of the teleconferencing system. First, most legislators also hold regular teleconferences with their constituents to field complaints or questions and to explain actions the legislature has taken. As distinct from legislative hearings, the electronic office hours offer the citizen the opportunity to define the agenda. Because the format is less structured, extended discussion and debate is more likely.

Reportedly, the participants in these constituent teleconferences come more often out of direct, individual interest than as representatives of an interest group or lobby organization.

Second, in order to draft legislation or hammer out compromises, representatives sometimes use the system to conduct working sessions, especially when the legislature is not in session. These usually involve small numbers of legislators and experts discussing issues in great detail. Though anyone on the system can listen in, the nature and substance of these meetings discourage most from doing so.

To complement the LTN, the state of Alaska also funds the Legislative Information Network (LIN) that provides citizens with pertinent and timely information regarding state government. A computer network allows citizens to trace the legislative history of any bill, to follow legislative development in particular subject areas, and to obtain copies of reports or bills. (The same computer network serves to coordinate the teleconferences, allowing the staff to exchange information on a "back channel.") Sites that combine the functions of the two networks are referred to as Legislative Information Offices (LIO); currently, fourteen LIOs staffed by full-time information officers dot the state while four other LIOs function on a part-time basis. Ideally, Alaskans who participate in teleconferences will also use the LIN to learn both the substantive and procedural issues affecting the topics in which they are interested.

Another important feature of the LIN allows citizens in distant locations to send their opinions on various legislative matters to legislators in Juneau through an electronic mail system. A concerned citizen can send a Public Opinion Message (POM) to a legislator or group of them through a computer network. The ease of using this system has made it very popular. When employed with the LIN, citizens can keep track of legislators' behavior on issues and prod them when they deviate from the citizen's own ideas.

Once it became clear that the LTN and LIN fulfilled a political need of legislators and citizens to communicate with each other, additional sites were gradually added. Besides the 18 Legislative Information Offices already mentioned, there are 28 full-time teleconference centers (LTN only) plus an additional 26 voluntary teleconference centers located in the homes and offices of people who have agreed to store and operate teleconferencing equipment for other people in the village.

Undoubtedly the most important reason for successful operation of the network lies in the efforts of those who run it. The crucial link in the system is provided by the field managers who actually run the scattered information offices and telecommunication centers. Not only do these people maintain the communications hardware but they also advocate its use to villagers who might be mistrustful of government, apathetic toward politics, or unaware of political disputes. If the field manager feels that village fishermen should be alerted to a bill concerning tax deductions for the purchase of business equipment, for example, he or she contacts the appropriate fishermen and informs them of the upcoming hearing. If the computer prints the requested information in the form of minutes of a committee hearing, the field manager often helps translate the information into a form that is useful for the citizen.

Thus the field manager walks a delicate tightrope between having to be strictly nonpartisan and yet wanting to stimulate interest in political issues so that the network receives use. Kedow and Baltes both said they selected the field managers with great care, trying to make sure that the new recruits move easily in the social and political circles of the communities they will be serving. Very often, the person chosen will be a former bartender, teacher or other central figure in the community who knows the intimate details of life in the community yet has managed not to alienate factions of the community.

Let us examine the quantity and quality of citizen participation. Alaska's small population is one of the most salient factors in state politics. Each representative has approximately 10,000 people in his or her district; the number of voters is much less. Very often, legislators know a high percentage of their constituents on a personal basis. In state races, elections are highly competitive. Moreover, the fact that many Alaskans work in subsidized or regulated industries also means that they appreciate the importance of speaking up for what they want.

Evidently, the LIN and LTN proved to be very popular within a short period of time. Legislators discovered that Alaskans wanted a greater voice in government and were willing to use the network. One can measure the popularity of the LTN and LIN in a number of ways. The expansion of LTN sites from an original five locations in 1978 to a total of 71 as of November 1984 indicates not only that demand among Alaskans for the system has increased, but also that legislators find the system provides a valuable contribution to their work. A series of better measures of growth in participation can be found in the data from Table 5.1 for the first four years of operation, provided by Kathy Baltes.

Other than in 1982, when there was a slight drop in the rates of participation because of internal politics in the legislature, use of the system has grown continually. In 1982, when a new majority coalition which crossed party lines came into being, much of the session was taken up with organizational matters. In addition, the push for adjournment came early that year, forcing attention onto budgetary

TABLE 5.1

Fiscal Year (July-June)	Total Tele-conferences	Gross Number Attending Tele-conferences	Legislative Public Hearings	Constituent Meetings
1981	412	8,745	72	114
1982	376	8,050	66	72
1983	589	15,726	123	186
1984	715	17,661	169	206

matters that usually do not provoke that much citizen interest. Both of these drove down the total amount of substantive legislative business and curtailed, as a consequence, the use of the LTN.

On the other hand, Baltes cautioned that the sharp jump registered between 1982 and 1983 in the total number of citizens attending teleconferences probably reflects tighter reporting procedures and an expansion in the number of teleconferencing sites from 5 to 28 more than a massive outpouring of citizen response.

The types of teleconferences of greatest interest to this research—legislative hearings or constituent meetings (versus those that deal with administrative matters or those conducted by executive branch agencies)—have both been rising rapidly in recent years. Moreover, the substantial growth in the number of teleconferences held each year indicates an expanding interest among legislators in the network. In 1985, when the decline in oil prices curtailed state revenue from the North Slope fields, the budget of the legislative information office was cut along with most other state agencies. As a result, many of the sites were downgraded to a volunteer basis, but the number of legislative teleconferences has not decreased. As previously mentioned, use of the LTN has now reached its saturation level. An average of three teleconferences a day are held when the legislature is in session. In part, this increased demand can be traced to (1) the value of the information legislators receive from the system, (2) the fact that more legislators are becoming more comfortable with using the networks, and (3) a feeling among legislators that citizens who want to participate will be disappointed unless they are included.

Even though only a few individuals can speak at each teleconference, some citizens find the discussions interesting or important enough that they will attend just to listen and be counted in the audience. One teleconference on highway regulations affecting trucking, for example, attracted over fifty truckers and their families, filling one site. Most of these only listened. Of course, their presence is noted and reported to the legislators in Juneau over the computer network.

During the five months of the 1984 legislative session, 11,451 "public opinion messages" (POMs) were sent by citizens to legislators. This figure constitutes a small decrease from that sent during the 1983 session that was slightly longer and considered several controversial measures. In that year, 14,202 messages were sent through this electronic mail service.

In theory, POMs are to be used by individual citizens to convey their views on policy matters to legislators. But the system has been partially appropriated by interest groups to send messages to the offices of all legislators at the government's expense. This can be seen in the number of addressees to which the above messages were sent; in 1984, POMs were sent to 178,511 recipients (an average of 15.6 legislators per message), compared to 190,789 (13.4 per message) the year before. Although the staff in Anchorage did not think that such activity violates the original intent of the network, such a convenient and free way of communicating with legislators has encouraged more frequent, organized communication. The high volume of POMs may eventually detract from the effectiveness of this type of participation. Legislators are aware of which messages are sent en masse, and they tend to disregard the results of mass mailings as merely the work of organized special interest groups.

In turning to the role of political elites, we must distinguish between how legislators use the system and the strategies of interest groups. Legislators can request that their constituents be heard on a particular teleconference and then notify people in the district of the opportunity, thus appearing to perform a public service for these people. In our talk with Representative Cowdrey, he openly described his efforts to be sure that interests with which he agreed were represented in the teleconference testimony. For example, if one of his committees was organizing a teleconference on oil pricing, he would alert some groups—in this case forestry interests—that normally might not pay attention to these matters but could well have a narrow interest in this particular bill.

Interest groups have begun to use the network in fairly sophisticated ways. For example, when the state was conducting teleconferences on regulating boxing, a political consultant with a side interest in boxing rounded up a busload of boxers and took them to the LTN site. Nobody opposed to boxing showed up, so virtually all the testimony the committee heard was in favor of abandoning state regulation of the sport. The same political consultant mentioned that several local church groups had publicized the LTN to their parishioners as a way to have their voices heard in Juneau on matters of interest to the churches.

Both Representative Cowdrey and Baltes admitted that the LTN could be used by lobbyists, enabling them to back up their position papers with popular support. Walter Parker, a former telecommunications official with the state, noted that the fisherman have used the system very effectively in pressing for support of their troubled industry. According to rough estimates we received from the LTN staff, about 30%–40% participate as individuals, while 60%–70% are affiliated with some group or organization. Even so, the LTN allows legislators to reach *members* of these groups rather than their lobbyists or organizational staff in Juneau. Moreover, the percentage of those participating under their own volition appears to be substantially higher during constituent meetings (as opposed to hearings) but the overall number of participants is often correspondingly lower.

The LTN has exerted an important influence on government accountability of Alaskan politics, a political structure that was necessarily closed to most citizens because of geography and climate. Certainly the LTN allows a widening of the pool of witnesses and greater diversity in viewpoints. This may force legislators to consider the broader public interest as well as the narrow concerns of directly affected groups. In the same vein, because they are open at all sites the teleconferences serve an educational role by demanding more sophisticated and well-thought out testimony from interest groups whose positions are also made more public and widely distributed among the citizens. Now they must sell their positions publicly to a more diverse, larger, and informed audience.

Some observers of Alaskan politics claim the networks also enhance the position of incumbents as against their opponents. The agenda for the LTN/LIN is controlled by legislators who can choose whether to attend or skip a hearing depending on how comfortable they feel with the subject matter. If the legislator plays his cards correctly, the LTN and LIN can effectively showcase his or her talents.

One must also note that opposing groups can more easily generate effective counterpublicity. They can seek information at the LIN about a legislator's record and then publicize their findings to the voters. Lobbyists and interest groups who have come to recognize the importance of the LTN/LIN have devised communication channels of their own in order to take political advantage of the system; these channels can be adopted to help opposing candidates.

In a more discreet way, the LTN and LIN have altered the political topography of the state. Because these networks offer such quick and easy contact with locations all over Alaska, legislators have expanded

their political activity beyond their own districts, particularly as it relates
to work they do to fulfill committee obligations. Lawmakers now seek
opinions from a cross-section of the Alaskan population, and the
networks have increased their familiarity with various interest groups in
the state. One cannot, however, ascertain whether the presence of the
LTN/LIN had sparked additional political mobilization in Alaskan
politics outside of the networks.

In the final analysis, the intelligent manner in which the LTN and the
LIN was grafted onto the existing political structure accounts for its
success. The tacit endorsement of these systems by legislators using the
system confers a legitimacy that encourages serious participation by all
parties.

NORTH CAROLINA'S OPEN/NET

In 1979, the State of North Carolina established The Agency for
Public Telecommunications (APT) within its Department of
Administration. In its early years, the Agency primarily served other
units of the State's Executive Branch, producing public service
announcements and other videotapes and establishing a "slow-picture"
teleconferencing network among seven sites in North Carolina plus
Washington, D.C. In addition to these services, APT has authority to
conduct policy studies of telecommunication issues facing the state.

In the spring of 1983, under the leadership of Executive Director Lee
Wing, APT undertook to improve contact between citizens and their
state government by staging an "Electronic Town Hall." On March 22,
51 cable systems, which reached 20% of the North Carolina population
in 116 cities and towns, simultaneously cablecast a two-hour meeting of
APT's Board discussing the local impact of deregulation of the
telephone industry. The videotaped meeting was followed by a one-hour
live call-in so that viewers could offer suggestions and raise questions. A
panel of state legislators and other officials in Raleigh responded to 19
phone calls during this hour.

In evaluating their experience, APT and other officials of the state
concluded that the format had successfully communicated to citizens
information about an important policy matter. Accordingly, they decided
to establish a regular series of weekly shows following the same pattern:
videotaped hearings or meetings of state government agencies followed
by a live show featuring decision makers on the receiving end of
telephone calls from around the state. The result is the North Carolina
Open Public Events Network (OPEN/net).

During the spring and summer of 1984, OPEN/net presented its first 16-week series of programs and call-in segments. APT rented a satellite transponder for three hours each Friday evening; the shows were taken by 48 cable companies scattered throughout the state. The first half of the program consisted of an unedited portion of a meeting or hearing of the relevant state agency; the second half followed a live call-in format. The substance of these sessions and the number of calls received in each call-in segment can be found in Table 5.2. An average of 10.9 calls per hour were handled by state officials, a rate that is roughly comparable with C-SPAN's national call-in shows which handle an average of 12.3 calls per hour. During the spring of 1985, OPEN/net's average moved up to 16 callers per hour. Evidently, this rate is limited more by the time needed to deal with each call than by the level of viewer interest. On one occasion, when legislative leaders came to discuss the upcoming legislative calendar, the telephone company reported to APT that incoming calls were running about 13% above the receiving capacity of their lines.

The number of calls varied according to the content of the show. Except for a special three-hour call-in program for people affected by a tornado disaster, the largest viewer response (in total number of calls) occurred on the night when the Hazardous Waste Study Commission hearing was aired. The fact that one town, Laurinberg, was being considered as a potential treatment site generated a considerable number of calls from viewers there. When state government action had direct consequences for a definable group of people, political organizations sprang up to use the vehicle of OPEN/net to demonstrate their concerns. We do not know what "behind the scenes" communication went on in Laurinberg before this show, but somehow those active in the dispute were able to generate viewers and callers from the town. Over the entire first series, OPEN/net received a total of 26 calls from Laurinberg; the vast bulk were recorded that night.

The problems that require discussion here are not related to technology. The OPEN/net concept has one major limitation that is easily recognized—it reaches a small percentage of the state's total population. In the spring of 1984, its shows were carried by approximately 50 cable systems that combined reached only about 20% of the state's population. Beyond that, the actual size of the audience is determined by the level of viewer interest. While no one can be precise as to the number of individuals who watch these shows, suffice it to say that the number is far, far below the total number of citizens. On the other hand, the same number is probably far above the number that travel to Raleigh to observe agency meetings and to register citizen opinion. The incremental gain

TABLE 5.2
OPEN/net Call-ins, Spring, 1984

		Total Number Calls	Call-in Length (hrs.)	Number Calls on air	Rate of Calls on air (hr.)
March 16	Council on Aging	19	1½	15	10.0
March 23	Legislative Study Commission on Agriculture, Forestry and Seafood	17	1½	17	11.2
March 30	Tornado Disaster Relief	65	3	53	17.7
April 6	Commission on Education and Economic Growth	22	1½	18	12.0
April 13	Community Colleges Board	32	1¼	16	12.8
April 20	Biotechnology Study Commission	15	1¼	11	9.0
April 27	Utility Review Committee	17	1¼	15	12.0
May 4	Western NC Tomorrow Conference on Mountain Subdivision Problems	6	1	6	6.0
May 11	Alcohol Beverage Control and Wildlife Commission	23	1¼	20	16.0
May 18	Waste Management Board and Hazardous Waste Study Commission	38	2	32	16.0
May 25	Legislative Research Commission's Committees on Public Health Facilities, Water Quality, and Telephone Deregulation	19	2¼	15	6.8
June 1	General Assembly Special on Appropriation, Education, and Other Major Issues	28	2¼	24	10.8
June 8	Child Day-Care Licensing Commission	11	1	10	10.0
June 15	Crime Commission/General Assembly Update	17	1⅚	6	3.3
June 22	State Health Coordinating	13	⅚	10	12.0
June 29	Courts Commission	7	⅚	7	8.4

over the functioning of existing institutions is sizable, but well short of utopian vision about letting the people govern themselves.

The OPEN/net staff noted a tendency for incoming telephone calls to occur near the hour and half hour breaks when entertainment channels normally run advertising. Ben Kittner, of the APT staff, theorized that at those times viewers were switching channels, happened to turn to OPEN/net, and were then stimulated to call. The fact that calls dropped off again after entertainment programming resumed, however, may indicate that many of these casual viewers lost interest and went on to other things.

OPEN/net's goal is, in Lee Wing's words, "to reach those people who live 4 to 8 hours from Raleigh, whose main source of news is from out of state, and who want to find out what's happening in their state." The factors that determine the success of this enterprise as a vehicle for political particpation are (1) the percentage of North Carolina homes wired for cable, (2) the willingness of cable system operators to carry their shows, (3) the attractiveness of the shows produced, and (4) the format of the OPEN/net productions. These factors are listed in inverse order of APT's capacity to affect them.

The last factor highlights a second problem from the viewpoint of this research: whether the citizen calls can be considered political participation. While participation facilitated by telecommunication technologies often involves an important educational component, through its design OPEN/net emphasizes the educational aspects over the exercise of citizen influence. This is true despite comments during a show by one week's moderator to the effect that, "Your participation is what makes OPEN/net special. No matter how far you live from Raleigh, OPEN/net gives you a chance to influence state government. So we want to hear from you." The substance of the show, however, concerned recommendations on future directions and commitments of North Carolina's community colleges that had been presented to the governor. In other words, these recommendations were in final form at the time of the OPEN/net broadcast. Although many still had to be approved by the governor and acted upon by the general assembly, they were still not very susceptible to citizen influence. The guests invited to respond to callers on OPEN/net were the president of the Department of Community Colleges and his assistant for policy. Clearly they had come prepared to discuss the community college system and their recommendations as an educational exercise in letting the public know what state government was doing. Their objectives were less to learn from the public about its perception of needs, problems, and priorities than to explain their recommendations. Most of the calls received were from viewers with questions; some had complaints; none of the callers told the guests what policies they thought ought to be followed by the community colleges.

Indeed, among those receiving OPEN/net there is some ambivalence as to whether it ought to offer citizens an effective political voice. Noting that OPEN/net was not instituted to rectify a perceived problem but to innovate at the frontiers of state government, Joel Fleischman, an APT Board member and cochair of the initial Electronic Town Hall, defined its purpose as, "not attempting to give citizens influence over state policy except that a more informed citizenry can participate better. More knowledge of the councils of government will lead to more influence."

While OPEN/net does lean toward the educational goals, citizen influence is not totally absent. In the discussion of community colleges, for example, one call brought to light a problem unrelated to the recommendations that the president had not been aware of previously. He left the studio asking his assistant to look into the matter. In addition, while most topics covered by OPEN/net in this first year dealt with policies in their end stage of development, some shows do concern matters at an earlier stage of policy-making when officials are still seeking information and input.

Consider a third problem: that of ensuring fairness and neutrality in the agency stimulating participation, a ubiquitous concern for all these efforts. OPEN/net illustrates the complexity of the problem and the great lengths to which Lee Wing has gone to ensure that fairness is preserved. The Agency for Public Telecommunications is governed by a board appointed jointly by the governor and the two houses of the state legislature. OPEN/net has a separate Coverage Policy Committee composed of private citizens who are "responsible for selecting meetings and ensuring objective coverage." The Coverage Policy Committee is balanced in terms of political persuasion and party affiliation, for Wing knows that if the project becomes too closely identified with one gubernatorial administration, it is likely to be terminated (or kept and used politically) by a new governor. In January 1985, OPEN/net survived the transition in governors from Hunt to Martin, from Democrat to Republican.

Lee Wing argues that underlying the political balance built into OPEN/net's board is an affirmation that its role is education not advocacy. To be sure, if the main purpose is to impart information so as to empower citizens over the long run, then a state agency must remain neutral or it will quickly become politicized. But it does not follow that vehicles for citizen involvement can maintain their neutrality *only* if they emphasize the educational aspects and avoid providing opportunities in which citizens can influence policy. The Alaskan LTN, for example, has demonstrated that it can serve as a conduit for highly charged arguments without losing the neutrality of open access.

Lee Wing argues that another protection for OPEN/net against outside influences comes from the fact that the committee selects the issues to be covered and the guests that will be asked to appear. If the state agencies or legislative commissions and committees themselves came to OPEN/net with an agenda, the process would quickly be politicized. Instead Wing arranges the substance of the shows and invites guests according to policy guidelines and specific instructions laid down by her committee.

In addition to guarding itself against becoming the tool of outside politicians, partisans, and bureaucrats, OPEN/net must also ensure that its own decisions do not affect policy outcomes. As Executive Director Lee Wing argued in our interview,

> In issue after issue, it is not our job to influence how that issue is managed by government—by the executive and legislative branches. It is our job to offer legislators and others the opportunity to hear from citizens and to offer citizens more information about policy before it is acted upon.

The most obvious way that APT could affect policy is through its decisions of what to cover, when to put an issue to the public, and who to invite to present it. It is not always possible to provide balance in the selection of guests. Ran Coble, director of a Raleigh policy research center, argued that the biggest potential flaw in the design was that the system could fall victim to state government insiders using it to sell their point of view to the public. He felt they might not give the public the full range of available policies, and concluded that opposing spokespersons were needed to ensure balance. Lee Wing countered that argument by noting that callers often provide the needed balance, raising objections and alternatives. Certainly that occurred in the show on hazardous waste policies. As OPEN/net becomes more widely recognized, it is all the more likely that proponents of alternative policies will find it in their interest to use the shows as vehicles for their viewpoints.

In order to avoid intruding into the policy process, OPEN/net does a minimal amount of editing of meetings taped for the initial half of each show. If the actual meeting runs longer than the available time, they select a segment that fits their time constraints, but they avoid any editing within the allotted hour and a half. In our interview, Lee Wing frankly admitted her debt to C-SPAN's coverage of congressional business, and asserted,

Once you start editing you become more like a broadcaster. Meetings are
boring in parts and interesting in parts. That's the way it is. If you came
to the meeting, that's what you would see. . . . In one show, a
microphone was knocked over and we had no sound for three minutes,
but we still put that segment on because we didn't want to edit.

OPEN/net's preference for policy decisions nearing completion may
also provide protection against the vehicle becoming politicized. For
most matters that OPEN/net brought to the citizens of North Carolina,
the latent political disputes had been resolved before the public discussion via OPEN/net. At an earlier stage of decision making, telecommunications may provide an instrument for effective citizen
participation, but the strategy aggravates the problem of preserving the
neutrality and fairness of the conduit through which citizen involvement
is to be channeled. OPEN/net demonstrates how sensitive and complicated those protections can be, and the project is exploring the frontiers
of how satellites and cable systems can be used to bring citizens and
their government closer.

MARKEY'S "ELECTURE"

In late 1983, Congressman Edward Markey of Massachusetts agreed
to participate in a computer conference discussing arms control policy
over a network provided by The Source Telecomputing Corporation.
The conferencing system on The Source is provided as a profit-making
product of Participation Systems, Inc., of Winchester, Massachusetts.
The president of this company, Harry Stevens, has both a political background and a long-term interest in the applications of technology to
politics, so it is not very surprising that he turned to a political figure to
initiate a series of electronic lectures or "electures." Though Congressman Markey was less involved than the ideal, the conception of an
"electure" is that a guest leader will stimulate discussion among Source
users by providing initial ideas and reacting to the contributions of
others. Markey, a Massachusetts Democrat, has been at the forefront of
the nuclear freeze movement and seemed a natural choice for a conference devoted to American strategic defense issues.

The computer conference consisted of a main branch and four principal subconferences devoted to different aspects of U.S. nuclear arms
policy. The main conference, entitled "Nuclear War," was used primarily for administrative notices such as announcing the start of a new sub-
topic for discussion. The branch-like structure of four subconferences
covered (1) the strategic balance of nuclear weapons vis-à-vis the USSR;

(2) the prospects and desirability of a freeze on new arms; (3) the deployment of nuclear arms in Europe; and (4) the feasibility of using nuclear weapons only against Soviet strategic forces. Each of these discussions was introduced by a long comment from Congressman Markey to which participants were expected to react. A staff member in Markey's Washington office entered these initiating remarks into the main conference.

Table 5.3 indicates the number and date of the initiating comment in the main conference (e.g. "Nuclear War"), the title and length of Markey's contribution and the number of subsequent comments generated among the participants during the subsequent two months of discussion.

In total, approximately 150 subscribers to The Source joined Markey's electure, reading at least some of the discussion in one or more of its subconferences. Of these, 46 or 31% actually made comments. The Source has a very large number of subscribers (45,000) but since most do not use the computer conferencing software, computing a participation rate is difficult. An estimated 10,000 subscribers make use of conferencing, but only some of these are regular active users. The participants in this electure are only 1.5% of the total users of the conferencing software.

In general, the level and sophistication of participation observed in this computer conference was much superior to that found in other public conferences dealing with political issues on The Source. Markey's presence appears to have stimulated a higher degree of interest and involvement. While such observations are difficult to quantify, it did appear that the contributions made by participants were more thoughtful and serious. The discussion did not contain the high level of unrelated or snide comments that frequently characterizes open conferences. Quantitatively, the comments appear to be longer than in other conferences observed, although figuring out what should be taken as the norm can be

TABLE 5.3

Date of Start	Comment No. in Main Conference	Title	Length of Initial Comment (# of char.)	Total Number of Comments Generated
12/1/83	—	Nuclear War	—	38
12/1/83	1	Nuclear Balance	5,000	90
12/4/84	4	Nuclear Freeze	6,000	51
12/8/84	10	Nuclear NATO	10,000	32
12/26/84	18	Nuclear Counterforce	7,000	6

difficult. Note, however, that many of those involved limited their participation to reading the collected comments without adding their own thoughts.

The pattern of discussion, however, resembled that of other public conferences that are "event triggered." That is to say, the discussion provoked by the opening comments of Markey were fast and furious. After a brief flurry, however, the frequency of responses dropped sharply, so that the conversation soon winnowed down to a few regular participants. This pattern also characterized involvement in the subconferences: The later they were introduced, the less participation they drew. The number of comments made, the number of subscribers who joined, and the number who actually contributed to the discussion dropped as the electure continued.

Congressman Markey limited his participation to the initiating comments, although his aide responsible for the electure, Ron Klein, stated that every few days he would go over a transcript of the comments with the congressman. Irving Learch, a doctor at NYU Medical School, served as moderator for the conference for Participation Systems. Most of the interaction enjoyed by the participants came from Learch, who made helpful suggestions and announcements and reacted to comments and questions posed by participants. Since Learch is a frequent participant in other conferences on The Source, however, interacting with him may not have had the same perceived benefits as the opportunity to discuss things with the congressman.

It is certainly plausible to suggest that Markey's lack of direct involvement was in part responsible for the sharp drop in participation rates. Those who joined the conference were not really able to interact with the congressman. Many may have felt that the electure offered them no more of an opportunity to be involved in policy-making than would, for example, reading the congressman's press releases. As a result, for the participants the electure may have represented just another open conference—albeit on an important topic and with a higher level of discussion—but not a real opportunity for input to the policy process.

Institutionally, while participants could react to Markey's initial thoughts and while the congressman was aware of the comments elicited, the demonstration did not really explore the interactive capabilities of this form of conferencing for the formation of policy. When asked in our interview if Markey learned anything by his involvement, aide Ron Klein replied, "There were two or three new angles that we hadn't heard before and those we had to rethink, but basically, no; we've been through the many arguments many times before." In other words, from Markey's perspective, the experiment was an exercise in sounding out arguments rather than subjecting oneself to citizen influence.

This lack of noticeable impact on policy reflects both the nature of the issue chosen for discussion and the legislator's conception of his or her role as a public figure. Arms policy is a major question on which Congressman Markey has become highly visible as a leading critic of the Reagan administration and as a prominent proponent of a nuclear freeze. Having declared his positions so publicly on these questions, Congressman Markey—and almost any other elected leader in the same position—was very unlikely to alter his views based on arguments from a scattered group of citizens, such as that linked together by The Source. Instead, Markey and his staff viewed this as an opportunity to experiment with a new medium and to acquaint a few concerned citizens with his positions on U.S. nuclear arms policy. "We wanted to try something new," explained Ron Klein during our interview. He added that those hooked up to the Source are not demographically representative of the population and observed that their response rate was not unlike that produced by direct mail. "This is not a way," he concluded, "to reach large numbers of people." Because the discussion did not involve a large or representative number, Markey's staff tended to dismiss the electure as a mechanism of citizen influence.

In many ways this electure demonstrated the strengths and weaknesses of this means of citizen participation. We should bear in mind the limitations of this medium: Markey's staff is correct in concluding that The Source is not yet (and may never be) a vehicle for reaching a large and heterogeneous audience. The limits of access need to be constantly reiterated. At present, only the affluent or those with an abiding interest in computers are members of The Source. Moreover, being a written medium, computer conferencing may never reach anything approaching a universal penetration.

Within these limitations, however, the Markey electure demonstrates that conferencing can provide an effective medium for policy discussion. To maximize these benefits, due care should be taken in the selection of an issue and the inclusion of public figures. Nevertheless, the seriousness and quality of the discussion in this electure demonstrate that computer conferencing can rise above the level of chitchat that characterizes many open conferences.

Open conferences, while not a means of mass participation, can be a valuable method of soliciting opinion from that segment of the population that now participates in commercial computer networks, for example, upper-income and educational groups with a high level of technical expertise. In other words, for public officials a more appropriate use of computer conferencing would be as an extension of the legislative hearing process rather than as a meeting with constituents or as an instrument of mass communications. Private conferences, rather than those open to all Source users, would remove the illusion that large or representative audiences can be reached through this medium. Conferencing can, however, allow the exchange of expertise and considered opinion—information that can be just as precious for a legislator, although they will treat it differently than that obtained through mass channels.

Discussion

We can now turn to an explicit evaluation of these experiments in teledemocracy along the institutional dimensions of participation laid out in Chapter Three.

ACCESS AND REACH

These projects demonstrated a very real and tangible benefit: Policy-making was opened to more citizens than normally participate through traditional institutions. These projects provided a greater reach than our normal governmental processes. While fifteen citizens speaking each week with the mayor of Reading or a member of the city council is not a large number of participants, from observations and interviews at various sites, it is clear that they do constitute a larger group than those who usually frequent city hall. The new mechanisms for participation do not replace the municipal corridors, but they do provide an expansive alternative or supplement.

In the process, the range of participants is probably broadened. Some of this growth undoubtedly permits the political incorporation of groups such as shut-ins, the elderly, or those whose occupations would not allow them to participate otherwise. In Reading, for example, the community and government access system, originally designed to facilitate communication among senior citizens, continues to have a strong orientation toward the elderly community.

I suspect, however, that the bulk of the additional participants do not fall into these special classes but are drawn from groups that normally find involvement in public affairs a little too burdensome given their other commitments in life. In these situations, technology has allowed the political elites to lessen some of the burdens and barriers to participation (especially those imposed by geography). Even so, the numbers additionally involved are small; this extension of the active population is far from a revolutionary transformation of political power. Those who visit city hall or employ the preexisting means of exerting influence still have their disproportionate access and power.

Strictly speaking, in determining the reach of these projects, I was forced to rely upon the statements of those conducting them in order to document the fact that the set of participants has been expanded. Independent observations, however, support their conclusions. Our own limited survey of 70 Reading households, for example, indicated that a fairly sizable proportion of viewers report watching BCTV programs on a regular basis. Moreover, the political community in Reading is small enough that government officials are able to recognize many callers. The number of repeaters from show to show and the overlap between those who call in to BCTV and those who show up in the corridors of city hall was judged to be minimal.

My confidence in the assertion that these mechanisms are extending the set of participants is increased, moreover, by the modesty of the claims made by the elites and the project initiators. Those managing these call-in shows did not claim to be wildly expanding the set of participants, nor even that those who did call in were somehow representative of the entire population. In the main, they recognized that the well-established inequities of participation rates affected their mechanisms.

A factor that partially determines the reach of these efforts is the degree of access to them by the general citizenry. Due to poor television reception, most homes in the city of Reading are wired for cable, and since there are only 12 channels on the system, it is difficult not to be aware of the programs featuring city officials. Of all these projects, BCTV had the broadest level of access. In North Carolina, less than half the adult citizens can receive OPEN/net. Access to the electures conducted over The Source computer network is, of course, the most severely constrained. Far too few individuals possess home computers and the financial resources that allow them to engage in extensive computer conferencing. The pool of potential participants, moreover, is completely atypical—upscale on economic and educational indicators. In all these cases, the technology employed proved to be the main factor limiting access.

The Markey electure sought to involve a limited and definable pool, the set of Source users. Since any participant can discover which users have joined a conference and all the comments bear the drafter's account number, the medium allows one to observe closely the actual achievements of this effort to involve citizens. Its actual reach graphically illustrates the limitations that are probably true of all these mechanisms: First, many of those eligible did not participate and, second, among those who did, the participants were stratified into a handful of those deeply involved, a larger group of those who added only one or two comments, and the majority who only observed the discussion.

This pattern of participation on The Source resembles that of the televised call-in shows. Certainly every viewer does not rush to the phone. Assumedly, the overwhelming majority of those who watch the discussion do so without initiating any further action. Most likely, a high proportion tune in for a short time and then move on, just as computer conferences draw sporadic attention from most of those who joined. Since television is so omnipresent, however, the reach of televised call-in meetings with public officials is larger than that of computer conferences.

In other words, while access limitations were important, other major factors affected the total number of citizens who become involved in these projects. These are related to limitations on (a) the ability of citizens to discover their opportunities to participate and (b) their interest in becoming involved. Both are significant limitations. The design of the Alaskan system mitigates one of these problems: Staff members in the separate communities are paid to inform citizens of upcoming hearings.

The Alaskan teleconferencing system appears to be the most successful from the perspective of the raw numbers of participants brought into politics through the use of technology. However, their results are probably not attributable to the higher level of communication technologies used in this endeavor but to the blending of these means with an organization designed to encourage participation. Without contact from the Legislative Information Office's personnel, the large number of teleconferences held on vastly different issues would probably discourage involvement; citizens would have to exert a good deal of self-initiative to find out what committee hearings were planned.

Another way of looking at this matter is to note that there exist persistent problems of communicating about communication. Advertising on the three television networks can be attractive to politicians precisely because they do not have to build their own audiences; they rent them from corporations that construct audiences on the basis of entertainment. But one effect of the emerging diversity in communication channels is that interested citizens may miss opportunities to participate simply because they do not know of the possibilities. If any of the projects other than the Alaska system had the same capacity for outreach to inform interested parties of opportunities to register their opinions, they would undoubtedly improve their performance in a purely quantitative sense.

Several qualifications are needed, however, to circumscribe our enthusiasm for the Alaskan LTN. First, counting the number of callers to a televised public official assumes a restricted definition of participation; those who do not call during the show may attempt to exert influence through some other channel or at some other time. While this systematic undercount also applies to the Alaskan Teleconferencing Network, one can more precisely count the number of individuals who attended the hearings but did not participate than one can estimate a television audience. Second, since much of the success in Alaska depends upon the human organization built around the technology, the effects we have observed may, as noted above, be primarily related to the impact of money. Of the projects examined, the Alaskan system was the most elaborate and the most expensive; the fact that it is also the most successful may not be unrelated.

DIVERSE PATHS OF ACCESS

In Chapter Three, we developed the notion of diversity of participation opportunities, recognizing that individuals differ in the intensity of their interest in policy matters and in their mastery of the skills required. Ideally, a project should incorporate a range of opportunities for citizen involvement, or multiple paths by which citizen's can achieve access. Even though each of the experiments studied provided some choice in participation strategies, in the main these alternatives were decidedly secondary to the primary participation link offered. As a result, we were not able to observe these alternatives effectively. For example, someone attending a legislative teleconference in Alaska may have spoken to a staff member, written a letter to the committee or sent a separate message through the electronic mail system even while refusing to step forward to offer public testimony. In most cases, however, the technology worked against diversity in participation. These projects were established with one form of citizen involvement in mind, and telecommunications media were made available to facilitate that form.

INDIVIDUAL OR GROUP BEHAVIOR

For the most part, citizens became involved in these projects as individuals, not as members of organized groups. However, groups are involved in these endeavors and the fact that one encounters group activity at all is all the more notable in contrast to the other variety of projects. Here real and significant public decisions are directly at stake. Since the structure of American politics is inevitably influenced by groups and organizations, it is natural that they can be found here trying to influence the government officials. The presence or absense of groups can be critical to the success of citizen participation, as Jeffrey Berry and his associates (1984) concluded after a review of 45 cases of public involvement in administrative hearings. Whether or not interest groups were involved proved to be significantly related to measures of the effectiveness of citizen participation.

Looking for those instances in which group involvement did occur turns one's attention to Alaska where some organizations were able to bring their membership to the hearing rooms in order to make their influence felt. These same groups appear to be using the electronic mail system to flood legislators with similar messages. In North Carolina, one of the most active shows concerned a policy that fell disproportionately upon a narrow population group. The citizens of Laurinberg mobilized to oppose a hazardous waste plan that would site a dump near their town.

The Alaska example shows that when citizens are required to come to a given location to participate, as in a teleconferencing site or hearing room, interest groups are often able to contact their members and ask them to attend. Thus there appears to be a complicated set of relationships between the degree of initiative required of citizens, the breadth of the audience reached, and the capacity of interest groups to affect participation. The more the project initiators assume the burdens of education and outreach, the broader the range of citizens who will become involved, and the more difficult the task for organized interest groups to use this mechanism for effective influence. When the initiative required of citizens is greater, interest groups are able to provide the incentives and stimuli needed to activate participation.

In projects employing television, for example, one can observe that technology works against group participation: Viewers at home are not easily mobilized by interest groups. In a small city such as Reading, for example, where a group such as the fire fighters might be tempted to monopolize the phone lines during a particular hearing, the public officials stated that this never occurred. They went on to argue that it would be easier for them to expose the group's demands as special pleadings in an open forum in which the general public was able to watch.

AGENDA SETTING

The degree to which citizens can influence and control the agenda of policy matters under consideration can be as important as the power to influence policy decisions. As a general finding, all of these projects studied reserved more control for initiators and elites than they awarded to the participating citizens.[3]

Those who called the mayor or councilor in Reading, for example, could raise any matter, but, because responsibilities for different city departments were spread among the public officials, some questions or complaints were more relevant than others. Moreover, when city government hearings are televised in Reading, the agenda is for all means and purposes established by their presence. The same can be said for the appearances on OPEN/net by state policymakers in North Carolina. They are interested in hearing from the public on one matter; other topics are usually treated as extraneous and directed elsewhere.

Elites exercise the highest degree of control in the legislative teleconferences in Alaska. The system was explicitly developed so as to preserve the power of committee chairs to determine the nature and timing of participation. In this system as a whole, however, citizens could decide what matters they wish to raise in electronic "public opinion messages" or during a legislator's constituency office hours. Assumedly, in large part the subjects of these communications are determined by the calendar of legislative business.

CITIZEN EDUCATION, EFFECTIVENESS, AND POLITICAL COMPETENCE

In this whole category of teledemocracy projects, the direct involvement of governmental officials demonstrates a concern for effective citizen influence. We should, however, consider the variations among them in the degree to which they educate citizens as well as allow them to have an effective voice in policy-making.

In most of these efforts, civic education was an important ingredient: Whether they watched public officials answering questions on television or listened to a legislative hearing, those who did so gained an enormous amount of information about governmental policies and processes. In the process, citizens may well have acquired information about and experience in the workings of the political system, so that they gained in political competence as well.

Education produces significant political effects. Over the course of five years of broadcasting hearings and office hours, those conducting the Berks County Television system in Reading have witnessed an appreciable gain in the sophistication of questions asked of government officials. In North Carolina, the cablecasting of commission and agency business has made accessible a great deal of information about governmental activity that simply was not available to those who could not travel to Raleigh. In Alaska, the legislators interviewed argued with a degree of confidence that the system was very successful in making the business of Juneau more intelligible to those outside the capital.

While the educational gain seems clear, it is very difficult to devise a simple measure of the effectiveness of citizen participation in these projects. Whether or not citizens are given real influence is almost exclusively the result of the project's design and the responsiveness of individual public officials, rather than the technology employed. Ultimately, effectiveness may be the most important test of success, but it can also be the most illusive. An extensive—but highly inconclusive—literature exists on those factors that explain legislative behavior, for example, party preference, constituency, expert testimony, lobbying pressure, and ideology. At the very least, these studies make clear that the attempt to measure, for example, the effects of teleconferences upon the Alaskan legislature in comparison with all these other possible influences would have constituted a major research effort by itself.

The government officials with whom we spoke were cautious in their claims that these mechanisms generated a pronounced impact on public policy. Reading provides some illustrations of this point. The mayor denied that BCTV had aided her rise to power, while other local political observers were quick to point out that her career coincided neatly with the existence of "government access programming" at which she was so adept. Whether they agreed or disagreed with the notion that technology had facilitated a transformation of the Reading political system, all those involved reported many instances in which the Reading municipal government has responded to individual requests made over the BCTV system. Complaints about garbage removal, potholes, downed stop signs, and the like are brought to the attention of higher officials, allowing them to ensure that the responsible agencies are performing their duties. On this most particular level, the city government is clearly more responsive because of BCTV. Many in Reading argue that the larger political system has also been affected in a substantial way. The city, which was described two decades ago in a study entitled *The Politics of Corruption* was functioning quite differently in the mid-1980s.

In North Carolina, both the participants from state government agencies and those who established the OPEN/net system placed more emphasis upon educating citizens about matters of state government than on allowing citizens an effective opportunity to influence policy. As mentioned above, the subject discussed was often a matter nearing completion in the policy cycle. As a result, the officials who came to respond to questions were in the position of explaining their policies to the public rather than soliciting citizen opinion or preferences.

In Alaska, legislators argued that teleconferences allowed them to gather information about the impact of legislation without relying upon lobbyists working in the state capital. They did not, however, go so far as to say that this involvement had radically transformed legislative hearings into a plebiscitory mechanism in which testimony determined the eventual legislation. Yet each one interviewed could cite examples in which testimony had helped modify the bill under consideration.

Despite the inability to measure precisely the effectiveness of participation allowed by these systems, my general impression is that, once again, the Alaska project appears to offer better prospects for systematically enhancing the weight of citizen involvement. In this case, the benefit grows out of the blend of hardware and the institutional structure that puts that technology to use. Specifically, the electronic hearings take place at early stages of policy formation and are embedded in a system (the legislature) designed to respond collectively to multiple influences.

Effectiveness in the other projects depended to a greater extent on the responsiveness of the individual officials involved rather than the institutional design. The best example of this can be drawn from the Markey electure. The congressman came to the project armed with long position papers stating his views on the issues to be discussed. As far as he was concerned, citizen education constituted the main intent of the experiment. The aide chiefly responsible for the project stated afterwards that the congressman himself had not learned a great deal about the substance of the issue, noting that the Congressman had already made his positions on arms control quite clear.

COSTS AND INITIATIVE

The costs of a participant system to individuals are not strictly monetary. The greater the personal costs in terms of time, energy, and commitment, the greater the degree of individual initiative needed to learn about and become involved in the system. Political activity is neither cheap nor easy. Watching a policy matter discussed on television is time consuming, as is attending a legislative hearing by teleconference. In both instances, these teledemocracy experiments demonstrate that the level of initiative required can be reduced by technology. Merely discovering that opportunities to participate exist may require diligence and considerable effort from citizens.

Strictly in terms of financial costs, by far the worst evaluations in this regard must be given to computer conferencing. Once the financial hurdle is surmounted, moreover, the mechanics of getting into the "Participate'' system on The Source, finding the correct computer conference, and following the discussion through various subconferences does impose significant time and learning costs upon the uninitiated. Even though The Source company featured Congressman Markey's electure in a monthly newsletter, I suspect its existence may have escaped the attention of many Source users.

A similar situation is faced by project initiators who would use cable television or other semipublic media to stimulate participation. As the number of channels of programming available to the consumer increases, it becomes less likely that viewers will become aware of their opportunities to influence public policy. Therefore, these projects require greater initiative on the part of citizens to seek out the available avenues for participating. Unfortunately, the existing lines of information and communication imply that knowledge of these opportunities is more likely to be gained by those already involved in political life.

It is possible, of course, that some interested citizens will serendipitously discover these televised discussions. The OPEN/net staff, for example, detected a tendency for the calls to flood in near the hour or the half hour when, during program changes and ads, more viewers are more likely to be changing channels.

The great advantage of the call-in projects is their convenience for a broad range of citizens. Television (though not cable) and telephones are almost universally available, so that participants do not have to leave their own homes to become involved. In fact, it appears that the costs of participation have been reduced to the reasonably practical minimum. Even at this minimum, these projects require that citizens initiate contact. They thereby impose a higher burden upon individuals than does, for example, a politician when she or he greets workers at a factory gate. Call-in formats also require verbal skills that are not uniformly distributed over the citizenry.

The Alaskan experiments indicate that it is possible to get citizens to leave their homes to attend political meetings. This project employed what I have referred to here as a semiprivate media. In so doing, the project design imposes higher costs upon the project initiators. Organization and outreach efforts are required to make the projects work. There is an important lesson here about technology that we noted earlier: Communications media cannot eliminate the costs in citizen participation but can serve to distribute them. By assuming greater burdens upon themselves, organizers can use technology to lessen the initiative required by citizens. A combination of television and telephones allows broad participation from home, minimizing costs for citizens. To be truly effective, however, project initiators have to assume correspondingly larger costs—financial and organizational—to notify viewers of the opportunity to participate. Video- and teleconferencing require that citizens move to central locations to participate; these semiprivate technologies have worked successfully in cases only when the project initiators were willing to engage in substantial outreach to solict citizen involvement.

Since they require a greater investment by citizens of time and effort, projects of this design are not likely to produce a set of participants representative of the broad citizenry. This effect goes beyond the well-established demographic pattern of greater participation from the upper end of education and income scales. These projects rely heavily upon individual and group interest to provide incentives for involvement; they are likely to draw participants who already know a great deal about the matter under discussion and have definite opinions and interests in the outcomes.

But the impact of this lack of representativeness is mitigated somewhat by the project's design. In projects that seek to entice citizens into dialogues, the initiators can afford to be somewhat less concerned with whether or not the participants were demographically and politically representative of the entire population. The whole exercise is not ruined if, for example, a hearing on highway taxes brings out only members of the trucking industry. Those who participate in these projects are motivated by self-interest to develop the initiative to participate. They represent only themselves and those similarly situated; they are not viewed as representing some amorphous conception of the common will or the general citizenry. More to the point, since citizen participation is not viewed as providing a definitive voice for the people, the policy preferences expressed through these mechanisms can be tempered by judgment of the interests of citizens who did not participate.

Conclusions

Practically speaking, the conception of teledemocracy imbedded in these government dialogic projects has proven more successful than that employed by the populist-plebiscitarian projects. These experiments are, nonetheless, open to a variety of attacks. For one thing, the vision of citizen involvement here is more circumscribed than the belief that through technology citizens will become their own direct governors. An important question is, therefore, whether or not the goals of these project organizers are high enough. Some observers will no doubt criticize these efforts as falling far short of the transformations in our politics they expect and want from "the communications revolution." They will point out that these projects only marginally surmount the inequalities now evident in participation by different social groups; they will complain that most of these projects encourage only a few more to become involved; and they will argue that participation mechanisms that are controlled by government officials are likely to be shams serving to co-opt the public into complacency.

Another line of possible attack on these projects can be directed at the sensitive balance between agenda-setting concerns and the level of initiative required of citizens. To what degree are these institutional arrangements subject to possible (or even likely) manipulation by the officials on the receiving end? As Laudon (1977) has forcefully argued, putting citizens in more extensive contact with political elites also places in the hands of those elites a greater capacity for manipulation.

Let us take up the latter concern first. While the dangers of elite manipulation are evident both in these projects and in private plebiscites, the dialogue projects do appear to contain more robust mechanisms of self-regulation. First, I have already observed that these project initiators have less control over the agenda of citizen participation. While the organizers did maintain the ultimate agenda-setting authority, that power was at least challengeable by rank-and-file participants who could use their participation to voice complaints or to change the subject. In some respects this is a function of size. As the number of participants rise, the agenda-setting capacity of citizens declines. Communications technology may be able to involve large numbers in instant plebiscites and may be useful in expanding marginally the number and diversity of those involved in agenda setting, but it cannot eliminate this basic relationship.

A second protection against elite manipulation of the dialogue projects results from the role which citizens are expected to play. Rather than being viewed as making decisions about public policy, citizens are seen as engaged in *influencing* policy. Although this arrangement may allow the project initiators to ignore citizen opinion, it also permits them to balance that participation with other considerations. For example, if the elites feel that only one side of a dispute has been heard, they do not have to treat that participation as the final word.

Third, in contrast to the plebiscitarian projects, most of the dialogue projects were ongoing mechanisms for policy formulation rather than one-time efforts to record the will of the people. That is, they sought to create a rolling discussion in which coalitions could form and change, new groups could raise issues, and policy with unexpected consequences could be adjusted. This process provides another bulwark against elite manipulation. Although we should guard against the naive conclusion that nobody ever loses in policy-making, nevertheless, if a stacked participatory process leads to policies that harm the interests of those who did not participate, the same mechanisms can be seized to redress the complaints of this emerging interest.

Recall that the general conception of political interest that lies behind the dialogue projects is one in which groups and individuals may differ dramatically in their awareness, level of concern, and information about politics. Once groups or individuals engage in policy making they may discover that their interests and desires collide rather than harmonize with those of others. Conflicting self-interest provides a self-regulating quality that helps contain abuse in projects based on dialogues.

Finally, a fourth protection can be seen in a noticeable and instructive contrast between OPEN/net in North Carolina and the Alaskan project. Clearly, in all these projects someone has to make authoritative decisions at some point about access and content. In Alaska, protection is provided by vesting these decisions in an overtly partisan institution (the legislature) that makes choices about these matters in other spheres all the time. Accountability for the participatory process is thus lodged within the broader institutions. In North Carolina, OPEN/net is housed within the Executive Branch bureaucracy that denies it the built-in partisanship of a legislature and the accountability through elections. Accordingly, the solution has been to build political neutrality into the Coverage Policy Committee and to reserve for it the capacity to decide substantive matters so that partisanship could not be thrust upon it. By contrast, the plebiscitarian projects did not have these institutional settings upon which to rely for overall accountability.

Let us take up the concerns of those who expect a significant transformation of our political system from technological advances. The initiators of the projects considered here seek to modify incrementally the existing political system and institutions; that is, they set out to use communication technologies to improve, rather than transform, the functioning of existing institutions. They wish to amplify the quality and importance of citizen participation, but they are less concerned with sheer numbers. In most of the projects studied, the number of citizens involved in policy-making has been expanded, often quite dramatically, over those normally engaged by existing institutions. The numbers involved are, however, much smaller than those incorporated through plebiscitory demonstrations. In short, the objectives of the government dialogue projects are far more limited than those envisioned by the plebiscitarian model.

Dialogue projects achieve this expansion by involving two types of participants: advertent and inadvertent. The balance between these two depends upon the media employed. In Reading and North Carolina, as well as nationally in the case of the Cable Satellite Public Affairs Network (C-SPAN), a substantial percentage of the audience appears to be drawn from a group of "regulars," a finite number of individuals who are interested generally in politics and public affairs. Robinson and Sheehan (1983) refer to this as an "advertent" audience. Added to this number is a second segment (probably smaller) that varies depending upon the content of the discussion.

Except for Alaska, these projects exhibited a noticeable shortcoming in their lack of communication external to the participatory channel and sufficient to alert potential participants that a matter of concern to them would be debated. As a result, in the main, expansion of the range of participants beyond the core group of active citizens occurred serendipitously rather than deliberately.

On the plus side, we should recall that, while the number of citizens involved in any one iteration tends to be finite, over time these projects can have a cumulative draw, so that the number of new participants can become quite numerous. This expansion comes about through the inadvertent audience, drawn to the project by the substance under discussion. The available evidence indicates that with these expanded numbers may come a broader range of interests and backgrounds than have been traditionally involved in politics. Certainly this is the case in Alaska with its particularly extreme problems of geography. In other instances, political officials reported that they encountered citizens in these projects who never became involved in traditional ways.

The complaint of the transformationalists goes deeper than their concern for mere numbers. Even while they might recognize the value of this expansion, those emphasizing the populist potential of emerging communication media are likely to be disappointed with incremental modifications of institutions that they consider inadequate. The more ardent would likely view these experiments merely as efforts to co-opt and dissipate citizen initiative and influence. While the use of communications media may promise citizens that they will have effective influence, in fact, participation will be channeled into ineffective avenues.

The best rejoinder to this argument is to demonstrate that this limited expansion does have actual effect on policy and policy making. In examining those projects initiated by government officials, I was able to uncover some evidence that expanded participation could influence the policy outcomes. In Alaska, legislation is often modified as a result of testimony that emerges over the teleconference. In Reading, municipal policy, from the location of stop signs to the allocation of revenue sharing funds, is affected by comments and questions telephoned to BCTV. In this sense, then, one can discuss the success of these projects.[4]

The critics of these incremental approaches would have a strong case if the policy matters covered in these newer participant systems were limited to trivial or "safe" issues (Bachrach & Baratz, 1963). Polsby (1963) and Frey (1971) have carefully considered the criteria under which issues ought to be deemed serious policy matters versus "non-issues." By this telling, the projects established in North Carolina, Reading, and Alaska qualify as subjecting significant issues to public pressure. For example, state budgeting matters, the handling of surplus oil revenues, the distribution of revenue sharing moneys, are questions that involve a significant percentage of all public funds and that affect a substantial proportion of the citizens. They cannot be considered trivial issues.

On a deeper level, our observation of these projects did indicate that long-run changes may occur in the functioning of the affected political institutions. This finding can be highly important, for as Frey (1971) has argued, the distribution of power itself is a highly significant issue at stake in all political systems. In Juneau, Alaska, and Reading, Pennsylvania, the political system appears to be undergoing change as a result of the increased level of citizen access. The evidence on this point, however, is very scanty and admittedly does not constitute a strong rebuttal of the co-optation argument. More research should be directed at this central thread of the argument. Beyond this survey of numerous attempts to use technology to facilitate participation, the next most appropriate step would be research focused intensively on whether changes in the functioning of political institutions result from the introduction of technology to facilitate citizen participation in one instance.

Notes

1. The original version of this section was written by my research assistant John Griffen.

2. The original version of this section was drafted by my research assistant John Griffen.

3. The Community Dialogue Project, studied in the course of this research but omitted from this analysis, provided the Massachusetts Governor's Office with the capacity to record and analyze systematically citizen complaints, problems, and requests expressed in phone calls, letters, and personal visits. Though the project never really became implemented, the planners hoped that it would allow them to pass agenda setting over to the citizens. A number of

similar complaints (spontaneous and unorganized) would signal problems in a given policy or administration area (see Arterton et al., 1984).

4. This observation, however, was not supported by a more statistically based effort to measure the impact of introducing public hearings into municipal decision making as to allocations of General Revenue Share funds (Cole & Caputo, 1984). Nor did another analysis (Berry, Portney, Bablitch, & Mahoney, 1984) conclude that the effectiveness of citizen participation could be strongly related to many institutional characteristics of the programs studied.

CHAPTER 6

EXPERIMENTING WITH REFERENDA

Conceptually, we can discern a third group of experiments in which government officials attempt to learn the will of their constituents through some form of plebiscite. Because public servants are on the receiving end of these expressions of citizen opinion, these projects constitute something of a middle ground between the two previous strategies of teledemocracy. Their results are likely to have a more immediate consequence for public policy than plebiscites staged by private or nongovernmental actors. On the other hand, even while they wish to involve "the people" in decision making, public officials are unlikely to surrender their ultimate authority to a real plebiscite. Rather, they are interested in involving citizens in discussion of policy, to give them some influence, but not to grant them decisive power. The government officials who initiate these experiments tend to emphasize the educational aspects in addition to the opportunities to hear from citizens.

Many states and countless municipalities do have the legal capacity to repose decision-making power in the voting public through the ballot referenda process. Why then have the projects studied here been undertaken in the first place, and what are their institutional differences from referenda campaigns? Fortunately, a recent and authoritative work on participation in referenda elections (Magleby, 1984) is available for comparison with the three ad hoc projects discussed here.

In some instances, public officials evidently deem these normal referenda process as inappropriate. Except in unusual circumstances, attention to referenda items is generally low and may be overwhelmed by the competition among candidates for office. A more significant reason may have to do with the substance of matters put to the electorate in referenda choices. Rather than being specific, discrete proposals, the matters taken up in the projects studied here were broad and complex policy areas—a voluminous municipal traffic plan, various strategies for health cost containment, and desirable objectives in long-term regional growth. Moreover, in two of the three cases, the topics under consideration were at the beginning of the policy cycle, well before specific policy proposals had been formulated. In these cases, public officials sought general advice and guidance from citizens rather than a definitive decision.

Accordingly, these public officials reached out for communications media that would help them create vehicles for exchanging ideas with citizens outside of existing institutions. Government officials are not always the initiators of these projects; in some cases, others conceive the idea and then entice the politicians into cooperating. In the first case presented below, for example, those managing the technology sought out a problem to which they could apply their new toy.

Whether the government officials are the creators of the project or are brought into it by others, however, the essence of this category of projects requires only that they be genuinely interested in learning citizen opinions in order to formulate policy. Ultimately, of course, they may or may not decide policy in conformity with the preferences voiced by the public.

The Government Plebiscites

With this introduction, let us now turn to a description of the three projects that fit this mold of teledemocracy.

UPPER ARLINGTON TOWN MEETING[1]

Because of its demographic profile, Columbus, Ohio has often been used as a test market by companies experimenting with new products. By investing huge sums of money, Warner-Amex hoped to build a model cable operating company and to generate showcase productions, which could be used to win franchises in other cities. Warner-Amex hoped to link its Qube cable systems across the country in a network headquartered in Columbus that would increase the commercial and entertainment potential of the entire system.

These dreams have been scrapped as the economic realities of the cable market have overtaken the lofty talk of cable's potential. Just as Warner's introduction of Qube technology sparked national debate about teledemocracy a couple of years ago, news of the system's troubles fueled talk about the failure of interactive cable. Sadly, all of this national attention on cable's difficulties has obscured the interesting and valuable political programming that has been produced in Columbus.

In addition to the northern and western parts of Columbus, the Qube franchise serves twelve other municipalities. Upper Arlington, a western suburb, has a population comprised almost exclusively of the upper middle class who vote overwhelmingly for Republicans. The town council and city manager cooperate in running Upper Arlington. Seldom do political controversies erupt and when they do, the city government is quick to resolve the dispute. Several people we talked to said Upper Arlington prides itself on its tranquil environment and shuns anything that might spoil that image. In fact, Upper Arlington agreed to the interactive town meeting only after learning that Warner-Amex planned to use the event as a showcase production to show to other cities. Priscilla Meade, currently a councilwoman and a former member of the Planning Commission, told us that the positive image of Upper Arlington likely to emerge from the meeting was an essential argument that convinced the town's political leaders to cooperate.

Like many other cable systems, Qube Columbus offers two tiers of service: one basic service such as the national broadcast networks plus cable networks like CNN and ESPN costs $9-$11 per month; and a second level offers a substantially wider variety of entertainment for an extra $11-$15 monthly. There are a total of 32 channels, all offering 24-hour service. Channel 1, the interactive channel, is available to subscribers who pay for it. In addition to this interactive channel, for which the Warner-Amex production crew does most of the programming, Qube makes available several access channels. Warner-Amex turns responsibility for these channels over to the Columbus Community Cable Association and provides that organization with the necessary equipment to create quality shows. The Columbus city government has its own channel and studio. Operating with a full-time staff of four, Ralph Squires, head of the Government Telecommunications Center, oversees the production not only of council and commission meetings but also of timely documentaries. Thus the Warner-Amex franchise is heavily involved in furthering local access programming, especially as it relates to political matters.

Interactive programming of two types occurs within the Qube system. First, a number of access shows have a call-in format. Several town meetings are staged monthly, giving citizens of Grandview, Upper Arlington, and other locations an opportunity to comment on the work being done by their town governments. The Government Telecommunications Center of the city of Columbus puts on a show once a week called *Connections*, which quite frequently deals with political issues.

The other, more controversial interactive capacity, involves the push-button console that allows Qube subscribers to record their answers instantaneously to questions posed on their TV screen. Relying on a large mainframe computer that scans viewers' homes every six seconds for responses, the Qube system can tally that information and flash it on viewers' screens within ten seconds. To respond to a question, a viewer pushes one of five possible response buttons located on his channel-finder console. The system cannot determine who is pushing the buttons, but only which homes are showing a response. In addition, each home can only vote once, even if there are a number of people in the room with differing opinions on the question at hand.

Warner-Amex has used Columbus Qube to test the strengths and weaknesses of various participatory programming formats: In addition to the meticulously planned and carefully conducted Upper Arlington Planning Commission meeting, the Qube system regularly broadcasts spontaneous phone interactive town meetings in Upper Arlington, Gahanna, and Grandview, and has aired regional broadcasts of the Mid-Ohio Planning Commission on air pollution (using both mail-in ballots and Qube interactive), programming of the Government Telecommunication Center in Columbus city hall, and access programming produced by political interest groups such as NOW and the Stonewall Union. Since these programs were broadcast to different parts of metropolitan Columbus and treated different issues, however, one must be careful not to ignore the difficulties that comparisons of these activities create. Most attention here will be directed toward the first of these efforts.

In 1978, distressed that a study they had commissioned to map out the future of Upper Arlington had gone virtually unnoticed, the city Planning Commission decided to broaden its engagement of the community before making recommendations to the town council. At the same time, Warner-Amex was searching for an event to demonstrate the potentials of its new Qube cable system. These two very different needs produced the Upper Arlington Town Meeting.

Both sides went to considerable pains to ensure the success of this event. Hours were spent deliberating which questions were most useful to the commissions and the participants. Warner-Amex flew in Alvin Toffler and other famous people to witness the event. Special hosts with considerable television experience ran the meeting. Patricia Ritter, telecommunications liaison for the city of Upper Arlington, recalled that Warner-Amex and the city went through extensive preparation to make sure a large studio audience turned out. Special invitations to those expressing interest in the system and to the media were mailed out. Local newspapers helped to promote the event and the *Upper Arlington News* ran several long articles on the subject being discussed and the process that would be used. A half-hour explanatory tape aired over a hundred times during the two weeks preceding the show. In short, the planning and production of the meeting required so much effort and expense that one would be hard pressed to make the case that this experiment could be reproduced on a continuous basis.

As a matter of corporate policy, Warner-Amex has taken a strong stand on the release of information from Qube voting; they will not divulge the number of viewers watching a show or the number responding to questions posed. Justified as a protection of the privacy of its subscribers, this policy makes particularly difficult any analysis of citizen participation. While it may be helpful to know that 80% of those who voted preferred a given alternative, it is also essential to know whether those voters constitute 80%, 40%, 8%, or .8% of the eligible population. One cannot use the Qube information as polling data, moreover, due to the self-selected sample and the fact that Warner will not reveal the demographic data necessary to check the statistical validity of the responses.

Although a precise figure for the audience is not available, people in a position to know the true figure placed the number of viewers for the Upper Arlington Town Meeting at about 2,500 out of a possible 32,000. Only about one-half of the homes viewing the show actually were engaged in the voting. They also observed that the viewership fluctuated significantly during the course of the show. In other words, different pools of people voted on various aspects of the final plan. We do know that not all the residents of Upper Arlington have cable and therefore many were either excluded from the proceedings or handicapped in their participation. While part of the population could participate from their own homes, others had to travel to the meeting site in order to be heard.

At the onset of the show, the hosts ran through a series of questions to give the Planning Commission a demographic profile of the audience. Though it is impossible to know whether the resulting slow pace had any effect on viewership, such inconveniences probably caused less interested watchers to exercise their option to leave the meeting by changing channels.

The character generator provided another limitation; it could only flash about twenty-five words onto the TV screen, restricting the level of complexity and the amount of information that could be designed into questions. Here we encounter a conflict between an entertainment format with its quest for large audiences and a meaningful effort to grapple with complex policy issues. The varying levels of familiarity and attention that exist among audience participants almost forces those running the event to favor a least common denominator approach. While this may have protected Warner-Amex from charges that it had overstepped its bounds, it may have also left some participants feeling that their contribution really had little meaning. For example, the first person in the studio audience who stood up to speak said that the questions asked by the Planning Commission mocked the intelligence of the participants because they asked the obvious. He cited the chairman's opening question asking whether the audience thought the commissioners should seek closer ties with town government.

Comparing this meeting with other political experiments over Qube, Kris Bailey and Carol Stevenson of the Qube staff (and others familiar with voting rates over Qube) emphasized the importance of the perception that the proceedings will have some direct effect on the political process. Viewers are more likely to feel the exercise is worthwhile if the public officials directly responsible for acting on the issue are part of the show. In addition to the moderators, the Upper Arlington Planning Commission members appeared on the screen so that viewers were aware that their comments would be considered in the final report. Evidently citizens also respond more frequently if their participation was solicited on specific matters. Both Meade and Bailey agreed that when a more general question—such as, for example, whether new economic development should be encouraged—was posed for the audience, a smaller percentage of viewers responded and more of those responding were likely to answer "not sure" or "do not know." However, when questions are presented in a specific, detailed form—such as whether a highway connecting the airport to the city should be built to encourage this economic development—participants can understand what the Planning Commission had in mind and respond by voting in greater numbers. Perhaps citizens can more easily visualize how their interests are affected by specific proposals.

Another important part of the Upper Arlington meeting can be found in the use of a second set of buttons so as to influence the course of the conversation. If a viewer at home wished to offer extended commentary (beyond just the simple voting), he or she could push a button that would indicate to Qube staffers that someone wished to speak. At the appropriate time, a Qube staff member in the studio would call up the viewer and have his or her comments placed on the air. A second button in the set was used to cancel the request to speak if the person's views had already been represented.

Furthermore, when viewers thought the conversation had slowed too much or needed to move on to other matters, they could press a third button letting the show's moderators know that the discussion no longer seemed useful. On the other hand, if someone felt the subject required more extended examination, he or she could press a final button to convey that opinion to the moderator. In other words, the interactive system was supplemented by a capacity that allowed those at home to influence the flow of discussion, if not the agenda of matters considered. Participants could not eliminate the planning report produced by consultants as the basis of the discussion, but they could focus their comments on the plan in those areas that meant the most to them. Those involved stated that these conversation cues did have an impact on the nature of the meeting.

According to Patricia Ritter, the politicians paid very little attention to results from Qube balloting. Ritter told us that the Upper Arlington Planning Commission shyed away from using the data they received from the town meeting because they had no idea whose views it represented. Priscilla Meade, an active member of the Planning Commission and former director of the Columbus Community Cable Association, disagreed with Ritter's assessment. She said that voting over the Qube system directly affected the commissioners' decision to recommend against the construction of an arterial highway in the oldest section of Upper Arlington. Especially noteworthy was the demographic data the commissioners were handed with each vote. In the case of the highway dispute, they could tell how people who actually lived in the older section voted as opposed to how people in newer and less affected areas cast their ballots. Meade also said that the final outcome of a controversial zoning provision was influenced by the Qube results gathered that night.

The Upper Arlington Town Meeting was an extraordinary event, not likely to be repeated on a continuous basis. Priscilla Meade mentioned that the Planning Board had been so exhausted by the work associated with this meeting that it took five years before anyone in the community could seriously suggest holding another electronic meeting.

In conclusion, Warner-Amex demonstrated understandable caution in the political uses of its Qube interactive technology. Their caution, however, undercut the successful application of Qube in two ways as demonstrated by the Upper Arlington meeting. First, the organizers had to spend so much time and effort on program development that enthusiasm for attempting similar projects in the future was considerably dampened. Second, the Upper Arlington example evinced a constant tension between useful participatory politics and entertainment values. Efforts to stage-manage the course of events so that the show would satisfy high entertainment programming standards stifled the ability to ask spontaneous follow-up questions that might have clarified the meaning of voting results. If the discussion indicated that a different question wording might have produced different results, for example, then those using the system might have asked a second question. Warner-Amex, which ultimately owns and controls the technology and the medium of communication, would only go so far in sacrificing the entertainment dimension, especially if innovating in the midst of a show might have produced confusion. To be truely useful to political participation, Qube needs the flexibility to respond to the desires of citizens as they surface during a meeting. Questions put to a vote have to reflect the thinking of participants. More in-depth questioning would not only prove more relevant to the needs of politicians but would give participants greater satisfaction that their true feelings were being solicited.

Thus we encounter here something of a contradiction: The medium with the highest plebiscitory potential among those studied was used in the most tightly controlled manner in terms of the agenda-setting dimension. In many ways, the policies of Warner-Amex run precisely counter to those that would be needed to test this mechanism as an effective instrument for participation.

THE DES MOINES HEALTH VOTE '82

During the fall of 1982, the Public Agenda Foundation conducted an extensive public relations campaign in Des Moines, Iowa. The effort sought to explain to the general population various strategies for controlling rising health care costs and their implicit trade-offs. After more than two months of public service announcements, the airing of a half-hour documentary, public affairs shows carried by radio and television stations, community meetings, and special newspaper supplements, ballots were mailed to all 125,000 households. Of these, 30,000 (24%) were returned.

The public was asked to register its views on 13 options or strategies through which health care costs might be contained. For each item, citizens were given a brief synopsis of the arguments for and against and were asked whether the proposal was something (a) that should be done now; (b) that should be done only if the problem worsened; (c) that should not be done; or (d) was something about which they were not sure.

As envisioned by its organizers, the project addressed a major policy problem about which there was evident widespread, but fairly uninformed, public concern. Daniel Yankelovich, president of the Public Agenda Foundation, and Jean Johnson, vice president and project director, describe "Health Vote '82" as a demonstration of how such mass opinion—confused, uninformed, and emotional—can be transformed into "public judgment." The latter represents, "the public's view once people have had the opportunity to confront an issue seriously, to wrestle with it, see its implications and consider alternative strategies for addressing it" (Johnson, 1983, p. 3). In other words, the project's originators placed a premium on the educative value of this communication campaign.

To evaluate their effectiveness, the Public Agenda Foundation conducted a random sample telephone survey before and after the public campaign. The answers registered in the post-project survey were compared with the results of the mail back ballot to demonstrate the representativeness of the self-selected sample in the actual Health Vote. As noted, 30,000 citizens of Des Moines recorded their opinions of different options for curtailing the health care cost spiral.

Evidently, the public relations campaign succeeded. In the second survey, 76% of those responding had heard about the Health Vote '82; 47% said they had read the supplement in the *Des Moines Register;* and 23% said they had seen the documentary broadcast on one of the three network affiliates, the public television station, or on the cable system. In addition, about 8,000 residents attended one of 200 community meetings in which the half-hour documentary was shown and a discussion ensued. An additional 1,000 were drawn to a series of "town hall" meetings or the panel discussions held in cooperation with Drake University. The postcampaign survey measured the attendance at these meetings as 4% of the general population. These meeting discussions were viewed, however, not as a separate instance of participation, but as part of the educative process leading up to the formal vote.

While there is no need to provide here a detailed examination of the results of the plebiscite on health care costs, the surveys taken before and after the public campaign do indicate that the general Des Moines public gained a better appreciation of the problem and potential solutions. This conclusion is amply demonstrated by the finding that in both the ballot and the postcampaign survey, residents reached different conclusions about alternatives for reducing health care costs from the views expressed in the early survey. For example, demand lessened for some measures such as modernizing the public hospital or requiring employers to provide dental insurance. In other cases, demand increased for some cost-cutting measures such as rising health maintenance organizations (HMOs) or increasing the deductable amount on health insurance. Meanwhile, the public remained adamantly opposed to other cost-cutting measures, such as cutting the health care budget for the poor or for medical research or disease research. In other words, public attitudes did not shift uniformly in one direction. The changes appear to document an increased degree of sophistication in understanding the details of this complex problem.

Jean Johnson separated out of the postcampaign survey a group of citizens that had been "exposed" to the campaign, those who had heard of Health Vote '82, and answered yes to at least two of four questions that asked whether they had read the supplement, voted, seen the documentary on TV, or attended a Health Vote meeting. About 40% of the full sample fell into the exposed group. As one might expect, those exposed were somewhat older (especially from 50 to 64), more likely to have college educations, earned higher salaries, tended to hold professional and executive jobs, and were more likely to be married. Thus the Health Vote '82 campaign reached an audience with more established interests and a higher socio-demographic status.

The Public Agenda Foundation (PAF) ran Health Vote '82 with significant help and support from the Des Moines community. In broad sweeps, however, the project was conducted almost entirely in a top-down manner: the essential decisions were made by elites not by citizen influence, and the Public Agenda Foundation retained much of the control. The Public Agenda Foundation picked the overall issue, decided what subtopics were important, staged the campaign, and timed the plebiscite. In short, PAF managed the agenda.

Many of these decisions were taken after consultation with a local advisory board. For example, several of the proposals placed on the ballot were not very significant national issues, but were important matters under discussion in Des Moines. Even though community leaders from Des Moines were involved in the project planning, as far as the citizens were concerned, the agenda was set by the project initiators. Citizens did not have an opportunity to modify the agenda, the information distributed publicly, or the mechanics of the voting.

In the context of the Public Agenda Foundation's control, it is not surprising that local elected government officials were only somewhat involved in the project. The initial press conference announcing the campaign was attended by the governor of Iowa, the mayor of Des Moines and Polk County board chairmen. Jean Johnson reported in our interviews that local political leaders, having lent their names to the endeavor, were very interested in the results of the balloting, and, interestingly, less concerned with the data gathered by the postproject, random sample survey.

Proving that Health Vote '82 had any direct consequences for public policy is difficult. Observations indicate that the leadership of Des Moines may well have been influenced by the plebiscite, but the evidence is suggestive and far from conclusive. In February 1983, shortly after the ballot results were publicly released, the Iowa state legislature passed almost unanimously a bill that required insurance companies to reimburse out-patient care as well as in-hospital costs. The proposal advocating this change was supported by 82% of the returned ballots; in fact, it received the highest level of public support registered in the voting. A year after the Health Vote, the total number of hospital beds in Des Moines had been reduced by around 150 and the recently opened health maintenance organization was experiencing a higher rate of participation than expected. A year and a half after the Health Vote, a number of efforts to contain the costs of health care were proving successful to such an extent that Blue Cross, Blue Shield announced a 5% decrease in health insurance rates in Iowa based upon declining numbers of hospital beds in use (Freudenheim, 1984).

While local business, community, and political leaders may have been looking to the results of the voting for guidance, it is less clear that the voting occupied such a pivotal role in the thinking of those at Public Agenda Foundation. That PAF is more centrally concerned with the educational effects upon citizen thinking is best illustrated by the fact that the major report summarizing the results of the Health Vote analyzes the data from the before and after surveys, but does not even contain the actual voting tallies. From the Public Agenda Foundation's viewpoint, the staging of a plebiscite appears to have been more of a device that focused public attention on the problem, forcing citizens to digest information in order to participate in the voting. "We didn't set out to do this project as a way of getting people to speak out," said Jean Johnson during our interview. "We were interested in moving public opinion over into public judgment." The ballot was necessary, she argued, because it seemed unfair to ask the public to learn about an issue without giving them an opportunity to say what they wanted.

In any case, once it was decided that the campaign would culminate in a mailed back ballot, the device served to peak people's interest. Local leaders became revved up by the idea of a citizen plebiscite and the symbol of "Health Vote '82" became the focus of the educational campaign. It might have been possible to stage an equally successful public communications campaign on health costs without leading up to a vote; but, in the absence of a plebiscite, it might not be possible to enlist so much help from the local media and community leaders.

Taking the project's goals as stated, two critiques of the educational process of Health Vote seem reasonable. First, the project's emphasis was on substantive gain in information and sophistication of views about health care costs. Less important was the teaching of a *process* of public involvement in matters of public policy. In some of the other projects studied, these twin goals receive equal emphasis. Second, to date, there has not been any attempt to examine whether Health Vote produced any

lasting effects in citizen judgment. While the evidence of an appreciable
gain measured immediately after the project is persuasive, we do not
know whether this has endured.

The Health Vote '82 campaign appears to be the most successful of
the plebiscitory projects we investigated. The citizens of Des Moines
became more aware of the problem of rising health costs and its
complexities. Many paid attention to the public discussion and
participated in the voting. Community leaders and governmental officials
cooperated in the enterprise; undoubtedly their support contributed to the
success of the project.

There are some important limitations, however. The first is cost. The
expenditures of $300,000 by the Public Agenda Foundation were but a
fraction of the total costs since so much was donated to the project in
the form of public service broadcasting and printing by the local
newspapers, radio stations, and television licensees. Whether such
resources could be available for a continued program of public involvement across a broad range of policy questions is doubtful.

Second, the available evidence indicates that in projects of this
variety subsequent iterations are rarely as successful (Orton, 1979).
Staging of votes on policy matters generates a degree of novelty which
can be an important incentive for citizen participation. Very quickly this
newness wears off and rates of participation decline. While the evidence
on this point is thin, it appears that the more a voting mechanism is
removed from actual policy influence, the steeper the rate of decline. At
one end, we have official ballot referenda in which citizens participate
repeatedly at close to the rates for candidate voting. At the other, the
decline in pushing the buttons in Warner-Amex's Qube system has been
most pronounced in formats that do not involve governmental officials.

Third, we should recognize that the issue of health care costs has
some characteristics that render it amenable to referendum-like participation, characteristics that not all issues share. Although there may be
diametrically opposed interests among the health care providers, the
cleavages among the general populace are not that intractable. In fact,
the Des Moines public refused to recognize or deem legitimate those
aspects of the problem in which different groups might have sharply conflicting interests, such as a proposal to provide lower-standard health
care for the poor or elderly. As the citizens of Des Moines viewed the
matter (and as it was presented to them), there was a public interest at
stake. Other issues might not be as tractable to this presentation or to
consideration in this form.

Notwithstanding these problems, Health Vote '82 remains a significant success along a number of important dimensions. The response

rate of 24% returned ballots is especially impressive in comparison to other projects (Orton, 1981) and particularly in that so large a population was involved. The Public Agenda Foundation was able to enlist the active participation of local public officials, community leaders, and news media organizations. The public communications campaign itself was conducted with a high degree of sophistication, and it worked. In the process, the campaign demonstrated that complex policy matters can be successfully "packaged" for the general public and, when this is done, a fairly sizable percentage of the public will pay attention. Finally, Health Vote '82 documented that when all those conditions are right, significant public learning can take place, at least in the short run.

ALTERNATIVES FOR WASHINGTON[2]

Alternatives for Washington (AFW) came about in 1974 through the efforts of Washington's three-term moderate Republican governor, Dan Evans. Several forces influenced Evans to establish a program that would involve as many citizens as possible in a long-range planning project for the future of the state. During this period, concern for the environment was growing nationwide and the citizens of Washington, a state still in relatively pristine condition, considered preservation of their "Northwest life-style" a top priority. Evans had been elected with the help of a strong grass roots organization, and he was especially sensitive to the voice of the people and to the importance of the government hearing that voice.

Briefly, AFW, which lasted from 1974 through 1976, took place in two phases. The first sought to define alternative futures for the state and preferred policies within those futures; and the second, in 1976, examined the costs, benefits, and trade-offs of the preferred policies developed in the first phase. Public participation in this planning project was encouraged through a combination of task forces, state and local meetings, media presentations, telephone and mail surveys, and a statewide newspaper questionnaire. Over 60,000 citizens participated in AFW, out of a total state population of 3,505,000.

In response to an invitation issued by Governor Evans in early 1974, over 450 business, labor, environmental groups, state legislators, local government officials, and others submitted the names of 4,000 individuals who might be interested in participating in AFW. From this pool, the membership of three AFW elements was drawn: the Statewide Task Force, the Delphi Study Group, and the Areawide Conferences. Every effort was made to make these panels nonpartisan, broadly representative, and balanced according to sex, age, and race, as well as geographically, demographically, and politically. Even so, the panels were criticized as not being representative of the state as a whole. The average income of the Task Force members, for instance, was $25,000, while the median family income in the state in 1975 was $14,962.

The core group, the 150-member Statewide Task Force, was asked to study and identify the alternatives for state growth and development. The Task Force met for four three-day seminars in which they examined a range of options, ultimately deciding on 211 regional policy goals that were later formulated into eleven alternative scenarios for the state's future.

Each of the 2,400 people participating in the Delphi Study Groups was asked, by questionnaire, to identify future trends and events that would have a major impact on the state in the next ten years. The data gathered in this manner served as input for the Statewide Task Force as well as for the Areawide Conferences.

The ten Areawide Conferences, held throughout the state in 1974 with 150-200 participants each, were designed to encourage discussion of the alternatives being developed by the Task Force and to add a local perspective to the planning effort.

Additionally, the AFW staff solicited the opinions of the members of various community and civic groups, and set up booths at county and state fairs, where they could describe the AFW project and ask for suggestions from the public. Over 5,000 Washington residents contributed their ideas in response to these outreach efforts. By mid-September, all of the ideas, concerns, and suggestions were catalogued, producing a comprehensive record of the sort of future the citizens of Washington envisioned for themselves. The Statewide Task Force then consolidated this information and began the process of presenting the policy options to the public.

Ten televison programs describing the various options were produced by Washington State University and aired on public television throughout the state. Several shows featured call-ins, allowing the public to question AFW panelists. The final show reviewed the growth and policy options, and asked viewers to express their preferences in a statewide questionnaire that outlined AFW's major options and alternatives. Over one million questionnaires were inserted in the state's 21 major newspapers in late October. Forty-five thousand of these questionnaires (approximately 4.5%) were completed and returned.

To measure the representativeness of the newspaper questionnaire response, a mail survey was conducted using a random sample of 5,000 people chosen from telephone directories. In total, 3,258 people completed and returned the detailed questionnaire. In yet another effort to validate the newspaper response, 727 of a sample of 1,000 were successfully contacted and interviewed by telephone.

AFW's second phase, in 1976, was devoted to analyzing the costs and benefits, and examining the trade-offs, of the alternative futures developed in phase one. During this phase, AFW primarily relied upon expert opinion and did not go to such lengths as to encourage citizen participation.

Six cost/trade-off study teams, comprised of interested citizens, state legislators and officials, business and technical experts, and AFW participants, met in early 1976 to consider the phase one recommendations in terms of their economic, social, and political impact and feasibility. These deliberations resulted in 14 committee reports that examined what was needed to implement the phase one goals, and identified the "hard choices," or trade-offs, necessary in realizing the goals. This information was then presented to the public for review and comment in a series of 21 community meetings held in the fall of 1976.

The 21 meetings, or Community Public Discussion Programs, were organized and conducted by local community groups working with the state's Office of Program Planning and Fiscal Management. Participation was open to the public, and encouraged through the use of posters, press releases, advertisements, public service spots, and personal contact. Close to 1,500 people attended the meetings. At each meeting, papers discussing the citizen recommendations were presented in conjunction with a film and slide show, and a questionnaire was distributed requesting feedback on the proposed policies. In total, 1,000 questionnaires were completed and returned. In this instance, the findings were not viewed as statistically representative of the population, but rather were considered to embrace the views of those politically aware citizens who were most probably community leaders.

During the same period, AFW conducted three random sample telephone surveys soliciting responses to the same questions, so that citizen opinion could be assessed as to the desirability of important trade-offs.

A final report published in late 1976 summarized the results of AFW's second phase. Because Governor Evans did not run for reelection in 1976, there was never enough time to develop and publish an overall final set of recommendations before Evans left office. Evans's successor, Dixie Lee Ray, showed little interest in involving the public in state planning and abruptly ended the AFW program when she took office.

All of these different efforts to involve citizens allow us to examine more closely the key question of representativeness of any one conduit.

In the course of their work, the Alternatives for Washington staff itself sought to determine how representative were the opinions voiced in telephone, mail, newspaper, conference, and Task Force surveys. In general, they concluded that the different measurements of citizen preferences produced roughly the same results. A reanalysis of the results, however, leads to a different conclusion. A rather simple statistical test dramatically reveals that the answers one receives to a survey depend to a very large extent on who is asked the questions. In short, pronounced differences in the preferences were expressed through the various channels by which AFW attempted to assess citizen opinion.

As indicated above, one should not expect the Task Force members or the conference participants to be representative of the population at large. At the outset, they were a highly selected and screened group. Politically active citizens are likely to be better educated and have higher than average incomes. If that were not enough, by virtue of their participation in the Alternatives for Washington program, they assumedly became more aware politically than their nonparticipating fellow citizens. These factors combine to give activists different political views and values than those held by other citizens.

Similarly, those who take the time to cut out and mail back a questionnaire from their newspaper are likely to be more politically motivated than those who do not respond. The differences between this group and the general population ought not to be as great, however, as those between citizens in general and the activists on the Task Force. One should also expect that citizens who go to the effort to respond to a mail survey are marginally more interested than those who throw the mail survey in the trash. Though by no means perfect, telephone surveys are probably the best measure of political views in the population at large in as much as they require the least effort on the part of the respondents.

Because the Alternatives for Washington surveys asked many of the same questions of respondents selected through these various sampling methods, one can compare statistically the political views expressed by the different groups of citizens contacted by the AFW team. Using only those questions that had identical wording in all surveys in which they appeared, we estimated that the responses in the different surveys are likely to have come from sample groups representing the same general population in only 21 of 89 possible instances.[3]

In other words, the AFW surveys could claim to have found consistent sentiment only 24% of the time that it asked the same question of more than one of its sample groups; fully 76% of the time the mail respondents, the Task Force members, the conference participants, the newspaper respondents, and the telephone respondents may have been drawn from distinctly different populations. When all five groups of respondents were asked the same question, they agreed as to what the appropriate policy option should be in only one instance out of 33 possible times.

Clearly the Task Force members and conference participants were highly selected and affected by their involvement in the project. The remaining three groups included in AFW, however, are all more or less representative of the general population. The three large samplings vary mostly in the degree of initiative required to participate: those responding to a telephone survey exercised the least, while more action and volunteerism was required of those returning the mailed questionnaire, and those who clipped and returned the newspaper ballots overcame the greatest resistance. There were 33 instances in which the same question was asked of three samples; statistically similar responses occurred in only 7 (21% of these).

While these findings may not be surprising, they are extremely important to the whole enterprise of registering citizen opinion in plebiscites. To the extent that projects like Alternatives for Washington claim to have captured the will of the people based upon participants rather than random surveys of the entire population, they are making highly questionable claims.

The results here indicate that the answers received to policy questions may really depend on the means employed to ask the questions. We suspect that the differences in answers are caused by discrepancies in who responds to these different means.

From this analysis, one cannot suggest, however, that one method is absolutely better than another, for really they serve different purposes. Ordinarily, we are accustomed to placing greater validity in the random sample telephone results, but the mailed questionnaire may resemble more closely that sample of the electorate that will actually turnout in elections. What is important to keep in mind is that each of these methods has some weaknesses when used as mechanisms of political participation.

This is a long-standing and more general problem for democratic institutions. It is well known, for example, that nonvoters often hold different preferences than the voting population. Inevitably, policy is more heavily influenced by the interests of participants. As a result, representative processes attempt to weigh into the balance some calculation of the interests of nonparticipants.

By allowing us to explore these comparisions, the AFW project has brought to the fore this basic problem in using participation as a substitute for representation: The class of participants is different from the general population. The AFW data provide clear evidence that even among participants, differences in opinion and outlook can be found according to the intensity of their involvement. In part, these differences are a result of self-selection; in part they relate to the experience and knowledge gained through participation.

Turning to an analysis of the political effectiveness of citizen participation through AFW, one must reach a mixed conclusion. From the beginning, the Democratic-controlled state legislature was suspicious of the AFW program. The legislators, often at odds with the Governor, accused Evans of going over their heads by appealing directly to the public. They viewed this as infringing upon their prerogatives as elected representatives of the people. Therefore, AFW received no support from the legislature and the options that were developed never evolved into specific legislative proposals.

An assessment five years after the project revealed, however, that many of its recommendations had ultimately worked their way into state policy, despite the hostility of Governor Ray and the legislature. Both supporters and critics of AFW agree that AFW had concrete long-term effects on the citizens of Washington. AFW got citizens involved, got them thinking and talking about issues. Many of those who were active in AFW went on to further involvement with planning, state government, and citizen activism. Liaisons that developed among citizens, community leaders, and government officials lasted well beyond the life of AFW. And the value of public input was made apparent to both citizens and the government.

Shelby Scates, a political reporter for the Seattle *Post Intelligencer*, feels that AFW's impact may have been subliminal: While nothing directly resulted from AFW, it gave a focus to controlled growth and conservation that was previously lacking. Scates claims that the general well-being of the area cannot be viewed without considering Alternatives for Washington. And while one cannot point to specific policy resulting directly from AFW, there does exist an AFW legacy in the influence the project had on the passage of the Forest Practices, Public Disclosure, and Agriculture Preservation acts.

Another frequent comment on the value of AFW is that it provided the first indication of the media's willingness to facilitate the exchange of information between the government and the public. Since then, television coverage of controversial issues facing the state and local communities has become commonplace. Seattle citizen activists Betty Jane Narver and Arlis Stewart agree that one of the most important consequences of AFW was that local groups became aware that the media were receptive to their needs. For example, in the wake of AFW, a group of environmental and energy groups came together to form the People Power Coalition. Many coalition members were involved in Energy 1990, a successful 1975 effort to dissuade Seattle from buying a share of the controversial and now financially troubled Washington Public Power Supply System (WPPSS). People Power produced several televison specials on the WPPSS controversy that aired on commercial and public stations, and played a major role in persuading the city council not to join WPPSS.

In addition to the Energy 1990 programs, KING-TV, the Seattle NBC affiliate, has subsequently aired several series of programs dealing with a variety of local and national issues such as the criminal justice system, national security, development of nuclear power in the Northwest, and the electoral system. Emory Bundy, the former public affairs director of KING-TV, set up a model for each series in which interest groups (churches, League of Women Voters, and so on) would publicize the programs and encourage their members to research a piece of the subject, a companion newspaper series would provide background information, and a questionnaire would be distributed through both newspapers and interest groups. Bundy's goal was to allow citizens to come to some conclusions on issues and take some action. In a series on the effects of nuclear war on Seattle, 3,000 people came to the studios to participate. An interactive program on the Washington Public Power Supply System linked TV stations and citizens in five states.

Metro, the city of Seattle's sewer and transportation authority, now uses technology for public information purposes. Metro has produced seven programs on topics such as the future of transportation, waste water treatment, sludge, the transit fare structure, vandalism, and urban pollution. The programs are produced with the support of one cable company, but are aired at the same time on all area cable systems. There are also public viewing centers for those not wired for cable. The programs are widely advertised, feature phone bank call-ins, and average a viewership of 2,500 per show.

Not all of this subsequent activity can be directly attributed to AFW. The state of Washington has traditionally had a high rate of citizen participation in the political process. Alternatives for Washington was conceived in and contributed to this environment. And while the involvement of 65,000 citizens out of a total state population of 3.5 million may not be an impressive rate of participation, from another perspective, involving 65,000 citizens in the public policy process is quite an accomplishment.

Discussion

ACCESS AND REACH

Governmental plebiscites have a tangibly broader reach than those teledemocracy projects aimed at encouraging dialogues. It is probably no accident, therefore, that two of these three efforts relied upon broadcast television as the principal means of communicating to citizens. The nature of the enterprise involves reaching the broadest possible audience and broadcast television is the most mass instrument available.

Of the three efforts studied, the Upper Arlington meeting conducted over Qube was the most restricted in terms of access. Even though the community does have a high rate of cable penetration, the medium is not as universally available as broadcast TV. The interactive system comes at an additional cost, so that not all cable subscribers could push buttons to inform the Planning Board of their opinions. Finally, cable channels certainly do not enjoy the huge audiences that network broadcasting mobilizes. The estimated audience of 2,500 constitutes only 8% of the adult population; the number of votes cast fluctuated around the 1,000 level.

In Washington and Des Moines, the principal technology employed for outreach was broadcast television. More importantly, in both instances the project team used multiple channels to contact citizens repeatedly, hoping to engage citizens repeatedly and to reach as broad a slice of the electorate as possible. The television shows and public service announcements placed on many channels were reinforced by similar formats on radio, by newspaper articles and ads, signs on buses, and by community meetings.

An evaluation of the actual reach of these projects can be made at two levels: those who became aware of the policy discussion and those who participated by engaging in some activity to communicate their preferences. In their survey after the Health Vote campaign, the Public Agenda Foundation discovered that 76% of the Des Moines citizens had heard about the project. In Alternatives for Washington, Orton (1980, p. 171) estimates that a third of the state's residents were reached by the campaign to discuss planning goals for the state. And, in Upper Arlington, Warner-Amex's cablecast reached only an estimated 8% of the city's residents, but undoubtedly more knew of the event and chose not to become involved.

In the first two cases, the number of active participants is a much smaller percentage of those who became aware of the campaign. In total 47,000 ballots were returned to the Alternatives for Washington staff, an estimated turnout rate of 4.5% of the ballots printed or 1.8% of the voting-age population of the state. In Des Moines, 30,000 citizens returned ballots constituting almost 25% of the number printed. Evidently, a higher percentage (40%) of the Upper Arlington audience participated by pressing buttons at the appropriate times, although the overall rate of participation was around 3% of the population. While low, these rates of involvement appear to be very respectable in comparison to other efforts to solicit widespread participation through mailed back ballots. Barry Orton (1980), who has examined a large number of these instances, reports that turnout rates usually are a good deal lower.

As in the dialogic projects, these numbers can be interpreted in two ways. On the one hand, they demonstrate that a substantial percentage of the general citizenry can be engaged by a referendum on public policies, conducted outside of the normal electoral processes. Yet, on the other, given the expenditures of effort and money involved, these figures do not provide much support for the notion of participatory democracy or direct teledemocracy.

DIVERSE PATHS OF ACCESS

All three of these projects provided some opportunities for citizens with diverse skills and levels of interest to participate. Task force discussions, community meetings, and discussions by the studio audience supplemented the mechanism of registering citizen votes. In most cases, however, these mechanisms were decidedly secondary; the attention of the project staff was focused more directly on the plebiscite. In the Alternatives for Washington project, however, the task forces and areawide meetings played an essential role in generating the ideas and propositions that subsequently became the basis of the voting. Intensive participation was available, therefore, to supplement the voting, a one-time choice between defined options. Participation in the task forces, however, or the Delphi Study Groups was not open to all citizens; individuals were nominated by interest groups and public leaders. Citizens could attend one of many community meetings where they could express their opinions, but the link between these soundings and policy making was not as well defined as were the roles of the task forces or the plebiscite.

AGENDA SETTING

The strength of the Alternatives for Washington project lies in the latitude allowed citizens to establish the project's agenda. This exercise was dedicated to the *creation* of broad goals from the preferences of citizens, not the selection or consecration of options identified by elites. Through the 150 member task forces, Delphi study groups with 2,400 participants and regional meetings attended by 1,500, AFW derived regional policy goals and alternative scenarios for growth that became the substance of the plebiscite. To be sure, participation in the first two of these mechanisms was not based on open access, but even so, the whole effort was to build upward to a statement of choices from citizen opinion.

By contrast, the agenda was most constrained in the Health Vote project. The reason for this lies in institutional choices rather than the technology employed; the Public Agenda Foundation, located in New York City, brought the issue to Des Moines and maintained control throughout.

Technology did provide citizens in Upper Arlington with some capacity to influence the pace of discussion if not the topics considered or the options presented. Reconstructing whether the citizen role proved to be very robust in the Qube production, however, proved impossible.

As a general statement, agenda setting in these projects was more tightly held by the organizers than the projects that involve dialogues. In part, this is a function of numbers of participants included; in part a result of the organizers' mindset that dictated a strategy of confining most participation to the capacity to choose among proffered alternatives.

EFFECTIVENESS

These three projects differed dramatically in the actual effectiveness of citizen participation upon public policy. In the case of Alternatives for Washington, Governor Evans's successor decided to ignore the proposals and eliminate the project. Even so, Alternatives left behind a legacy to the Washington area; many of its recommendations subsequently worked their way into state policy and the project legitimized innovative methods of gauging citizen opinion to inform the policy process.

While the Upper Arlington Planning Board was careful not to suggest that the Qube voting would be decisive, it appears that in several specific instances the final decisions were influenced heavily by the town meeting conducted that night. Similarly, there was no direct connection between the Des Moines Health Vote and consequent public policies. Nevertheless, anecdotal evidence suggests that the political decision makers considered the voting results in their subsequent decisions and that citizen behavior changed as a result of the public education campaign so that the health cost spiral was, in fact, broken (Freudenheim, 1984).

EDUCATION

The Health Vote project demonstrated that a large-scale public education campaign can be successfully managed. The final report is repleate with examples in which public attitudes were changed and public understanding was deepened; citizens became more aware of the difficult trade-offs in curtailing health costs. From the point of view of the sponsoring Public Agenda Foundation, if not for the local political elites, the whole purpose of staging a plebiscite was to give the public a reason to pay attention to the information campaign. They were more interested in mass public education, and they were successful in achieving that purpose. We do not know, however, whether the demonstrated effects lasted very long after the campaign's conclusion.

Gauging the educational achievement of the other two projects proved to be impossible as the organizers failed to record or publish sufficient data to permit reconstruction years later. However, the subsequent adoption of many of the proposals in Alternatives for Washington came about because of the continued presence in politics of a knowledgeable cadre of activists educated by the experience in AFW.

COSTS AND INITIATIVE

In these plebiscitory projects, citizens either filled out and mailed paper ballots or they pushed buttons connected to their cable television receivers. In comparison to involvement in a dialogue, the plebiscitory projects do not impose substantial demands upon citizens; they require less initiative. Thus broad-scale participation was achieved by lowering the costs and burdens associated with the participant act. This relationship appears to constitute a working assumption for much of this experimentation: the greater the burdens and costs necessary to participate, the smaller and more unrepresentative the set of participants (Milbrath, 1965).

Costs were not absent entirely, but the direct costs were those of the time needed to watch the Qube show or to learn about the issues at stake and to fill out the ballots. These costs, while minimal in comparison to many other projects studied, are undoubtedly the principal reason why rates of involvement are far from universal (Orton, 1980).

INDIVIDUAL OR GROUP BEHAVIOR

There is no evidence of group participation in any of these projects. Except for the nominees to the task forces in Alternatives for Washington, citizens became involved as individuals, not as members of groups or organizations. Even so, opinion leaders for different interests probably exerted some influence on the thinking of citizens. In the Des Moines Health Vote, for example, several community meetings and broadcast public service discussion formats featured spokesmen for various points of view who quite likely exerted influence on those who heard their arguments. But this process is quite different from organized involvement as a deliberate effort to affect the voting results.

Several explanations may account for the lack of organized groups. In addressing the public at large, these projects impose substantial costs on any organized group that might wish to influence the outcomes. Since we know that, upon occasion, referenda issues on election ballots do evoke major efforts by interest groups, the mass base of the electorate cannot, however, be considered a total barrier. The fact that these projects are both innovative and one-time events may also be partially responsible for the lack of group activity. Presumably, if these attempts to register public opinion were institutionalized and became an effective route for influencing policy, then group organization would result. On the other hand, we must recognize that, in general, the broader the medium employed to reach citizens, the harder it will be for interest groups to affect the outcomes. They are, therefore, less likely to assert themselves in plebiscitarian contexts.

These considerations shed light upon the relationship between costs to the participants versus costs to those who would influence the outcomes. As noted above, an increased number of participants can be achieved by lowering the burdens that citizens must bear to become involved. Outreach through television, as opposed to a hearing or meeting, is one example of this expansion. As numbers increase, however, the costs—financial and administrative—also increase for both the initiators and those who might try to shape the result. Where the costs of participation are high, as in the teleconferences discussed earlier, interest groups can themselves try to lower these costs for their members, informing them of the meeting, encouraging attendance, providing transportation, and so forth.

This chain of reasoning amounts to another way of stating the basic differences between plebiscitory projects and those that seek to promote dialogue. The latter are instituted in the belief that meaningful politics involve parochial interests that must be negotiated and accommodated. Interest groups provide a concrete expression of these compartmentalized and sometimes antagonistic points of view. The plebiscitory efforts, on the other hand, derive from a conception of political decision making that seeks to minimize or ignore the role played by these special interests. By extending the set of participants, they hope to curtail the ability of narrow interest groups to affect public policy.

Conclusions

In order to supplement this discussion of the empirical differences between dialogue and plebiscitory projects, I also examined the levels of turnout that occur in referendum voting in numerous states. What are voting rates like when public participation does indeed determine policy? As it turns out, participation in this plebiscitory context appears to be lower than turnout for candidates (Magleby, 1984).[4] When both appear on the same ballot, many voters opt to ignore the referenda questions. Furthermore, turnout also is generally lower when referenda are held without candidates on the same ballot. Thus the real draw for turnout in election campaigns appears to be provided by the candidates for public office rather than referenda questions.

The argument that a referendum's direct impact on policy will draw more voters to the polls also suffers when it is tested by evidence of the types of individuals who vote in referenda elections and those who do not. The smaller electorate for referenda elections is not made up of a large number of citizens who fail to participate in candidate elections. Even though their input on policy can be said to be more direct, referenda elections do not pull to the polls those disenchanted with representative processes. In fact, the two pools of nonvoters look roughly similar, only one—that for referenda—is larger. Therefore, the available evidence contradicts the assertion by advocates of direct teledemocracy that once citizens realize their actions will really determine outcomes, rates of participation will rise.

Another argument might cause us to doubt that universal participation in a plebiscite would ever occur. Since one's vote is only a single tally out of many cast, few voters will believe that their vote will decide the outcome (Frolich, Oppenheimer, Smith, & Young, 1978). Accordingly, they might question whether it is worth the trouble. Even so, referenda are still a more direct means of policy control than are candidate elections. Therefore, for Wolff (1982) and the others to be correct, rates of participation in referenda should be the same or at least marginally higher than in candiate elections. Instead, they are significantly lower.

In some of the plebiscites studied here—Alternatives for Washington, Choices for '76, the Des Moines Health Vote, and the Hawaii Televotes—the project organizers sought to establish that those who did participate were representative of the entire population. Data on gender, educational levels, income rates, and geographical dispersion were gathered to support the argument that the substantive outcomes of full participation would have been similar since those who did become involved looked very much like the general citizenry. One can question, however, whether a group that is demographically representative of the general population is indeed politically representative. Those who participate at their own volition are, by definition, likely to be drawn from the activist strata in society: They are more likely to be members of organizations, to be interested in politics, to engage in political discussions with their peers, to pay attention to news and public affairs, and so forth. As the data from the Alternative for Washington project make clear, arguing that this group will have the same opinions and values of those who are not so involved is a leap of faith, even if the groups share similar background characteristics.

Theoretically, of course, not even the staunchest advocates of direct democracy would contend that representative participation constitutes a satisfactory level of involvement for deciding public policy. The argument that the opinions of these activists reflect those of the population as a whole if nonparticipants did become energized to activity is suspect.

Daniel Yankelovich distinguishes between "public opinion," consisting of surface and comparatively uninformed attitudes, versus "public judgment," when citizens understand the complexities and trade-offs involved in an issue. It is always possible that if the general population became interested in a policy question, public opinions might change, moving into line with those expressed by the demographically similar activists who participate in these kinds of projects. But this idea remains to be demonstrated empirically. While the notion of public judgment may be very useful as a goal of public education, relying upon it as basis for deciding public policy is more problematical if it includes an assertion of hypothetical public attitudes.

The discussion thus far has revolved primarily around the difference between the plebiscitarian and dialogic conceptions of citizen involvement. I will conclude this chapter by giving some attention to the other major distinguishing feature among these projects, the role of government officials. Comparing projects in which government officials were involved to similar endeavors without them, one discovers that an important consequence of the involvement of public officials is to boost the number of citizens who participate. In about half of the projects that involved government officials, these decision makers had, in fact, instigated the experiment as a means of reaching out for citizen opinion. A slightly smaller percentage of the projects were initiated by others, who then enlisted the cooperation of government officials. But whether or not the officials were themselves the instigators of the project appears to make little difference in the amount or nature of citizen involvement stimulated. Their involvement alone appears to stimulate participation.

Considering the reasons why this relationship might exist brings to light several intertwining arguments that relate to the dimensions of participation we have been discussing. Overall, one suspects that the effect of public officials is to lend an air of legitimacy and credibility to the enterprise. But to say that one project appears to be a "serious" attempt to solicit citizen participation while another seems less so, is inevitably an argument that relates back to the perceived impact on public policy. We have not advanced much beyond a restatement of the basic conceptual differences among project types. Let us turn to some related arguments.

Considering both plebiscitarian projects and those that set out to encourage dialogues, the efforts initiated by government officials are more likely to stretch out over time, while those established by others tend to be one-time occurrences. Longevity may, in turn, affect the rate of participation. While novelty can be an incentive for some to participate, it may well be a mixed blessing. Newness can create public uncertainty, whereas citizens may recognize more readily their role in established mechanisms. Continuing efforts are also likely to be accorded greater legitimacy.

Longevity is undoubtedly intertwined with financing. In some cases, especially the Alaskan teleconferencing network and Alternatives for Washington, the project's length can be attributed to a secure source of funding provided from public treasuries. While financing has, in other cases, been patched together from a variety of contributions and grants, governmental projects generally have been able to draw upon greater resources than the nongovernmental efforts, suggesting that fund-raising is also facilitated by the legitimacy that the participation of government officials imparts to these endeavors.

Longevity, legitimacy, effectiveness, and the rate of participation are all intertwined. As novelty wears off in continuing projects, moreover, the importance of the effectiveness of participation may be accentuated.

Citizens want to get something out of their involvement, and the educative values and self-enhancing aspects of participation are not likely to be strong incentives for many citizens. Evidence presented by Orton (1980) indicates that in nongovernmental projects the number of individuals who will participate in subsequent interations of a project drops sharply. The data from Choices for '76 was a major element of Orton's conclusion. Similarly, the research staff at the Qube system in Columbus, Ohio reported that after initial enthusiasm, their subscribers' willingness to register opinions declined precipitously. They found two exceptions that could stimulate higher levels of participation: when prizes were awarded or when the person asking a question was a public official who could actually decide a matter at issue. These are all indications that encouraging political participation can be a fragile undertaking; citizens can always exercise their option of refusing to become involved, particularly when they cannot see a purpose served by participation.

To some extent, this finding is analogous to the assertion that if direct democracy were instituted, citizens would take more interest and become involved in greater numbers. If one is willing to accept the proposition that the involvement of public officials can be used as a measure—albeit a crude measure—of effectiveness, then the effectiveness of a participatory endeavor does appear to be a stimulus to involvement. But we are talking in relative degrees of poor turnout. In no case, does participation reach to the levels of citizen involvement that would make direct democracy feasible.

Notes

1. The original version of this section was drafted by my research assistant John Griffen.

2. The original version of this section was drafted by my research assistant Monica Andres.

3. We began by assuming that the people responding to one of the surveys were drawn from a population that was, on the average, just like the group of citizens from whom respondents were drawn to answer another of the five AFW surveys. Statistically, we calculated the range within which we could be confident that the true answer would lie if we were to poll the entire population, the 95% confidence interval for each question. If the confidence intervals overlap for the same question asked of different sets of respondents, then we could say that our original assumption is probably correct: The different respondents are all representative of the same group. If, however, the confidence intervals do not overlap, then we must question our original assumption and consider the pos-

sibility that the different surveys were conducted among distinctly different populations. (This data analysis was conducted by Edward Lazarus.)

4. A background report on referenda elections was compiled by Edward Lazarus. I have drawn from his arguments in writing these paragraphs.

CHAPTER 7

TEACHING CITIZENSHIP
THROUGH TECHNOLOGY

A democracy, if it is more than a cruel hoax, brings forth a rich cornucopia of efforts to mobilize citizens. The vitality of our system of government springs from attempts by political leaders to use the democratic processes to secure benefits and policies for themselves and their constituencies. Political parties, candidates for elective office, interest groups, and social movements reach out to engage citizens in political activity. As the means of communication have changed, these groups have quickly adapted their strategies for catalyzing citizen action. In today's politics, policy advocates are on the forefront of efforts to exploit the potential of emerging communications media (Arterton, 1983; Hadden & Swann, 1981).

Even when we turn from advocacy to attempts to involve citizens in policy discussions without regard to desired objectives, we find a lengthy list of endeavors. As Oliver (1983) has noted, the varied history of these efforts stretches back to the beginning of the Republic. Of the four categories of projects discussed in Chapter Three, these are undoubtedly the most numerous. Everything from Quaker meetings to neighborhood associations to the future goals projects established by environmentalists to high school civics classes could be counted as efforts by someone to stimulate public discussion about politics and community.

Coping with this diversity and abundance constitutes something of a problem for this research. The list is sharply reduced if we draw a line between those endeavors that have used telecommunication technologies and those that have not. Even so, since many of the goals projects conducted during the 1970s used television to explain their work to citizens (Bezold, 1978), the number remains too numerous to examine completely.

Private (Nongovernment) Dialogues

Ultimately, I resolved this issue by studying only two such projects, selected not, of course, as a representative sampling but to provide illustrations of a broad strategy of citizen engagement. They are typical but by no means representative of the range of activities that could legitimately be considered here. It turns out, moreover, that only the first of these is truely a project in the formal sense, so it will have to suffice as an example. It is, in fact, an exemplar.

DOMESTIC POLICY ASSOCIATION:
NATIONAL ISSUE FORUMS

The Domestic Policy Association (DPA) is a joint project of several foundations and scores of convening institutions across the country led by the Kettering Foundation (Dayton, Ohio) and the Public Agenda Foundation (New York City). The process, repeated annually, begins when a steering committee selects three policy areas that they deem to be ripe for citizen learning and public discussion. The Public Agenda Foundation prepares for each issue a booklet describing in considerable detail the pros and cons of the three problems and stressing the trade-offs that must be considered in reaching a sophisticated and responsible policy response. The booklets also contain questionnaires that are to be answered by participating citizens before and after their involvement in DPA.

The selected topics become the subject matters of National Issue Forums held in many communities throughout the country. These meetings are largely created by local organizations. The network of local contacts, maintained by the Kettering Foundation, then reports back the substance of citizen opinions expressed in these meetings to the DPA staff in Dayton, using questionnaires, convener reports, and direct observation by DPA staff. From this feedback, the results of the local meetings are compiled and aggregated in Dayton in time for a single national meeting held at one of the presidential libraries. The national gathering allows citizens from across the country to exchange views with each other and with those policy-makers as can be convinced to attend.

In each cycle, participation in the Domestic Policy Association has grown. In the fall of 1982, 10,000 citizens went to 313 meetings organized in 145 communities in 17 states to discuss social security, inflation, and job productivity. The second cycle brought together more than 23,000 participants gathered in communities in 33 states, considering nuclear arms and national security, the federal budget and deficit, and education. Topics debated by more than 33,000 citizen participants in 43 states during the fall of 1984 included health care costs, the environment, and the work environment. During 1985, more than 100,000 citizens in 45 states attended 200 community meetings on taxation, welfare, and U.S.-Soviet relations.

During the 1983 iteration, the DPA experimented in several different settings with the use of telecommunication technologies to conduct these local meetings electronically. Attempts to involve radio stations were mostly unsuccessful, but televised call-in formats were organized in Reading, Pennsylvania, in Charlotte, North Carolina, and over the C-SPAN network, and interested Qube viewers in Dallas could push their interactive buttons in response to questions posed from the studio.

At an evaluation meeting in February 1984, however, the DPA staff concluded that the massive amount of work required by these trial efforts with technology could not be justified in terms of the number of citizens engaged or the quality of participation achieved. Despite the recognized difficulties of getting people to attend a meeting in person, the quality of discussion and personal contact could not yet be duplicated through televised outreach to viewers at home. Accordingly, they decided these efforts did not warrant a vigorous commitment of resources in the third cycle but a continuing marginal effort of experimentation with technology-mediated meetings. DPA has also explored the use of videotaped presentations to take the place of the booklets now prepared on each policy issue. If successful, these videos could be used both to stimulate discussion at face-to-face meetings and to promote the telecommunicated meetings.

The Qube experiment in Dallas was particularly disappointing. While the technology permits those at the "head end" to make a precise count of viewership and the number responding to questions, for reasons discussed in Chapter Six, the Qube staff refused to give the DPA precise figures as to audience size or participation rate. An examination of the pattern of percentages preferring different options appears to suggest, however, that only a handful were pushing their buttons. Because they believe in public education, the DPA normally establishes a baseline by asking participants the same series of questions before and after each meeting. When they did so in the Dallas experiment, however, they were cautioned by Qube personnel that the audience at the end of the broadcast was composed almost entirely of different viewers from those watching at the beginning. If the results of the Dallas test are generally illustrative, the ease of tuning in to a DPA discussion in one's living room is offset by the ease of tuning out.

On the other hand, by most accounts their experimentation in Reading was more successful. Since Reading has the thriving public access system in Berks Community Television (see Chapter Five), one must conclude that a factor more important than technology is the level of preexisting organization that can be thrown into a series of DPA metings.

The DPA put together another successful adaptation of communication hardware in the use of videoconferencing to link different points at which participants gather. A televised portion of the February 1983 national meeting, which convened in Ann Arbor, Michigan, was distributed by satellite to locations around the country, capitalizing on communities in which the local response to DPA had been particularly strong. Thus the small number (N = 16) of grass roots participants who traveled to Ann Arbor to represent the views of all who participated in community meetings could be expanded by around 450 people gathered at 14 sites. Those in remote locations were able to telephone questions and comments to those attending the national meeting and hear their reactions. In one hour, panelists in Ann Arbor responded to 12 questions of which 7 were posed from the remote locations. In March of 1984, the teleconference from the Johnson Library in Austin, Texas, was beamed to 24 sites from which over 1,000 people could share in the proceedings. The length of the teleconference was expanded to two and a half hours, allowing time for the national participants to respond to 52 questions and comments from the field. And the 1985 national meeting held at the Kennedy Library in Boston also included a two-hour teleconference that linked 25 sites. From an additional uplink location in Washington, a senator, two congressmen, and a White House aide could participate in the discussion and respond to 22 calls from the citizens scattered across the country.

Beyond a sense that the numbers of citizens involved in the fall meetings is large and growing (10,000 in 1982, 23,000 in 1983, 33,000 in 1984, and over 100,000 in 1985), evaluating the quality of participation in DPA is quite difficult. The DPA is a decentralized network of local initiators; for example, in the 1984 cycle 145 organizations sponsored forum discussions, aided by leadership, encouragement, and materials from Dayton and New York. As a result, the nature of each meeting is unique, depending upon the conception of the convener, the temperment of moderators, and the personality of the panelists. In some meetings—those deemed less successful by the national staff in Dayton—citizen participants are lectured to by a panel of experts. Others involve a high degree of discussion and exchange of views without domination from the podium. Some meetings end in consensus, while dissension and controversy mark others.

The willingness of citizens to participate in more than one local meeting would be quite revealing as to the perceived value of participation to citizens. Unfortunately, the DPA staff has not systematically measured return rates either from year to year or from one meeting to the next in a single cycle. Some of the participants are probably attracted by a single subject under discussion and may not take a similar interest in other topics. When asked, however, the conveners estimated impressionistically that between 50% and 70% attend all three meetings in one year (Kinghorn, 1984). Another indication so far is that 90% of the communities that have held DPA forums in one year are similarly active the next year. Conveners report that they start each year with a core of participants who have been active in years past.

The express purpose of the National Issues Forums is to build an enlightened and interested citizenry. In meeting with fellow citizens, participants are expected to learn both about the topic discussed and to acquire a sense of the legitimacy of public involvement in national policy issues. For its motto, emblazoned on all its literature, DPA uses a quotation from Thomas Jefferson, that captures the basic assumption of their orientation toward citizen participation:

> I know no safe depository of the ultimate powers of the society but the people themselves; and if we think them not enlightened enough to exercise their control with a wholesome discretion, the remedy is not to take it from them, but to inform their discretion by education.

For the DPA, public enlightenment predominates over a direct impact of citizen opinion on public policy.

Not surprisingly, the connection between DPA discussions and the policy process is weak. While efforts are made to sum up the feelings expressed in community meetings and to convey those to leaders gathered at the national meetings, the very diverseness of the DPA complicates this task. In the first place, with so much data drawn from local meetings, the DPA staff undoubtedly has a difficult time extracting and distilling a "citizens view" of the policy in question. Second, while some participants from local meetings are invited to attend the national gathering, the criteria for selection are not clearly specified and the selection process is controlled by the DPA staff. Third, the citizens' role at the national meeting is deliberately vague. While they certainly are viewed as representatives of the American public, they have not been selected by constituents who attended the local meetings. As a result, the linkage between the discussions held around the country and the recommendations given to policy-makers is tenuous at best.

It is possible that the educative process extends to public leaders as well. That is, rather than providing a mechanism for conveying precise citizen needs and opinions to policy-makers, the DPA permits political leaders (in addition to citizens) to reflect upon policy in a broader context provided by citizen discussion. Perhaps, the political leaders learn a great deal from the discussions that take place at the presidential libraries. While they may not come away with policy guidance in a directly usable form—how many voters prefer which option, which groups support which alternatives—they may have their own thoughts stimulated by the experience and, in the process, acquire a deeper conception of the nature of the problem, the priorities within it, the urgency of a solution, and so forth.

For this process to develop into a significant, long-term impact, however, the reputation and visibility of DPA must continue to expand such that they are able to attract a greater number of political leaders who are in actual control of the policy process during the time of their involvement in DPA. Former Presidents Carter and Ford led the group of policy-makers at the first national meeting in 1983, including seven former cabinet secretaries, six former advisors to past presidents, and one incumbent congressman. Of eight "policy-makers and dignitaries" at the LBJ Library Conference in 1984, only three held office at that time (two congressmen and the governor of Texas). The 15 public officials invited to the 1985 meeting at the Kennedy Library in Boston came mostly from state and regional levels, since the issues considered were more relevant to their authority. In addition, the teleconference linked them with a senator, two congressmen, and a White House aide located in Washington, D.C.

Sensitive to the criticism that the connection to the policy process is too weak, the DPA has added to its design a "Washington Week" during which citizens can come to the nation's capital to discuss the issues with policymakers. In 1984, 20 individuals were invited to attend; in 1985 and 1986 anyone could come if they had taken part in the local meetings and could pay their own way. In each year, 50 citizens signed up to meet with members of Congress and Washington opinion leaders. While this is an important addition to the program, the role of the citizens and the relationship between local discussion and policy advice conveyed to the public officials remains somewhat unspecified.

The implied criticism of the DPA in this analysis is based on my normative preferences for tangible and immediate policy impact. The primary goal of the DPA is to create "forums where those concerned, disinterested citizens who form the ballot of a democratic nation come together to address the common good" (DPA, 1983). To their credit, the leadership of the DPA, Donald Mathews, president of Kettering, and Daniel Yankelovich, president of the Public Agenda Foundation, have avoided the temptation to claim that the DPA will allow citizens to shape policy. Instead, their speeches are full of phrases such as: "There must be a meaningful quality of public discussion out in the grass roots" (Mathews) and "We're quite effective in raising people's consciousness about the issues . . . [but] *not* a method for making a place for the public at the table where policy is formulated" (Yankelovich). Both express the hope that DPA can become that instrument in the long run, but recognize that it's immediate impact is lacking.

In the meantime, the continuing success of DPA in widening its circle of participants demonstrates that citizens can be involved in the discussion of national issues and that technology can facilitate that process. Again the water-in-glass analogy applies. From one perspective, the numbers involved are a minuscule fraction of the national electorate; from another, the organization is providing an opportunity for collective discussion among a larger number of citizens than might otherwise consider and debate the complexities of public policy.

The DPA provides an important lesson in the uses of communication technologies. The life blood and ethos of this organization is "low tech, high touch": citizens engaging their peers in face-to-face meetings. Grafting electronic media on to this process has only proved successful where technology amplifies and extends the normal functioning of the organization; for example, by linking several sites so that a national discussion among those active in the organization can be held. Where public access to cable television is already firmly established, then the DPA can provide fruitful material for discussion. However, when technology is picked up for its own sake and used to engage citizens not otherwise involved, then the results are less encouraging.

COMPUTER CONFERENCING

Several software systems are currently available through which scattered home computer operators can carry on a continuing discussion over a computer network. Each participant must have a computer or a terminal that can send and receive text messages several lines long. These are connected through telephone lines to a central computer that stores the comments made in each conference, grants access to them for qualified participants, allows them to compose messages that can be sent to individual participants or added as an open comment available to all who join the conference, and otherwise facilitates the flow of messages. An evergrowing list of comments by participants can be read or briefly scanned by anyone who has joined a conference, and the central computer tells each participant if new messages have been added since his or her last session.

Computer conferencing exhibits several general characteristics that must be considered before turning to its uses as a medium of political participation. Like all media, use of computer conferencing is largely determined by the values and needs of the individuals communicating.

Egalitarianism. The central computer files each comment in the order it is received. Although the software allows one to scan the first few lines written by others, the medium almost forces participants to pay equal attention to each comment. Though regular participants become quite skilled at moving around in an evergrowing file, at the very least, participants must deal sequentially with each comment. Although they can dispense with a whole sequence in a batch, they do so without much sense of whether the discarded comments are valuable or trivial.

The result is that the comments of each participant must be given near equal attention by the others involved in the discussion. In a face-to-face meeting, speakers can outshout each other, the chair can refuse to recognize a waving hand, and nonverbal cues are exchanged that signal that further discussion by the group or further participation by one member is unwelcome. These checks are weaker in this medium.

Engineered Hierarchy. The egalitarianism and interactivity of this medium can be strong points for political participation, general discussion, and intraorganization communications in which hierarchy is a barrier. For many uses, however, software has been designed to allow users to introduce a degree of hierarchy into a conference. Basically, a moderator serves as gatekeeper, denying some access to the conference and allowing others a "read only" (i.e., observer) status. The moderator can also exercise editorial functions, paring or eliminating some comments. The software allows any member to put an issue to a vote by all participants, but the moderator can limit that capability as desired.

Terseness. Even with allowances for the moderator's duties, the medium places a premium upon terse comments. Long contributions translate into greater "connect time" and longer periods while others sit gazing at a cathode-ray tube. Since most services charge customers based on their connect time and since eye strain can be a problem, the medium and social pressure push participants toward succinctness. Often nuance and detail are traded-off for brevity.

Anonymity. Conferences are either open to all subscribers to a network or closed to all except those admitted by the moderator. In open conferences, the participants normally do not know each other except through their computer-mediated contacts. Each subscriber can make available such information about herself or himself as desired. Even so, it appears to me, from having read numerous open conferences, that the bounds of restraints are weaker than those normally found in social contact. More often than acceptable in face-to-face contact, participants will make snide and biting comments directed toward individuals they do not know or toward the whole group discussion. Glossbrenner (1985) argues, however, that anonymity has many positive effects upon communication through this medium, including the absence of cues as to gender, age, race, or ethnic origin that can stereotype individuals and thereby distort communication.

Anonymity, terseness, and egalitarianism do, however, result in a conversation rather resembling that of a CB radio, a series of "one-liners" exchanged among strangers, many of whom hide behind a code name and all isolated from each other. Also, like CB radio, a great deal of the conversation is centered upon what the participants have in common—road conditions and equipment in the one case, computers, high tech and conferencing in the other. Thus many of those engaged in computer networking naturally spend more time discussing the capacities of different home computers or the advantages of various software packages over others than they do on more personal matters or, for our purposes here, on public policy. In the conferences observed in this research, which did deal with policy matters, a fairly high proportion of the comments were largely off the subject being discussed. Keeping the conversation on track proved to be a significant problem. Perhaps this is not so surprising given that the conferences studied were composed of people who had no underlying common organization or integrating contact beyond the conference itself.

An "asynchronous" medium. The strongest advantage of computer conferencing is the capacity for interaction without the requirement that the communicator and the audience be engaged simultaneously. Written text, although instantly available to everyone who has joined the conference, can be read to them at any subsequent time. While this feature can result in a spasmodic style of conversation in which the topic keeps shifting back to matters broached earlier, those groups led by a skilled moderator have learned how to divide the conference into numerous subtopics covering different aspects of the central conversation. The strength of this characteristic for participants should not be missed: One can participate in a meeting at a time and place of one's choosing. When joining an ongoing meeting, moreover, one can catch up by reviewing the entire conversation that has already taken place.

This discussion of computer conferencing differs from the other reports of this study in that we will not be considering a demonstration project or experiment per se. Rather, I sought to observe the nature of political discussion that had spontaneously taken place over two computer networks. I selected two of the most elaborate, successful, and heavily used computer conferencing systems now available: the Electronic Information Exchange System (EIES) maintained at the New Jersey Institute of Technology and the "Participate" package available to users of The Source, an "information utility" owned jointly by *Reader's Digest* and the Control Data Corporation. The Participate system, a popular feature of The Source, is owned by Participation Systems Inc. (Winchester, MA) and is, so far as I could determine, the most widely used conferencing package. EIES links primarily an academic roster of subscribers and is itself the center of research and experimentation on computer conferencing.

Subscribers to either The Source or EIES are also not average citizens. The costs of home computers, modems, and connect time put this form of communication well beyond the means of all but the most affluent or dedicated technology buffs. Many appear to belong to organizations, companies, or institutions that will pay for their conferencing time. While I did not conduct a study of the background of participants in these conferences, I suspect that, in addition to high incomes or institutional connections, this population has an educational median far above national norms. Conclusions about the usefulness of computer networking as an instrument of mass political participation, therefore, need to be advanced highly tentatively. We simply do not have enough valid data to speak with any confidence as to how computer conferencing might be used politically if it gained widespread acceptance (Henderson & MacNaughton, 1980; Hiltz & Turoff, 1978). For example, the verbal and written character of this medium will inevitably create a limitation that can not be overcome; those with poor verbal skills will be handicapped if computer networking becomes a principal means of influencing public policy. That fact alone may curtail the breadth of acceptance of this medium both by different social classes and by those who strongly insist that participation mechanisms must be open to all citizens (e.g., reasonably universal access).

While it is accurate to note that the computer conferencing I observed did not constitute a project explicitly designed to encourage political participation, many of those actively engaged in conferencing, including some of the service providers, are very interested in encouraging discussion of politics. The president of Participation Systems, Chandler Stevens, for example, has himself been active in elective and legislative politics and remains committed to stimulating political discussions over his system. He is the convener of several conferences on The Source in which political matters are debated and he is a frequent participant in those discussions. As a result, to observe the level and nature of political involvement in these conferencing systems is not quite as unfair as would be, for example, faulting an art school for lack of consideration devoted to public policy.

Of 46 open conferences taking place on EIES in the spring of 1984, only 5 (10%) were devoted to matters that could be subsumed under the broadest possible definition of politics or public policy. For comparison, 18 conferences, or about 40%, dealt with subjects relating to computers, information sciences, and computer conferencing itself. Similarly, on The Source, 10% (16 out of 155 conferences examined) were broadly political, while 36% (55 conferences) focused on the technology. The number of "political" conferences would have been lower, around 6%, if the count had not included six conferences organized by Participation Systems as part of the Markey electure (see Chapter Five).

On EIES, participation in the "political" conferences ranged from a low of 40 members (approximately 3% of the total EIES membership) discussing food and population problems to a high of 96 individuals (6%) sharing their reactions to ABC's special on the effects of a nuclear bomb on an average American city entitled *The Day After*. In all, a little over 12% of the EIES membership (N = 197) engaged in one open "political" discussion or another. Among those who were involved, the vast majority (65%) specialized in only one topic, while slightly more than one-tenth engaged in three political matters.

Calculating the same figures for the 45,000 individuals who subscribe to The Source would be misleading since many of them do not participate in computer conferencing at all. Instead, they use other features such as games, news, stock market quotations, travel information, and the like. Suffice it to say, however, that our basic conclusions as to the pattern of usage are the same: Of all conference users, only a finite number become actively engaged in discussing policy and politics.

Moreover, when we use a stronger lens and examine the pattern of participation within the conferences in which politics is discussed, the results are quite similar. A few individuals account for most of the comments, while a plurality either make a single comment or merely read the remarks of others. In one conference analyzed in detail, 40% of the comments were contributed by only 3 individuals, versus 21 participants who broke into the discussion only once. In another conference of almost 100 people who became involved in a discussion of ABC's show *The Day After*, only one-third of these participants read all the way through to near the end of the conference discussion; only 40% of all participants contributed to the discussion; and more than half of that 40% made only one comment. These rates of involvement are very similar to those recorded in closed conferences (Henderson &MacNaughton, 1980).

Rates of participation also appear to be affected by the passage of time. In several conferences examined, participation followed the same declining pattern: a precipitating event generated a flood of interest and discussion that rapidly evaporated, so that within a few days the discussion amounted to a trickle of approximately one new comment added each day. For example, the reaction on EIES to the ABC show dragged on for more than two months, but over half the comments were made within 48 hours of the show. Similarly, the shooting down of a Korean airliner produced an intense reaction measured by the number of comments added to the "Politics" conference on The Source (Mohl, 1983), but that interest waned rapidly.

To examine the substance of these conferences more systematically, I developed a very simple coding scheme. In one example, fully 22% were off the stated topic of discussion. The remainder divided about equally between those who merely voiced their own opinions on the matter at hand and those who responded interactively to the comments of others (answering questions, posing questions for others, or commenting on another's remark). Those who participate more heavily tend to be more responsive to others—they get caught up in an evolving discussion. Those who only voice their own opinions tend to be one-time participants; they "say their piece" and then desist.

These remarks should be placed within a context: The conferences observed were all open to participation from any EIES or Source subscribers. As such they may have some unique characteristics that do not carry over to all conferences. In particular, the difficulty of keeping a conversation going is certainly related to the fact that the participants are essentially strangers without a group purpose beyond the discussion itself. Use of conferencing by an established group to accomplish a collective objective might be less sensitive to fall off over time. In preparation for a 1983 White House Conference on Productivity, for example, the American Productivity Center in Houston, Texas organized a series of conferences on seven subtopics in which 175 senior leaders from business, labor, academia, and government participated. In five months of conferencing, they generated 2,170 conference comments (177,335 lines) and exchanged 12,600 private messages. Given a deadline instead of a triggering event, the rate of contributions did not appear to taper off dramatically.

As an instrument of mass participation, computer conferencing is not that promising, especially given that we are hardly dealing with a mass phenomenon yet. By virtue of the great detail that this medium can carry, even the highly verbal often run out of things to say to each other if they are strangers. The above observations cause one to wonder whether there is a real need for a medium that connects a large number of speakers with a large number of listeners.

This medium is often described by its promoters as a many-to-many instrument (Stevens, 1981); in practice, a maximum of about 40 people can conveniently conference together (Hiltz & Turoff, 1978). "Some-to-some" is a more accurate description of its capacities. Even so, 40 is more participants than can easily communicate in an egalitarian fashion through any other media, especially when large distances may be involved.

This preliminary review, conducted at this early stage in the development of a medium, leads to the conclusion that computer conferencing will prove better suited to communication within established groups than as an instrument through which strangers will engage each other. While my conclusion denigrates the capacity of computer conferencing to facilitate mass citizen participation—in comparison to, for example, televised call-in shows—the medium could easily become a highly useful tool for stimulating dialogue among interested groups of citizens. Such uses—either lateral contact among citizens with the ultimate aim of changing public policy or electronic lobbying with public officials on a finite policy terrain—would emerge from a pluralist conception of political processes rather than a plebiscitarian norm of mass involvement.

Discussion

Given that the two teledemocracy experiments reviewed here differ dramatically in the level of technology employed, one should not be too surprised to discover that they also differ in many institutional aspects. The DPA is primarily a "low tech" or even "no tech" project; citizens are encouraged to come to face-to-face gatherings to discuss a series of policy questions.[1] On the other end of the spectrum, computer conferencing calls forth the highest of hi-tech: home computers linked to a large machine over phone lines. Computer participation demands familiarity and comfortableness with the workings of computer software. The number of participants in the DPA is large and growing, while participation in computer conferencing is limited and concentrated, although growing as well.

ACCESS AND REACH

While theoretically anyone can attend a DPA meeting, access to computer conferencing is severely restricted. Home computers may spread rapidly in our society and citizens may be willing to pay for the information services available through corporations offering networks or videotex but we cannot be sure of this trend. One astute analysis concludes that this access problem will remain very severe for a long while (Blomquist, 1984).

Once we put aside the access dimension, the limitations in the reach of these two efforts appear to be similar. Only a small percentage of the total population is interested enough in politics to become involved in educative discussions, whether it takes place electronically or in face-to-face meetings. The fact that only a very small percentage of subscribers to The Source use this medium for discussions of politics or policy is not very striking. The same is certainly true of the public's responses to the efforts of the DPA. These trends may simply be more visible in computer conferencing because the information publicly available about conference joiners on The Source or EIES affords us better documentation of how individuals respond to opportunities for discussion of political topics.

While the DPA has attracted a large number of citizens to its local meetings, the percentage of the general population so engaged is minimal—less than 1/10th of 1%.

DIVERSE PATHS OF ACCESS

Interestingly, these two teledemocracy projects, which are vastly different in the technologies they employ, bear some noticeable similarities in their pattern of involving people. For example, both projects allow diversity in participation skills. Just as individuals attending meetings (such as those arranged by the DPA) can listen while saying nothing, many of those participating in computer conferences merely read the contributions of others. In both formats, one encounters a small number of citizens who become very vocal and account for much of the conversation and another small set who become involved in so many meetings or many conferences that they take on the label "activist."

Finally, just as meetings can employ a "show of hands," so computer conferencing allows any participant to arrange a vote on any topic. In the conferences observed, however, participants used this option in only one. Conceivably, expressing opinions by voting could be used to resolve an issue of some disagreement or could allow participants to steer their discussion along lines preferred by the majority. But voting—at least in our political culture—is normally a means of ending discussion and resolving questions. Similarly, we suspect that a show of hands vote in a face-to-face meeting is rarely used to stimulate discussion but to resolve and conclude matters. Because these projects are primarily interested in encouraging discussion, there may be informal disincentives to use voting procedures. Moreover, if the voting mechanism becomes extensively used as a means of participation in computer conferencing, then the medium will probably begin to resemble videotex; rather than an egalitarian discussion, hierarchy will emerge. Participants who are most active will naturally begin to define issues and questions for the rest to express their opinions.

AGENDA SETTING

A major difference between these projects occurs in the degree to which participants can influence the agenda of discussion. The egalitarian nature of computer conferencing carries over into agenda making. Once someone is allowed to participate in a conference, he or she is able to comment on any matter. In one conference closely observed, for example, the result was that almost one-third of the contributions were departures from the stated purpose of the discussion. This could be a great strength: The initiators cannot tightly control the agenda, while rank-and-file participants can move the discussion in directions they believe more fruitful.

Meanwhile, the agenda of National Issues Forum meetings is sharply defined by decisions made well in advance by the project staff. Deciding upon three topics for discussion allows the DPA to prepare materials that will, it hopes, be stimulating and educative. Even though participants may bring other information and knowledge with them, the DPA does assume higher burdens of fairness, access, and balance such as are usually associated with the plebiscitarian efforts. The strategy of the DPA is to generate the roughly similar discussions in numerous localities, so that they standardize the agenda as a means of incorporating larger numbers of citizens. Once these meetings are opened, the attending citizens probably have a greater capacity to define for themselves the range of proposed solutions than do participants in a plebiscite.

EDUCATION AND EFFECTIVENESS

The degree to which these projects educate or have effective direct impact on public policy proved impossible to assess, so that only sparce comments on these points are in order. Given their position on our four-fold grid of projects, it is obvious that these endeavors (nongovernmental dialogues) are the longest-term efforts involving the most minimal direct impact on policy. Therefore, their success is most appropriately measured in terms of their educative aspects: whether citizens learn about the policy matter at hand and, in the process, acquire the skills and a predilection for future involvement.

The Public Agenda Foundation endeavors to measure the learning and attitude change that results from attendance at its DPA meetings. However, in view of the great variation in types of meetings and in the collection of pre- and postmeeting questionnaires, a detailed examination of the educative value of these experiences has been difficult to achieve. Suffice it to say that the Public Agenda Foundation staff—a group with considerable professional experience in public opinion measurement—has been convinced by their results that learning does take place among many who attended DPA meetings.

COSTS AND INITIATIVE

The projects impose remarkably different costs upon would-be participants. Enough has already been said about the financial costs of computer conferencing and resulting social stratification now evident among its users. Since it is highly unlikely that anyone would purchase a home computer or subscribe to a service like The Source simply to participate politically, the immediate financial costs of participation via The Source are smaller than might first appear.

Once past the threshold of access to computers, the costs and inconveniences such as one encounters in attending the Domestic Policy Association meetings are *minimized* by the technology of computer conferencing. Rather than travel to attend a lengthy meeting in which one has little control over the content or timing, the skilled computer user can determine the time in which to particpiate in a conference and can proceed through the discussion at an individually determined rate. Moreover, the interactive capacity allows the participant to determine the content, or at least the subject matter, in which he or she will partake.

On the other hand, we should not overlook the costs of participation in the Domestic Policy Association: Citizens are urged to purchase the explanatory booklets that contain detailed information about the policy matters to be discussed. Most likely, a larger burden for most is the act of attending a meeting. Despite awareness of this problem and efforts to mitigate its effects, the DPA meetings are probably less representative of the general population than are electronic meetings conducted over the television.

The level of initiative required by both these projects is high. Involvement in DPA meetings may well be encouraged by personal contact with the enthusiastic arrangers of separate events, so that the initiative required to find out about a DPA meeting may be minimal for many citizens. But participants must travel to the meeting site, a burden that is eliminated by conferencing. The experience of computer conferencing is rather like attending a set of meetings in which a different topic is being discussed in each room and where one can move freely and instantaneously from one room to another. Upon entering a room, moreover, one can pick up the conversation taking place at that moment or review the entire transcript of the discussion up to the present.

The strengths of this technology appear to come at a cost in terms of their practical use. Since the initiative required to join a given discussion is lower, the commitment to sustained participation is likely to be less. In discussing the differences between the Alaska system and those governmental efforts in which the dialogue took place over television, we noted that home viewers could easily turn away from the political discussion and back to more entertaining pursuits. The same applies here. Computer conference participants can jump quickly from subject to subject. In some of the discussions monitored closely, those who became disgusted with the comments of others frequently quit the conference while venting their anger in snide remarks, rather than pursuing a resolution to their differences through dialogue.

Conclusions

In terms of the quantity of participation that these projects generate, they appear to be on the losing end of both of the major dimensions that differentiate projects. On the one hand, since government officials are mostly absent from these engagement efforts, citizens are not attracted by the prospects of actually influencing public policy. Nor do they possess the aura of legitimacy that may be cast upon ad hoc events by the active involvement of public officials.

On the other hand, consider the fact that involvement in dialogue takes more time than casting votes in a plebiscite. To be sure, informed participation in a vote may require as much preparation costs as attending a community meeting. But as observations made in the Health Vote '82 and Choices for '76 indicate, frequently citizens cast votes without having attended to any of the informative communications that preceded the voting. By requiring more from citizens, dialogue projects suffer reduced participation.

These endeavors must be judged on the quality of their educative and competence building process, which are, unfortunately, difficult concepts to measure. But we can be fairly well assured that success here is determined more by idiosyncratic factors such as project design or the responsiveness of the organizers than by the technology employed. The terseness of comments in computer conferencing, however, should give us grounds for reserve in evaluating the capacity of this medium to educate. One may discover that terseness is offset by the interactive nature of the dialogue nurtured by the technology, but, at present, the question is very much in doubt. Predictably, we must conclude that the medium is too young for one to be able to resolve the quality issue with any precision.

Note

1. DPA was considered in our study because they have been experimenting with the use of communication technologies such as holding meetings over cable using a call-in format and with national videoconferences.

CHAPTER 8

LESSONS FROM THE TELEDEMOCRACY PROJECTS

The thirteen teledemocracy experiments examined in the last four chapters were divided conceptually based upon two conceptual dichotomies. First, some projects placed government officials on the receiving end of citizen participation, while others did not. Where public figures were involved, the organizers appeared to be interested in setting up the conditions in which citizens might directly influence public policy. When public officials were not involved, the project initiators were most likely to emphasize the value of civic education. The second dichotomy involved the nature of the participant act: Some experiments encourage dialogues and others staged plebiscites. This distinction reflects differences in the project organizers' belief about the nature of politics. Some feel that its essence involves disputes among competing groups that must be harmonized; others believe that a common will exists among the citizenry and must be made manifest by citizen participation in plebiscites.

Behind this schema lies the formative principle that the goals and values of teledemocracy organizers are more important in understanding the differences among projects than are the technologies employed. I could have described these projects according to the media used (broadcast television versus cable versus computer networks). But a technology-based schema would not have been nearly as insightful.

In any case, an effort to evaluate thirteen projects—grouped under four rubrics and employing six different technologies—along eleven different dimensions of participation is not likely to yield a single, simple conclusion. Can telecommunication technologies be used to improve the quantity and quality of citizen participation in politics? Yes. Can these uses also mitigate the inequalities now found in the rates of participation of different social groups? Yes. Do these projects collectively point toward one technology that best facilitates participation? No. Does this research suggest that technological change will produce an inevitable transition of our political institutions toward direct democracy? No. Can teledemocracy contribute to the functioning of America's political institutions? It depends upon what you mean by "teledemocracy."

The most straightforward manner of summarizing our conclusions from these investigations is to group them according to whether they are consequences of the technology or derived from the social planning of the project initiators.

Before doing so, however, I should restate succinctly the major limitations of the research. First, I have not examined all applications of technology to political communication. I have observed only instances designed to elicit citizen participation. The internal use of videoconferencing by interest groups, or the rapidly increasing sharing of data across levels of our federal system, to cite two examples, fall outside our purview. Second, the projects selected for study are all instances in which the organizers took an "outcome neutral" posture; they sought to encourage involvement as a value in its own right. The electronic ministers, the Chamber of Commerce, or the expanding apparatus at the Republican National Committee were excluded from this analysis. Third, rather than predicting the use of communication technologies that may become available in the future, I have tried to remain empirical, studying actual situations in which technology has been used. While some of the projects studied are on the forefront of technological developments, many of them are really jury-rigged efforts to use existing technologies, rather than experiments in "hi-tech" politics.

The Consequences of Technology

In truth, I cannot maintain a tidy separation between developments induced by hardware and those produced by the initiator's objectives. Abstractly, we confront a range of causes from those that are more dependent on the physical capabilities of technology to those that are primarily a result of the values brought to the exercise by participants and organizers. There is no pure case of technological imperative; when we speak of a communications medium, we refer to more than hardware. For example, beyond the transmission of sound, the telephone as a medium refers to private messages exchanged between individuals, near universal service, and monopoly utilities regulated as to rates and service, protected from liability for the messages they transmit, and unable to determine or limit access. In short, a huge number of value choices are already implicit in the regulatory policies under which a medium is established. Those who would use a given media such as the telephone to encourage participation must accept these inherent value choices as their starting point. But one should not pretend that those uses are purely a product of the technology of telephony. The most one can do in this situation is to discuss here those factors that *primarily* depend upon the capacities of the technology and the characteristics of the communications media.

Each medium has a distinctly different capacity to reach people. Some succeed in engaging a large, diffuse audience; others reach a much smaller group with definable characteristics; still others can be used to contact almost everybody, but they do so one at a time. Many of the new media are "semipublic" in that they are available to the broad public but, practically, because of choices made by receivers, they reach only limited segments of their potential audience. Others are "semi-private" in that the sender can designate recipients, but the emerging technology can include vastly more people in these conduits than can a point-to-point medium. Political actors use these different media for accomplishing different tasks, according to these characteristics.

Plebiscites demand broad-gauged mass media. For these purposes, the communications media as they currently exist in the United States are less than ideal. Recent events such as the attempted assassination of Ronald Reagan amply demonstrate that the mechanisms do exist to communicate to all our citizens relatively rapidly. But an analogy drawn from times of crisis does not conform to the requirements of a functioning political system. As currently structured, the media available in the United States simply cannot be used to conduct the extensive and more-or-less continuous efforts that would be necessary to allow citizens to express their views of policy questions on a daily basis.

Among the projects examined, competition for the attention of potential voters has been the most persistent problem encountered by project organizers, especially by those who have sought to conduct plebiscites. The plethora of media is the single most difficult institutional barrier they face. The organizers of projects such as the Honolulu Electronic Town Meetings, Alternatives for Washington, Choices for '76, or the Des Moines Health Vote, have commandeered broadcast television because that medium has the most extensive reach to the citizenry. Their experience, however, documents that despite the capabilities of the medium, repetition and the use of multiple channels are necessary to involve anything approaching all the people. The most successful of these plebiscitarian projects, the Des Moines Health Vote, relied upon frequent public service advertisements, newspaper articles, radio talk shows, and even billboards and bus placards in addition to top public affairs broadcast programming. Yet even Health Vote had sharp limitations that circumscribe the degree to which it met the requirements of an effective, ongoing political system. It was a one-time effort staged over a lengthy time interval (to allow more opportunity to reach citizens and stimulate their thinking). It was concentrated upon a single policy area in a definable media market. And it proved to be expensive and taxing. The project amply demonstrated the capacity of technology to involve citizens in policy discussions, but it also documented how costly and extensive are the exertions needed to achieve even a 25% rate of involvement.

Can these projects serve as a model for a fully developed, effective political system? Evidently not. Consider the fact that, at present, broadcast channels require "roadblocking" and considerable repetition, which necessitates either substantial financial expenditures or a level of cooperation from private broadcasters that seems unlikely.

Moreover, the direction of change in the communications industry appears to be in a direction that will complicate the management of effective plebiscites. That is, competition for the communications industry is expanding the number of available channels. A larger number of conduits will aggrevate the problems of getting the public's attention.

Perhaps the communications revolution will, as Barber (1984) suggests, allow society to establish a completely separate conduit reserved for political information exchange and voting. The problem then will become whether citizens are interested enough in public affairs to pay attention to this conduit, given all the other streams of information and entertainment available. These projects emphatically illustrate that public life is in a severe, and often losing, competition with other aspects of individual and social activity.

The evolution of the communications industry appears, on the other hand, to be improving the prospects for "pluralist" forms of teledemocracy. For example, in North Carolina and Reading, public officials reach out to solicit constituent opinions using semipublic cable channels. While the technology may look much like a plebiscite (television programming out, telephone calls in), the difference is really one of expectation. Since everyone knows that the cable medium reaches a small audience, the organizers cannot pretend that they are receiving back the "voice of the people."

The more innovative experiments involve the political uses of semiprivate media. The legislature of Alaska, for example, holds committee hearings over a voice-only teleconferencing network and citizens who wish to testify must go to one of 71 sites located throughout the vast state where those state-owned facilities are located. Computer conferences have been arranged allowing a congressman to discuss arms control policy with a limited group of citizens. Another congressman held videoconferences with constituents back home in California.

In addition, the evolving mix of communications media appears to be more conducive to the development of stronger interest groups; they will be able to use these narrower, private links to mobilize their membership. For example, several national interest groups now hold strategy sessions with affiliate state-level organizations to map out a lobbying strategy by a videoconference. As a result, any effective mechanism for embracing citizen participation will have to build into its design a positive role for interest groups and pluralist politics.

At present, however, there is still a long way to go before we reach the point at which the available media will be ideal for pluralist dialogues. Many of the efforts studied here employed cable television and a call-in format—mechanisms that are not totally satisfactory. The televised call-in has the potential of reaching large numbers of citizens, yet the number who can voice their opinions via the feedback loop is quite small.

If the currently available conduits are inadequate, what of the future? Audio- and videoconferencing hold better prospects for the few-to-few pattern of communication that is needed for a detailed, interactive exchange of views. In the process, they also give citizens much greater agenda-setting powers than does network television. But they impose additional burdens upon citizen participants over the convenience of cable television: They require that those who would become involved travel to a meeting site. The Iaskan example demonstrates that in order to surmount (or reduce) these burdens, systems employing video- or audioconferencing need to be backstopped by a staff specifically responsible for reaching out to potential participants.

Videotex and computer conferencing may become a suitable middle ground. Videotex can certainly convey outward a substantial amount of information about policy matters and can collect inward opinions from a substantial number of participants. The "voice" given participants may range from a simple yes/no choice to the opportunity for an individual citizen to poll the opinions of everyone else. That citizens have greater control over the timing and extent of information provided them is another benefit of these systems. Computer conferencing, moreover, facilitates horizontal exchange of information permitting citizens to organize politically or negotiate a set of common interests.

Videotex and computer conferencing systems, however, will also exhibit limitations as vehicles of political discourse. As a medium of dialogue, each of these vehicles may be conveniently used by modest numbers of communicators; the emerging technologies do not promise that everyone can have his or her individual say in a national dialogue. Another major problem, shared with cable television, is that videotex and computer conferencing carry material pertaining to a wide variety of human activity. As a result, in a single medium, politics comes into direct competition with these other facets of life for the attention of citizens. Many citizens may choose to spend their time in front of the computer screen engaging in commercial activity or being entertained rather than discussing or influencing politics.

At present, moreover, access to these systems is so severely limited by cost that they cannot be considered practical, and this condition will probably last for a substantial period of time (Blomquist, 1984). Yet they do promise a reduction in the inconveniences associated with the present state of audio- and videoconferencing, and, at the same time, they will permit a more extensive amount of feedback than systems employing the telephone. While they may greatly ease the mechanical problems of conducting plebiscites, they provide no solution to the political problems that this research has documented in plebiscites. Instead, they offer the prospect of facilitating genuine government-to-citizen dialogue patterned on the pluralist model of politics generated by self-interest and self-initiative rather than the populist-plebiscitarian perspective.

The principal observed impact of the use of technology for democratic politics is to reduce the costs and burdens of participation for citizens. These costs may be financial or they may be associated with time, travel, and information necessary to participate politically. Technology does not, however, reduce these costs and burdens across the board. In financial terms, communications technology can be very expensive.

Another important point, however, can be gleened from the relationship between technology and the costs of participation. Across the range of project designs, technology served to distribute the burdens between those who would elicit participation and citizens who might become involved. Generally speaking, the lower the burdens placed on citizens, the greater the demands (both financial and in an obligatory sense) upon project organizers. For example, where the news media are used to "spoon feed" citizens the information they need to consider a policy matter, the initiators must assume consequentially higher duties of inclusiveness, fairness, and balance in presenting that information. Similarly, through electronic voting systems, a much larger number of citizens can be induced to participate in a plebiscite than will attend a discussion; but the organizers of plebiscites must be held to higher standards of openness in view of their more substantial control over the agenda of policy considered.

I am speaking conceptually of costs and burdens, and accordingly cannot come to any simple additive notion of whether the costs to society as a whole are reduced or simply redistributed by technology. Clearly, if institutions that have functioned quite smoothly through direct human contact now begin employing technology to conduct communications, they may incur additional costs of operation. There is no evidence that technology can open up the political process while saving money.

But since citizen participation has been rather low in these traditional mechanisms and inequitably distributed across social classes, the advantages of using the emerging communications technology to allocate costs and burdens away from citizens appear rather clear. The principal questions involve the nature of participation that can be encouraged and the institutional patterns that are most successful for generating citizen involvement. To this discussion we now turn.

The Organization of Participation

The organizers of these four types of teledemocracy projects held sharply different views as to what constitutes appropriate participation, differences that proved to be quite important in determining the whole nature of their projects. The number of citizens involved, the breadth of their representativeness, the meaningfulness of their activity, the extensiveness of the educational or confidence-building processes, these and the other dimensions of participation were directly affected by the goals of the project initiators. Technology helped accomplish these objectives, but never supplanted them.

Because populist visions of direct democracy offer more radical departures from the existing pattern of politics, their novelty may well make them easier to organize on an experimental basis. Yet the outreach costs for universal involvement are so high and burdensome that these efforts tend to be single-shot events. They retain, therefore, an experimental nature that may not meet the requirements for a functioning political system.

In contrast, the advocates of using technology to modify current institutions may have difficulty persuading political leaders to accept their ideas. Since they start off by implying that the existing machinery is not adequately responding to citizen needs, they may insult the performance of those in power whose help they need. Initially, these projects may appear to threaten the position of these elites; experience has shown, however, that once in place they often prove so valuable to government officials that they become solidly institutionalized.

This research brought to the fore many political problems implicit in the conduct of plebiscites that will not be easy to cure. As noted above, when a large number of participants are involved, the elites or organizers are more likely to exercise unrestrained control over information available to citizens and the agenda of issues on which their involvement is sought. In the projects studied, none of the organizers were interested in promoting their own view of appropriate policy. As a result, none of the plebiscitarian projects had to contain a robust, self-interested advocacy; rather they experimented with a somewhat sanitized version of politics. They may have demonstrated techniques of staging plebiscites electronically, but they have not successfully explored the very real political problems encountered in managing elite conflict. Nor have they probed the institutional arrangements necessary to circumscribe these conflicts.

The projects that attempted to use technology to stimulate discussions and negotiations among citizens or social groups, on the other hand, proved to be more successful in reaching their goals. Those goals were, however, far more limited than the vision of electronic plebiscites, both as to the number of citizen participants sought and the transformative nature of the experiment.[1] A wide range of experiments have been conducted including office hours held on cable television, citizens discussing policy matters via videoconferencing, legislative hearings extended geographically by audio teleconferencing, electronic mailings to legislators, and political dialogue by computer conferencing. By alleviating the burdens associated with intense political activity, these experiments involve many more individuals than normally become involved through traditional channels such as calling upon public officials or attending legislative hearings.

A different conception of politics and participation underlies the design of these experiments. Citizens who become involved in these projects are viewed as primarily self-interested; they represent only themselves or a group of which they are a part. They are not perceived by public officials as representing "the citizenry" as a whole. In these instances, the mechanism of citizen involvement is intended to allow expression of legitimate interests; differences among them must be negotiated, balanced, and compromised in the political arena. Those who organize these efforts recognize that not everyone will participate through their project and that, therefore, the interests expressed by participants need to be balanced against estimates of the needs of groups and citizens who did not become involved.

If raw numbers of participants mobilized over a short time span were the ultimate goal, those who promote plebiscites would be entitled to claim superiority. But this cannot be the whole story; several problems exist with the numerical comparisons between plebiscites and dialogues. First while the numbers of participants are larger in voting projects, so far they have been substantially less than would be desirable as a basis for an effective political system. Second, there may be a tendency for plebiscitarian involvement to drop in subsequent trials after the novelty has worn off. Third, since the dialogue projects promote a continuing discussion reshaping policy, the numbers of citizens involved at various points over the long run may be a good deal higher than would appear from observation of any one iteration.

It may well be that the different models of politics employed by those who hold plebiscites versus those who stimulate dialogues are relevant to different policy problems. Establishing broad social goals for future growth of government services poses a very different political question, raises a different structure of constituency relations, and triggers a different kind of political interest, than does, for example, deciding where a highway should be located or how to provide social security programs for the elderly (Lowi, 1964). In the former, the assumption that a common will exists and institutions are needed to stimulate and register the wishes of the people may be more valid. In the most successful plebiscitarian effort, the Des Moines Health Vote, the issue of concern—finding a way to limit the cost spiral in health services—had this characteristic; it was amenable to collective agreement. But most of the intractable policy problems are so difficult precisely because social and economic interests are pitted against one another and must be compromised and accommodated. For these problems we have uncovered ample demonstrations that communication technologies can be harnessed to stimulate and improve the political dialogue between governmental authorities and the competing interests.

Two final notes about conditions that increased participation in all projects will conclude this section. First, financing proved to be an essential component of success. With one exception (Choices for '76), the better funded projects were able to encourage more citizens to become involved and to give them more meaningful experiences. In some of the instances studied, the direct costs were minimal because citizens had already made major investments in technology (e.g., television) for other purposes. This factor is constantly changing. In the 1940s and early 1950s, the political use of television (and even telephone) would have been distorted by differential access. So while it seems absurd to propose now that the costs of a successful videotex project might not be substantial, that day may come.

Second, comparing similar projects of both the dialogue and the plebiscitarian molds reveals that those efforts that bring citizens into contact with government officials are generally more successful in encouraging participation. This finding appears to be related to an aura of legitimacy conveyed by the involvement of public officials and, possibly, to the more substantial financial resources that they bring to the experiment.

This observation provides yet one more difficulty for those who argue that technology is transforming our politics into a direct democracy. It appears that, for the present at least, more citizens are interested in participating in processes in which their opinions are expressed to public representatives. They are more likely to avoid projects that lack the trappings of legitimate government authority. Perhaps the inducement to participate is the opportunity to have some impact on actual policy. That is a point to which we will return in the concluding chapter.

Note

1. One commenter on this research, Russell Neuman of M.I.T., referred to this as the "buddha solution: want less and you'll be much happier."

CHAPTER 9

DEMOCRACY AND TECHNOLOGY

Democratic institutions must constantly adapt to changes spurred by technological innovation. The industrial revolution, telephones, automobiles, tractors, airplanes, medical advances, and television, to cite some major examples, have all generated social and economic forces to which our political institutions have inevitably had to respond. Human behavior—particularly that of political leadership that shapes political processes—has been the primary vehicle through which these changes have occurred. That is to say, values embedded in patterns of behavior and culture substantially modify the force of technological determinism. Two hundred years of political change has been necessitated by the social consequences of technological innovations. But the continual recasting or adaptation of institutions that conduct the public's business has been determined by enduring political values.

The canvas of American political history—if one is willing to paint with sufficiently broad strokes—depicts a major intellectual conflict between republican and democratic principles, philosophical doctrines that are only partially congruent with the policies of our two major parties. In addressing institutional questions, republicans have asserted the value of representative democracy and leadership invested with the capacity to make independent judgments on behalf of the interests of society.[1] Much of the Constitutional architecture erected by the Founders and their supporting arguments advanced in the Federalist Papers enshrines these values. They quickly became and remain the reigning political wisdom, the departure point for many conflicts over political processes and institutions.

From the moment the Constitution was enacted, however, democrats—whose thinking was flamboyantly manifest in the Declaration of Independence—have mustered both philosophical and practical political challenges to this prevailing view. The major drift of institutional change in American politics has been a grudgingly slow series of concessions to the advocates of more direct democracy.[2] The Federalist party floundered by being caught on the wrong side on this basic question. After seizing power, Jeffersonian Democrats were able to extend the franchise and establish the principle that presidential electors should

be popularly elected rather than selected by state legislators. By the
1840s, more broadly based national conventions became accepted as the
vehicle for nominating presidential candidates, replacing the more
indirect selection by congressional caucus. At the turn of the century, the
Progressives successfully promoted participation by rank-and-file party
members in nomination decisions; primaries were instituted in most
states. Under their prodding, many states and municipalities instituted
provisions for initiatives, referenda, and recall procedures, designed to
give citizens a more direct role in policy-making. Pressure from the
Progressives also eventually lead to the direct election of senators and
extension of the franchise to women. The long decline of political
parties—a trend evident across all levels of the election system during
much of this century—has been accompanied by stronger campaign
organizations that attempt to institute direct ties between the candidate
and voters. More recently, this trend acquired new life: In the last fifteen
years, the presidential nomination system has been recast to permit
greater public participation, and the power of committee chairmen in the
Congress has been decentralized to a host of subcommittees. Finally, if
one questions the American people today for their opinions as to desired
political reforms, large majorities support further "democratization"
such as direct election of presidents or a simple national presidential
primary. In short, small "d" democrats come from a long tradition in
American politics; the vigor of this tradition is hardly sapped.

   Amid all this democracy, however, in the past twenty years rates of
participation in electoral voting have declined, the inequalities across
social and economic classes that accompany these lowered rates have
intensified, and the related attitudes of cynicism and alienation expressed
in many national opinion surveys have escalated. These undesirable
trends have produced something of a crisis for the proponents of greater
democracy. Their solution? Many of them agree with Al Smith: The
only cure for the evils of democracy is more democracy. In arguing that
communication technologies will make possible a vast expansion in the
power wielded directly by citizens in policy-making processes, these
advocates of "teledemocracy" draw upon a potent intellectual heritage
that originates with Jefferson. Conversely, the tradition in American
thought that descends from Madison regards the potential of electronic
plebiscites with strong misgivings, emphasizing instead the value of
deliberation and judgment vested in representative processes.

   This argumentation is essentially normative. Nevertheless, empirical
research may add something to the debate. In fact, the advocates of
teledemocracy—Barber (1984), Becker (1981, 1984), Hollander (1985),
Naisbitt (1982), and Toffler (1980)—frequently cite observations drawn

from some of the same projects studied here to buttress their conclusions that technology is propelling political change in the direction of direct democracy. By systematically examining those instances in which communications has been used to underwrite citizen participation, we have gained some understanding of the context in which this enduring argument has most recently become manifest.

Teledemocracy Reconsidered

For the sake of argumentation, I have drawn the differences between two perspectives of politics rather more sharply than the advocates of either side would feel justified. The modern version of the Jefferson versus Madison argument surrounding the discussion of teledemocracy pits the populist vision of politics against the pluralist theories of political interest. To enact their concept of democracy, one group of projects staged plebiscites, while others engaged in stimulating dialogues. In the process of "pigeonholing" the work of project organizers and political theorists in this dispute, I may have unfairly simplified some of their thoughts. The Des Moines Health Vote, for example, involved considerable community discussion before the voting. Benjamin Barber's book *Strong Democracy* (1984) proposes many institutions for involving citizens in politics, only some of which would enlist the community as a whole in the direct determination of public policy. Recognizing the present unequal levels of political interest, Barber also suggests mechanisms to involve citizens first through self-interest and then to stimulate a general pattern of participation in politics.

Thus far, however, most of those who use the term *teledemocracy* refer to the expected and desirable prospects for plebiscitory democracy. These proponents believe that the arrival of new communications technology will permit a different solution to the problems of size, problems that have limited the realization of pure democracy. We will no longer need representative machinery, they argue; citizens themselves can engage directly in policy-making through the marvels of instant, extensive, interactive communications. The information required by them for decision can easily be communicated outward, and interactive technology will allow citizen preferences to be aggregated instantaneously.

This examination of seven plebiscitory projects suggests that technology can indeed solve the problems of rapidly coordinating the simultaneous behavior of large numbers of citizens. Very soon reliable mechanisms will be available that could perform the functions necessary for an ongoing national plebiscite. Consumer acceptance of and investment in this technology undoubtedly will take a much longer time to develop to the point of practical feasibility. But whatever the time lag in the development of media necessary to conduct plebiscites, this research indicates that the real problems are political in nature.

These investigations also formulate a response to those who argue that we are *inevitably* headed in the direction of more plebiscitory politics. Looking across a range of projects, I discovered that institutional choices were more important than technological capacity. The nature of participation evoked was a product of the values brought to the endeavor by the project organizers. Technology was not determinative. The design of most of these projects began with a goal that directed project initiators toward a given media to fulfill their objectives. Only in the instances in which the initiators were the owners of the media— Qube in Upper Arlington, Participation Systems on The Source—could it be said that the technology determined the political use. While different media are better suited to different communications tasks, a given piece of technology could be used to reach toward various objectives. A similar conception of participation could, moreover, be pursued by using various media.

Thus I feel justified in concluding that the future of our political institutions will be determined by the value choices we make about our political process. Any changes in store for our political institutions will not be thrust upon us without choice; the actions of those who care about safeguarding and reinforcing the democratic processes can have a profound impact on how these forces affect our politics. Because of the intellectual force and political pressure of the Jeffersonian tradition, the change they seek may well occur. We may yet evolve into a plebiscitarian democracy; certainly, there are those who argue vigorously in favor of the concept, and their ideas may enjoy broad popular support. But such a change will not be thrust upon us inexorably. The problems of plebiscitarian democracy boil down to two: citizen interest and control of elites.

Those who predict or advocate a transformation to direct democracy believe that when policy is actually at stake, citizens will find it worthwhile to pay attention, to educate themselves, and to participate. The observations collected in this research do not provide a basis for such optimism. Principally, I found little support for the notion that citizens have the interest necessary to sustain near universal participation; in practice too few are interested enough in politics to make plebiscites a feasible means of policy-making. No doubt many become involved when they feel their interests are at stake. But politics as an avocation of public service is not a strong motivation for many. Most citizens, probably around two-thirds, will not participate. The increasing number of competing media or channels of communication available to citizens will only exacerbate this problem.

Given the nature of the argument raised by the defenders of plebiscites, however, the teledemocracy experiments investigated here do not provide definitive data. None of them had the real-life quality that is viewed as necessary to stimulate participation. But to follow that logic through to its conclusion is to argue that only by establishing plebiscitarian teledemocracy will we be able to learn whether it works.

Another possibility is to examine citizen participation in statewide referenda elections where real issues and real power are at stake. A cursory examination of participation in these instruments of direct democracy also does not offer much support for the plebiscitarian point of view. The number voting on these ballot issues is frequently smaller than the votes cast on the same ballot for candidates. When referenda questions alone appear on the ballot, moreover, turnout is usually well below those elections in which candidates are running for office. In most cases, the real pull for turnout appears to be the choice of candidates (i.e., representative democracy) rather than the prospects of direct citizen determination of policy through referenda.

If conceived from a pluralist perspective, however, teledemocracy can address this problem. Through the use of emerging communications technology, more citizens will become involved in policy-making and policy implementation than traditionally take part through our existing machinery. Lowering the burdens of participation can, moreover, broaden the class base of those involved in political processes. These achievements will, however, fall short of the requirements of direct plebiscitory democracy: The number of nonparticipants will remain large and the well-known inequalities will persist, albeit in mitigated degree.

Turning our attention to the second political problem with plebiscitarian politics, this research has illustrated how severe the problems of controlling elites are for this school of teledemocracy. In most instances, agenda-setting powers were exercised only by the project organizers— they chose the subject matter, proposed the options for citizen choice, dictated the nature and timing of votes, and provided the information upon which citizens were supposed to act. The larger the number of participants, the more citizen involvement had to be structured by the initiators. Among these projects, I found no experimentation with mechanisms for containing abuses by elites.

The advocates of plebiscites showed little recognition that political disputes often involve passionate, self-interested advocacy and partisanship that will challenge the very process rules that define the boundaries of fair play. I also found little appreciation of the complexities and difficulties that have arisen in one body of law and regulations that does attempt to impose burdens of fairness, balance, and equal access upon elites. I refer, of course, to the regulation of broadcasting through the Federal Communications Act, which has not had an overwhelmingly successful history. All of these are political, not technological, problems of plebiscitory teledemocracy, but I found no instances that offered hope that they could be mitigated by technology.

On the other side of this picture, a strong argument can be mobilized against devoting major resources to endeavors that merely serve to reinforce the status quo. If technology is used to give government officials greater contact with citizens, critics will point out that there are no guarantees that citizen involvement will actually affect public policy. These projects can become co-optational, deluding people into supporting an unresponsive system. Consider the Alaskan Teleconferencing Network, for example; some will surely note that legislative hearings are a facade hiding the nasty politics of self-interested lobbying that really determine policy. Political elites who set up these projects are not about to allow citizen participation to affect substantially their prerogatives and latitude. Ultimately, the structure of government and the existing processes of decision making go unquestioned.

These objections do not square with my observations and impressions. In the projects researched most intensively, the public officials involved were genuinely open to citizen participation. Moreover, these experiments in teledemocracy gradually gained support from those governmental officials who were initially dubious. City Councilors in Reading, who four years before had been extremely awkward and reluctant on BCTV, appeared regularly and handled unsophisticated and sometimes hostile questions with unexpected skill and responsiveness. Where some state legislators initially opposed the Legislative Teleconferencing Network, its history has been one of marked expansion pressed on the system by legislators who have discovered how useful it can be. And in North Carolina, the OPEN/net project is expanding its support within the state government as more agencies and commissions learn what it can do for them. In sum, it appears that these mechanisms were initiated in a genuine spirit of openness rather than cynical manipulation, and they have been sustained when they proved valuable.

While elites certainly control the agenda in most of these projects, the matters under consideration were not limited to trivial questions. This is an important finding since a major piece of evidence that could be cited to support the "facade argument" is that the matters resolved in a participatory system are insignificant (Bachrach & Baratz, 1962; Polsby, 1963).

I recognize that these arguments do not disprove the co-optation hypothesis; it could be that my observations are naive, that I failed to pierce the veil of elite manipulation, and that reluctant elites became supportive only when they realized the project would not threaten their control. Notice, however, that this line of attack comes close to being untestable, since one must be part of the elite conspiracy to comprehend its potency (Wolfinger, 1971). Rather than accepting the assertion of elite manipulation as a postulated truth, we have the right to ask its proponents to specify concretely the mechanisms of collusion and suppression and to document empirically their strength (Frey, 1971).

Teledemocracy and the Problems of Representative Government

Technology can make teledemocracy, in the sense of pluralist dialogues, possible. In every case where communications media were used to allow citizens to interact with public officials, the results were beneficial. The citizens certainly became better informed. The number and breadth of those who could be said to be politically active was increased. In many of these cases, the available evidence suggests that citizen involvement had a tangible effect on the public policies enacted. And finally, in a few instances, I tentatively concluded that the political system itself was modified by the expanded role of citizen involvement. The broadening of citizen participation itself created pressures upon public leaders to accept those influences.

The communications revolution promises citizens more than mere electronic voting. Regular interaction with fellow citizens and with political authorities constitutes a more complete and educational form of participation. Applications of technology in this manner allow incremental modifications of the existing political machinery. There is, moreover, great vitality to these existing institutions; by and large over the years they have proved capable of handling a host of thorny political problems, such as control over the agenda, elite manipulation of process to their own ends, elite conflict over outcomes, accountability of elites, vast differences in citizen interest in politics, unequal rates of participation, disparities in the intensity of preferences among citizens, and the inevitability of conflicting interests among social groups. The developing communications media can improve the functioning of this machinery; teledemocracy can refer to the strengthening of these institutions rather than to their supplantation.

Despite the strengths of representative democracy, our current governmental institutions do endure a plethora of difficulties that technology might diminish. The inequalities of participation across social groups, for example, should be a matter of grave concern, for they constitute an empirical refutation of our deepest convictions of appropriate government: "of the people, by the people, and for the people."

In addressing this contradiction between our vision of democracy and the fact of nonparticipation, the general strategy of pluralist theory is to concentrate on open access. As long as the legal barriers to participation are minimal, pluralists can be reassured by the knowledge that, should they become politicized, citizens can easily move into political institutions and exert effective influence. Regardless of how one feels about their politics, the rapid mobilization and organization of Boston housewives opposed to school desegregation in the early 1970s was a concrete demonstration of the capacity of citizens to move across the boundary from inactivity into activism.

But there are several reasons why promoting the ideal of a democracy that actively engages citizens is better than accepting the reality of poor performance. The politics resulting from passive governmental institutions may be unnecessarily reactive and conflictual. Individuals and groups move into activity when their interests are affected; they do so most often in a confrontational mode. When they do become engaged, they are very likely to be at a significant disadvantage of rebutting both established policy and accepted political practices—what Schattsneider calls "the mobilization of bias." Reactive politics misses the very real opportunities to address different political interests early in the policy process when conflict may be ameliorated.

Participatory teledemocracy can help. In Alaska, for example, legislators found that a major contribution of electronic hearings came in the venting of political considerations before policy was enacted. By reducing costs and burdens that must be born by participating citizens, communications media can provide political leadership with an early warning system, a proactive capacity to judge the effects of proposed policy.

The idea of subsidizing political activity is a departure from traditional pluralism that adopts a laissez-faire attitude toward the reality of low participation rates. But the strategy is not unknown in the American political system. The states pay the costs of primary elections held by political parties, which are private associations, and, in many cases, they keep enrollment or membership lists for the parties. In many states, brochures are sent to all registered voters containing information drafted by the competing candidates and the proponents and opponents of ballot questions. Broadcast regulations force television stations to underwrite political discussion. More explicitly, under the Federal Election Campaign Act, presidential candidates and national political parties receive public funding. So the idea of establishing regular mechanisms of teledemocracy to mitigate the unequal participation rates is not entirely unprecedented.

Another reason why we might wish to subsidize political participation can be found in the layers of insulation that the complex machinery of government packs around political leaders. Executives in all levels of government require bureaucracies to implement their policies. But these agencies can also become a buffer, filtering information, defining problems and alternative policies, and, in the process, isolating leadership from citizens. For executives in Reading and North Carolina, teledemocracy means a way of bypassing these bureaucracies and learning directly from citizens the effects of government actions or proposed public policies. Legislators have a similar problem in the layers of lobbyists and staff that cluster around them in an effort to circumscribe their actions. In Alaska, this inevitable process is at least partially offset by the reach to citizens. In this context as well, the effort of public officials in Washington and Des Moines to conduct ad hoc plebiscites to learn the policy preferences of citizens can be seen as quite appropriate responses—as long as these mechanisms are advisory and interpreted in light of their pronounced political limitations discussed above.

The importance of policy-making (by both executives and legislators) and implementation may have been accentuated by a growing incapacity of the electoral system to cope with the complexity of American politics. When Jefferson, Madison, and the other Founders drafted the electoral machinery into the Constitution, politics was simpler. Since then, American society, economic structure, and political interests have become increasingly complex, and the scope of government action has become vastly greater than envisioned 200 years ago. Both processes have complicated the capacity of the electoral system to offer citizens a meaningful choice, one that mirrors their interests, their agendas, and their priorities, especially when that choice is compressed into one of two candidates. The present drift, moreover, appears to magnify the organization of political interests that transcend geography, while the electoral system is irretrievably locked into geographical constituencies. These contradictions are not new. They have, however, intensified in the last 50 years.

At the outset of this book, I referred to the unfulfilled promise of television, a medium that might have produced a knowledgeable, concerned, efficacious, and active citizenry. Much of the research here demonstrates the naivete of that idealistic view. The problem is not simply that television has become an entertainment medium dominated by three private corporations that deliver high audiences to advertisers. Except in extreme circumstances, large numbers of Americans avoid public affairs programming and discussion. Furthermore, the medium turns politics into a spectator sport in which citizens passively receive political information as autonomous individuals rather than as active members of collectivities. A public television monopoly that set out to ''force feed'' political information to the populace would do little to rectify citizen individuation, inattention, cynicism, and noninvolvement. Finally, the First Amendment principle of a free press not only prohibits such a governmental monopoly but also warns of the dangers to liberty of a press provided or regulated in content by the government.

On the other hand, any mechanism of communication that costs money to use will necessarily produce inequalities of access among social and economic groups. When these media become conveyors of political participation, differential access, both as to speakers and listeners, can become unduly restrictive from the viewpoint of a democracy. The goal of political equality, or at least something approaching a near equal opportunity to be heard and to listen, is probably not achievable in an absolute sense, but public policies need not reinforce those inequalities. For example, recent moves in Washington and several state capitals to turn over to private companies the collection and distribution of public policy information will exacerbate the problems of differential access to communication.

An alternative approach to political inequality can be found in attempts to use government power to enact limitations upon political activity. Recently, however, legislation of this variety—such as ceilings on campaign expenditures—has been struck down as unconstitutional (*Buckeley v. Valeo*, 1975).

By subsidizing political participation, the emerging electronic media may diminish inequality by underwriting the access of excluded groups. While public affairs programming may never compete for attention with entertainment media, it can convey substantial amounts of political information to citizens and create mechanisms that empower them in governmental processes. If some of the costs of involvement can be transferred to government, then a larger number and broader array of citizens can be encouraged to become involved in public policy-making. Not all of the citizens; not all of the time; but still an improvement

Teledemocracy cannot be justified by rhetoric that suggests ''the people'' are going to be empowered by technology. Episodic attention to politics and individual agendas will give this participation a ''lumpy,'' pluralistic character in that some individuals will be involved only in education matters, others in foreign policy disputes. Many will remain inactive over the whole gamut of policy matters. These inequalities are a reality. They constitute, moreover, the major reason why television has failed to deliver an involved, informed, participatory citizenship. Recognizing them as a political fact does not, however, necessitate surrendering to their inevitability. They can be mitigated by exploiting the potentials of communication technologies in appropriate institutional structures.

These investigations of thirteen different experiments provide greater support for a conception of teledemocracy in which technology is used to underwrite representative processes and a pluralist conception of political interest. Ultimately, of course, the choice remains a normative judgment. But where does this leave us? The use of communications technology to promote this notion of teledemocracy offers us only a slight improvement over the widely recognized difficulties that characterize our present political institutions. On the whole, however, settling for modest improvements may be more satisfactory than yearning for a miraculous technological fix for these problems. On the basis of evidence presented here, such a dramatic cure appears to be largely unfounded. Instead, we may take some comfort from the finding that technology can ease some of the major problems in American democracy. Teledemocracy offers us improvements in democracy, not a major transformation nor a final fulfillment.

Notes

1. I use the term *republicanism* here in a very different sense than the meaning developed by historiographers such as Pococh (1975), Wood (1972) or Appleby (1974). They refer to theories of classical political liberalism, whereas I am discussing a republic as a representative democracy.

2. I emphatically reject the notion that the only acceptable vision of democracy involves direct participation by citizens. Nevertheless, for the purposes of this discussion, it is useful to perpetuate this definition.

REFERENCES

Abelman, R., & Neuendorf, K. (1985). How religious is religious television programming. *Journal of Communications, 35*(1), 1 98–110.

Alaska Growth Policy Council. (1977, September). The Alaska Public Forum year end report. Anchorage: Author.

Appleby, J. O. (1974). *Materialism and morality in the American past: Themes and sources, 1600–1860.* Reading, MA: Addison-Wesley.

Arlen, G. (1983). Videotex goes on line. *The 1984 Field Guide to the Electronic Media, Channels Magazine, 3*(4), 40.

Arlen, G. (1984, June). Viewtron's $3995 deal. *International Videotex and Teletext News,* p. 2.

Arlen, G. (1984). Videotex: shifting from keypad to keyboard. *The Essential 1985 Field Guide to the Electronic Media, Channels Magazine, 4*(4), 22–23.

Arnstein, S. (1969, July). A ladder of citizen participation. *Journal of the American Institute of Planners, 35,* 216–224.

Arterton, F. C. (1974). *Political participation as attempted interpersonal influence.* Unpublished doctoral dissertation, Massachusetts Institute of Technology.

Arterton, F. C. (1983). *Communication technologies and political campaigns in 1982: Assessing the implications.* Washington, DC: Roosevelt Center for American Policy Studies.

Arterton, F. C. (1984). *Media politics: The news strategies of presidential campaigns.* Lexington, MA: Lexington Books.

Arterton, F. C., & Hahn, H. (1974). *Political participation.* Washington, DC: American Political Science Association.

Arterton, F. C., Lazarus, E. H., Griffen, J., & Andres, M. C. (1984). *Telecommunication technologies and political participation.* Washington, DC: Roosevelt Center for American Policy Studies.

Bachrach, P., & Baratz, M. (1962). Two faces of power. *American Political Science Review 56*(4), 947–952.

Baker, D. (1976). The states experiment with "Anticipatory democracy." *Futurist, 10*(5), 262–271.

Barber, B. J. (1982). The second American Revolution. *Channels, 2*(1), 21-15, 62.

Barber, B. J. (1984a). *Strong democracy: Participatory politics for a new age.* Berkeley: University of California Press.

Barber, B. J. (1984b, June). Voting is not enough. *Atlantic Monthly, pp.* 45–52.

Barnes, S., & Kaase, M. (1979). *Political action.* Newbury Park, CA: Sage.

Becker, L. B., McCombs, M. E., & McLeod, J. M., (1975). The development of political cognitions. In Chaffee (Ed.), *Political communication.* Newbury Park, CA: Sage.

Becker, T. L. et al. (1976). *Un-vote for a new America: A guide to constitutional revolution.* Boston: Allyn & Bacon.

Becker, T. L. (1978). *American government: Past, present and future.* Boston: Allyn & Bacon.

205

Becker, T. L. (1981)   Teledemocracy: Bringing power back to the people. *Futurist, 15*(6), 6-9.

Becker, T. L., & Scarce, R. (1983). *Teledemocracy: Past, present, future.* Honolulu: University of Hawaii. mimeo

Becker, T. L. & Scarce, R. (1984, August 30–September 2). *Teledemocracy emergent: The state of the art and science.* Paper delivered at the APSA annual meetings, Washington, DC.

Bell, D. (1979, May/June). Communications technology: For better or for worse. *Harvard Business Review*, p. 20.

Benjamin, G. (Ed.). (1982). *The communications revolution in politics.* New York: American Academy of Political Science.

Berry, J. M., Portney, K. E., Bablitch, M. B., & Mahoney, R. (1984). Public involvement in administration: The structural determinants of effective citizen participation. *Journal of Voluntary Action Research, 13*(2), 7–23.

Bezold, C. (Ed.). (1978). *Anticipatory democracy: People in the politics of the future.* New York: Random House.

Blomquist, D. (1984, August 30–September 2). *The more things change . . . Videotex and American politics.* Paper presented at the annual meetings of the American Politial Science Association, Washington, DC.

Blumler, J. G. (1983). Communication and democracy: The crisis beyond and the torment within. *Journal of Communication, 33*(3), 166–173.

Blumler, J. G., & McLeod, J. M. (1974). Communication and voter turnout in Britain. In T. Leggett (Ed.) *Sociological theory and survey research.* Newbury Park, CA: Sage.

Boyd, R. (1981). Decline of U.S. voter turnout: Structural explanation. *American Politics Quarterly, 9*(2), 133-159.

Bretz, R. (1975). Public access cable TV: Audiences. *Journal of Communication, 25*(3), 22–32.

Bretz, R., with Dougherty, L. (1984, April). *Two-way TV teleconferencing in government: The MRC-TV system.* Santa Monica, CA: Rand.

Brody, R. & Tufte, E. (1964). Congressional constituent mail. *Journal of Communication, 14*(1), 34-49.

Brooks, M. P. (1975, September). Review of *Participation, planning, and exchange in old and new communities: A collaborative paradigm,* by David R. Godschalk. *Journal of the American Institute of Planners*, pp. 359–360.

Brotman, S. N. (1981). New campaigning for the new media. *Campaigns and Elections 2*(3), 32–34.

Burke, E. M. (1968, September). Citizen participation strategies. *Journal of the American Institute of Planners, 34*, 287–294.

Burke, T. J. M., & Lehrman, M. (Eds.). (1981). *Communication technologies and information flow.* New York: Pergamon.

Campbell, V. N. (1974). *The televote system on civic communication: First demonstration and evaluation.* Palo Alto, CA: American Institute for Research.

Carey, J. (1982, Spring). Videotex: The past as prologue. *Journal of Communication, 32*(2).

Castleman, N. (1974). *An electronic town hall meeting in the center of apathy.* New York: Columbia University, Center for Policy Research.

Champion, P. (1974). Town meeting on the tube: People planning in southwestern Virginia. *Appalachia, 7*(5), 1–11.

Channels. (1983). The 1984 field guide to the electronic media, 3(4).

Chaplin, G., & Paige, G. D. (Eds.). (1973). *Hawaii 2000: Continuing experiment in anticipatory democracy.* Honolulu: University Press of Hawaii.

Chisman, F. P. (1973). Politics in the new mass communications. In G. Gerbner & L. P. Gross (Eds.), *Communications technology and social policy.* New York: John Wiley.

Cole, R. L., & Caputo, D. A. (1984, June). The public hearing as an effective citizen participation mechanism. *American Political Science Review, 78*(2), 404–416.

Commission on the Future of North Carolina. (1983). *The future of North Carolina: Goals and recommendations for the year 2000.* Raleigh: Author.

Comstock, G. (1980). *Television in America.* Newbury Park, CA: Sage.

Czitrom, D. J. (1983). *Media and the American mind.* Chapel Hill: University of North Carolina Press.

Czitrom, D. J. (1984). Context: Remembering the future. *The essential 1985 field guide to the electronic media. Channels, 4(4),* 75–77.

Dahl, R. A. (1956). *Preface to democratic theory.* Chicago: University of Chicago Press.

Dakin, J. (1973). *Telecommunications and the planning of greater metropolitan regions.* Toronto: University of Toronto Press.

Danziger, J. N., Dutton, W. H., Kling, R. & Kraemer, K. L. (1982). *Computers and politics: High technology in American local governments.* New York: Columbia University Press.

Dator, J. (1983). The 1982 Honolulu electronic town meeting. In W. Page (Ed.), *The future of politics.* London: Frances Pintor.

Davidson, W. P. (1978). Public opinion research as communication. *Public Opinion Quarterly, 36*(2), 206–221.

Dillman, D. A. (1978). *Mail and telephone surveys: The total design method.* New York: John Wiley.

Dizard, W. P., Jr. (1982). *The coming information age.* New York: Longman.

Domestic Policy Association. (1983). *A report on its first year.* Dayton, OH: Author.

Dutton, W., Streckenrider, J., Ross-Christensen, D., Lynch, L., Goldfarb, B., Hirschberg, L., Bancroft, T., & Williams, R. (1984). Electronic participation by citizens in U.S. local government. *Information Age, 6*(2), 78–97.

Elstain, J. B. (1982, August 7–14). Democracy and the Qube tube. *The Nation,* 108–110.

Etzioni, A. (1972). Minerva: An electronic town hall. *Policy Science, 3*(4), 457–474.

Etzioni, A. (1978). *The active society.* New York: Free Press.

Fagence, M. (1977). *Citizen participation in planning.* Oxford: Pergamon.

Frank, R. E., & Greenberg, M. G. (1980). *The public's use of television.* Newbury Park, CA: Sage.

Frantzich, S. E. (1982). *Computers in Congress.* Newbury Park, CA: Sage.

Freudenheim, M. (1984, June 14). Iowa plans to lower health costs. *New York Times, p. B19.*

Frey, F. W. (1971). Comment: On issues and nonissues in the study of power. *American Political Science Review, 65*(4), 1081–1101.

Frohlich, N. J., Oppenheimer, A., Smith, J., & Young, O. R. (1978). A test of downsian voter rationality: The 1964 presidential voting. *American Political Science Review, 72*(1), 178–179.

Ganley, O. H. (1979). *The role of communications and information resources in Canada.* Cambridge, MA: Harvard University, Program on Information Resources Policy.

Ganley, O. H. & Ganley, G. D. (1982). *To inform or to control: The new communications networks.* New York: McGraw-Hill.

Gardner, J. A. (1970). *The politics of corruption in an American city.* New York: Russell Sage.

Gerbner, G., Gross, L. P., & Molody, W. H. (Eds.). (1973). *Communications technology and social policy: Understanding the new "Cultural Revolution."* New York: John Wiley.

Gitlin, T. (1981, October). New video technology: Pluralism or banality. *Democracy,* pp. 60–76.

Glaser, W. A. (1965). Television and voting turnout. *Public Opinion Quarterly, 29*(1), 71–86.

Glass, D., Squire, P., & Wolfinger, R. (1984). Voter turnout: An international comparison. *Public Opinion, 6*(6), 49–55.

Glossbrenner, A. (1985, November/December). A new medium in the making: How people are shaping (and being shaped by) on-line communication. *Rain,* pp. 28–31.

Goals for Dallas. (1966, 1969, 1970). *Proposals for achieving the goals, achieving the goals* (3 vols.). Dallas: Excellence in Education Foundation.

Godschalk, D. R. (1972). *Participation, planning and exchange in old and new communities: A collaborative paradigm.* Chapel Hill: University of North Carolina, Center for Urban and Regional Studies.

Goldbeck, W. B. (1975, January/February). Choices for '76: A metropolitan experiment in resident education and communications. *Public Administration Review,* pp. 74–79.

Gotlieb, C. C., & Zeman, Z. P. (1980). *Towards a national computer and communication policy: Seven national approaches.* Toronto, Canada: Institute for Research on Public Policy.

Graber, D. (1965). *Verbal behavior and politics.* Urbana: University of Illinois Press.

Greenfield, J. (1982, December). *1984 candidates ready to bow on cable television.* New York: Syndicated column.

Grewlich, K. W., & Pedersen, F. H. (1984). *Power and participation in an information society.* Brussels, Luxembourg: Commission of the European Communities.

Groombridge, B. (1972). *Television and the people.* Harmondsworth, England: Penguin.

Gross, L. S. (1983). *The new television technologies.* Dubuque, IA: William C. Brown.

Gusdorf, N., Little, J.D.C., Stevens, C. H., & Tropp, P. (1971). *Puerto Rico's citizen feedback system.* (Tech. Rep. No. 59). Cambridge: MIT Operations Research Center.

Hadden, J. K. & Swann, C. E. (1981). *Prime time preachers: The rising power of televangelism.* Reading, MA: Addison-Wesley.

Hansen, J. M. (1985). The political economy of group membership. *American Political Science Review., 79*(1), 79-96.

Hansen, J. M. & Rosenstone, S. J. (1984). *Context, mobilization and political participation.* Unpublished manuscript, Yale University, New Haven, CT.

Havlicek, F. J. (Ed.). (1985). *Election communications and the election of 1992.* Washington, DC: American Bar Association.

Henderson, M. M. & MacNaughton, M. J. (1980). *Electronic communication: Technology and its impact.* Boulder, CO: Westview.

Henninger, D. (1973, July 14). Three million attend town meeting. *The National Observer.*

Hiltz, S. R., & Turoff, M. (1978). *The network nation: Human communication via computer.* Reading, MA: Addison-Wesley.

Hollander, R. (1985). *Video democracy: The vote-from-home revolution.* Mt. Airy, MD: Lomond.

Homet, R. S., Jr. (1984). *Getting the message: Statutory approaches to electronic information delivery and the duty of carriage.* Washington, DC: Roosevelt Center for American Policy Studies. (Also published in *Federal Communications Law Journal, 37*(2), 217–292.

Hoover, J. H., & Altshuler, A. A. (1977). *Involving citizens in metropolitan region transportation planning.* Washington, DC: Government Printing Office.

International City Management Association. (1984). The surprising revolution: Final report of the 1983–1984 ICMA committee on telecommunications. *Public Management, 66*(5), 7–14.

International City Management Association. (1982). *Telecommunications for local government.* Washington, DC: Author.

Iyenger, S., Peters, M., & Kinder, D. (1983). Experimental demonstrations of the "not-so-minimal" consequences of television news programs. Unpublished paper, Yale University, Department of Political Science. (memeo)

Johansen, R., Valee, J., & Spangler, K. (1979). *Electronic meetings, technical alternatives and social choices.* Reading, MA: Addison-Wesley.

Johnson J. (1983) *Curbing health costs: The public's prescription.* New York: Public Agenda Foundation.

Jordon, D., Arnstein, S., Gray, E., Metcalf, W., Mills, F. (1976). *Effective citizen participation in transportation planning, Vol. 1: Community involvement processes: Vol. 2. A Catalog of Techniques.* Washington, DC: U.S. Superintendent of Documents.

Kay, P. (1976, July). *Social services and cable TV.* Washington, DC: Cable Television Information Center.

Keeter, S., & Zukin, C. (1983). *Uninformed choice.* New York: Praeger.

Kinghorn, J. R. (1984, July 20). Personal interview.

Klapper, J. T. (1960). *The effect of mass communication.* New York: Free Press.

Knight, F. S., Horn, H. E., & Jesuale, N. J. (Eds.). (1982). *Telecommunications for local government.* Washington, DC: International City Management Association.

Kowinski, W. (1979, November). Talking back to television. *Penthouse,* pp. 125–131, 190.

Krasnow, E. G., Longley, L. D., & Terry, H. A. (1982). *The politics of broadcast regulation.* New York: St. Martin's.

Kraus, S., & Davis, D. (1976). *The effects of mass communication on political behavior.* State College: Pennsylvania State University Press.

Kulakow, A. M. (1974). *Interactive media: Beyond open access, the real communications revolution.* Dayton, OH: Kettering Foundation.

Langton, S. (1978) *Citizen participation in America.* Lexington, MA: Lexington Books.

LaPalombara, J. G., & Hagan, C. B. (1951). Direct legislation: An appraisal and a suggestion. *American Political Science Review, 45*(2), 400–421.

Laudon, K. C. (1977). *Communications technology and democratic participation.* New York. Praeger Special Studies.

Laudon, K. C. (1978). Information technology and participation in the political process. In A. Mowshowitz (Ed.), *Human choice and computers* (pp. 167–191). Montvale, NJ: North-Holland.

Laudon, K. C. (1984). New possibilities for participation in the democratic process. In K. W. Grewlich & F. H. Pederson (Eds.), *Power and participation in an information society.* Luxembourg: Commission of European Communities.

Lazarsfeld, P. F., Berelson, B., & Gaudot, H. (1944) *The people's choices.* New York: Columbia University Press.

Leary, M. E. (1977). *Phantom politics: Campaigning in California.* Washington, DC: Public Affairs Press.

Lehman-Wilzig, S. (1983, March). Teledemocracy from the top. *Telecommunications Policy,* pp. 5–8.

Lemert, J. B., Mitzman, B. N., Seither, M. A., Cook, R. H., & Hackett, R. (1977). Journalists and mobilizing information. *Journalism Quarterly, 54,* 721–726.

Licklider, J.C.R. (1980). Computers and government. In M. L. Dertouzos & T. Moses (Eds.), *The computer age: A twenty year view.* Cambridge: MIT Press.

Little, J.D.C., Stevens, C. H., Sheridan, T. B., & Tropp, P. (1972, June). *Citizen feedback components and sytems* (Tech. Rep. No. 76). Cambridge: MIT Operations Research Center.

Little, J. D. C., Stevens, C. H., & Tropp, P. (1971). Citizen feedback system: The Puerto Rico model. *National Civic Review, 60,* 191–198, 203.

Lowi, T. (1964). American business, public policy, case studies and political theory. *World Politics, 16*(4), 689–690.

Lowi, T. (1969). *The end of liberalism.* New York: W. W. Norton.

Lowi, T. (1983). The political impact of information technology. In T. Forester (Ed.), *The microelectronics revolution: The complete guide to the new technology and its impact on society.* Cambridge: MIT Press.

Magleby, D. (1984). *Direct legislation: Voting on ballot propositions in the United States.* Baltimore: Johns Hopkins University Press.

Malbin, M. (1982, June–July). Teledemocracy and its discontents. *Public Opinion,* pp. 57–58.

Manheim, J. B. (1976). Can democracy survive television? *Journal of Communication, 26,* 84–90.

Martin, J. (1978). *The wired society.* Englewood Cliffs, NJ: Prentice-Hall.

Marvick, D. (1970). Some potential effects of the information utility on citizen participation. In H. Sackman & N. Nie (Eds.), *The information utility and social choice.* Montvale, NJ: American Federation of Information Processing Societies.

Marvin, C. (1980). Delivering the news of the future. *Journal of Communication, 30*(1), 10-20.

McCauley, C., Rood, O., & Johnson, T. (1977, November–December). *World Future Society Bulletin.*

McLuhan, M. (1964). *Understanding media.* New York: New American Library.

McManus, M. (1976a, July). Back to the people: Dallas' blueprint for the future. *Civil Engineering,* pp. 57–60.

McManus, M. (1976b). What American needs is a voice for the people. *Planning, 42*(6), 28–31.

McManus, M. (1985, January). Creating 20th century town meetings. *National Civic Review,* pp. 9–20.

McPhail, T. (1981). *Electronic colonialism: The future of international broadcasting and communication.* Newbury Park, CA: Sage.

Meadow, R. G. (1980). *Politics as communication.* Norwood, NJ: Ablex.

Meadow, R. G. (Ed.). (1985). *New communication technologies in politics.* Washington, DC: Annenberg School of Communications, Washington Program.

Meyrowitz, J. (1985). *No sense of place: The impact of the electronic media on social behavior.* New York: Oxford.

Milbrath, L. (1965). *Political participation.* Chicago: Rand McNally.

Mohl, B. A. (1983, September 9). Computers abuzz with talk about downing of plane. *Boston Globe,* p. 11.

Mosco, V. (1982). *Pushbutton fantasies.* Norwood, NJ: Ablex.

Moss, M. L. (1978). Two-way cable television: An evaluation of community uses in Reading, Pennsylvania. Final report to the National Science Foundation. New York: NYU Graduate School of Public Administration Alternate Media Center.

Mueller, C. (1978). *The politics of communication*. New York: Oxford University Press.

Naisbitt, J. (1982). *Megatrends: Ten new directions transforming our lives*. New York: Warner Brothers.

Neuman, W. R. (in press). *The future of the mass audience*. Cambridge, MA: Harvard University Press.

Neustadt, R. E. (1982, March 14). Watch out, politics—technology is coming. *Washington Post*.

Nie, N. (1970). Future developments in mass communications and citizen participation. In H. Sackman & N. Nie (Eds.), *The information utility and social choice* (pp. 217–230). Montvale, NJ: American Federation of Information Processing Societies.

Nimmo, D. (1978). *Political communication and public opinion in America*. Santa Monica, CA: Goodyear.

Oettinger, A., Berman, P. J. & Read, W. H. (1977). *High and low politics: Information resources for the 80s*. Cambridge, MA: Ballinger.

O'Keefe, G. J. (1975). Political campaigns and mass communication research. In S. Chaffee (Ed.), *Political communication*. Newbury Park, CA: Sage.

Oliver, L. (1983). *The act of citizenship: Public issue forums*. Dayton, OH: Kettering Foundation.

Orton, B. M. (1980). *Media-based issue balloting for regional planning* (Doctoral dissertation, Rutgers University, 1980). (University Microfilms No. 80–13, 177)

Orton, B. M. (1982, June/July). Pseudo-polls: The pollster's nemesis. *Political Opinion*, pp. 56-60.

Parker, L. A., & Olgren, C. H. (1980). *Teleconferencing and interactive media*. Madison: University of Wisconsin Extension, Center for Interactive Programs.

Patterson, T. E. (1980). *Mass media election*. New York: Praeger.

Pederson, F. H. (1984). Power and participation in an information society: Perspectives. In K. W. Grewlich & F. H. Pederson, *Power and participation in an information society* (pp. 249–289). Luxembourg: Commission of the European Communities.

Perlman, J. E. (1978). Grassroots participation from neighborhood to nation. In S. Langton (Ed.), *Citizen participation in America*. Lexington, MA: Lexington Books.

Perloff, H. S. (Ed.). (1971). *The future of the United States Government: Toward the year 2000*. New York: George Braziller.

Pococh, J. G. (1975). *The Machiavellian moment: Florentine political thought and the Atlantic republican tradition*. Princeton, NJ: Princeton University Press.

Polsby, N. (1963). *Community power and political theory*. New Haven, CT: Yale University Press.

Polsby, N. (1983). *The consequences of party reform.* New York: Oxford University Press.

Pool, I. de Sola. (Ed.). (1973a). *Talking back: Citizen feedback and cable technology.* Cambridge: MIT Press.

Pool, I. de Sola. (1973b). Citizen feedback in political philosophy. In I. de Sola Pool (Ed.), *Talking back: Citizen feedback and cable technology.* Cambridge: MIT Press.

Pool, I. de Sola. (1981). The new technologies: Promise of abundant channels at lower cost. In E. Abel (Ed.), *What's news: The media in American society.* New Brunswick, NJ: Transaction.

Pool, I. de Sola. (1983). *Technologies of freedom.* Cambridge, MA: Belknap.

Pool, I. de Sola, & Alexander, H. E. (1973). Politics in a wired nation. In I. de Sola Pool (Ed.), *Talking back: Citizen feedback and cable technology.* Cambridge: MIT Press.

Porat, M. A. (1979). The U.S. as an information society: International implications. In U.S. Department of State, *Selected papers: International policy implications of computers and advanced telecommunication in information systems.* Washington, DC: Government Printing Office.

Ranney, A. (1975). *Curing the mischiefs of faction.* Berkeley: University of California Press.

Ranney, A. (1983). *Channels of power.* New York: Basic Books.

Reeves, R. (1983a, May 5). *Finding political parties' future.* New York: United Press Syndicate.

Reeves, R. (1983b, April 25). *The signal fires of the future.* New York: United Press Syndicate.

Reidel, J. A. (1972). Citizen participation: Myths and realities. *Public Administration Review, 32,* 211–220.

Robinson, G. O. (1978). *Communications for tommorrow: Policy prospectives for the 1980s.* New York: Praeger.

Robinson, M., & Clancey, M. (1985, January 14). Who watches C-Span? *C-Span Update.* Washington, DC: Cable-Satellite Public Affairs Network, Special Supplement.

Robinson, M. J., & McPherson, K. A. (1977). Television news coverage before the 1976 New Hampshire primary: The focus of network journalism. *Journal of Broadcasting, 21,* 177–186.

Robinson, M. J. & Sheehan, M. (1983). *Over the wire and on TV: CBS and UPI in campaign '80.* New York: Russell Sage.

Rosener, J. B. (1975, December). Citizen participation: A cafeteria of techniques and critiques. *Public Management,* pp. 16–19.

Routh, F. B. (1971, March/April). Goals for Dallas: More participation than power-sharing. *City,* pp. 49–53.

Rubin, R. (1981). *Press, party and presidency.* New York: W. W. Norton.

Saldich, A. R. (1979). *Electronic democracy: Television's impact on the American political process.* New York: Praeger.

Sanoff, A. P. (1984, March). ABC's phone-in polling: Does it put credibility on the line? *Washington Journalism Review,* pp. 48–49.

Satin, M. (1979). *New age politics*. New York: Dell.

Schockly, J. S. (1984, August 30–September 2). *Direct democracy, campaign finance and the courts: Can corruption, undue influence and declining voter confidence be found?* Paper presented at the annual meeting of the American Political Science Association. Washington, D.C.

Schudson, M. (1983). *The news media and the democratic process*. New York: Aspen Institute for Humanistic Studies.

Seymore-Ure, C. (1974). *The political impact of mass media*. London: Constable.

Shaw, D. L., & McCombs, M. (1977). *The emergence of American political issues: The agenda-setting function of the press*. St. Paul, MN: West.

Sheridan, T. B. (1975). *Technology for citizen participation in planning*. Massachusetts Institute of Technology, Cambridge. (mimeo)

Sherrill, R. (1968, November). Instant electorate. *Playboy*.

Shore, W. B. (1965). Public consultation in the planning process. *Planning, 31*, 148–157.

Shore, W. B. (1975, January). Choices for '76: The results and lessons. *National Civic Review*, pp. 6–20.

Shore, W. B., Anderson, R. T., McManus, M. J., Goldbeck, W., & Hack, P. H. (1974). *Listening to the metropolis: An evaluation of the New York region's choices for '76 mass media town meetings and handbook on public participation in regional planning*. New York: Regional Planning Association.

Singer, B. D. (1973). *Feedback and society: A study of the uses of mass channels for coping*. Lexington, MA: Lexington Books.

Smith, A. (1979). *Television and political life: Studies in six European countries*. New York: St. Martin's.

Smith, A. (1980). *Goodbye Gutenberg: The newspaper revolution of the 1980s*. New York: Oxford University Press.

Solomon, R. (1984). *The growth of the electronic media* (report to the Future of the Mass Audience Project). Unpublished manuscript, Massachusetts Institute of Technology.

Stevens, C. H. (1981). *Many-to-many communications* (CISR No. 72). Cambridge: MIT, Center for Information Systems Research.

Stevens, C. H., Barwig, F. E., Jr., & Haviland, D. S. (1974). *Feedback: An involvement primer*. Troy, NY: Rensselaer Polytechnic Institute.

Toffler, A. (1971). *Future shock*. New York: Bantam.

Toffler, A. (1980). *The third wave*. New York: Bantam.

Turn the dial to "citizen participation." (1974). *Planning, 40*(9), 26–29.

Turoff, M., & Hiltz, S. R. (1982). Computer support for the group versus individual decisions. *IEEE Transactions on Communications, 30*(1), 82–91.

Tydeman, J., Lipinski, H., Alder, R., Nyhan, M., & Zwimpfer, L. (1982). *Teletex and videotex in the United States: Market potential, technology and public policy issues*. New York: McGraw-Hill.

U.S. Bureau of the Census. (1985). *Statistical abstract of the United States, Participation in elections for president and U.S. House of Representatives: 1932 to 1980*. Washington, DC: Government Printing Office.

U.S. Congress, Committee on House Administration. (1979). *Information policy: Public laws from the 95th Congress.* Washington, DC: Government Printing Office.

Valaskakis, K., & Arnopoulous, P. (1982). *Telecommunitary democracy: Utopian vision or probable future.* Montreal: McGill and Montreal Universities, Gamma Research Service.

Verba, S. (1967). Democratic participation. *Annals of the American Academy of Political and Social Science, 373,* 53–78.

Verba, S., & Nie, N. H. (1972). *Participation in America: Political democracy and social equality.* New York: Harper & Row.

Verba, S., Nie, N. H., & Kim, J. (1971). *Modes of democratic participation: A cross-national comparison.* Newbury Park, CA: Sage.

Verba, S., Nie, N. H., & Kim, J. (1978). *Participation and political equality.* New York: Cambridge University Press.

Washington State, Office of Program Planning and Fiscal Management. (1975). *Alternatives for Washington* (Vols. 1, 6, 9, 10, 11). Olympia: Author.

Weissberg, R. (1976). *Public opinion and popular government.* Englewood Cliffs, NJ: Prentice-Hall.

White, G. (1978). *A study of access to television for political candidates.* Cambridge, MA: Harvard University, Institute of Politics.

Wicklein, J. (1982). *Electronic nightmare: The home communications set and your freedom.* Boston: Beacon.

Williams, F. (1982). *The communications revolution.* New York: New American Library.

Wing, L. (1981). State government application and telecommunications productivity. In M. L. Moss (Ed.), *Telecommunications and productivity* (pp. 296–315). Reading, MA: Addison-Wesley.

Winner, L. (1983). *Autonomous technology.* Cambridge: MIT Press.

Wolff, R. P. (1976). *In defense of anarchy.* New York: Harper Colophon.

Wolfinger, R. (1971). Nondecisions and the study of local politics. *American Political Science Review, 65*(4), 1063–1080.

Wolfinger, R., & Rosenstone, S. J. (1980). *Who votes?* New Haven, CT: Yale University Press.

Wolfson, L (1986). *The untapped power of the press: Explaining government to the people.* New York: Praeger.

Wood, F. B., Coates, V. T., Chartrant, R. L., & Ericson, R. F. (1978). *Videoconferencing via satellite: Opening Congress to the people.* Washington, DC: George Washington University, Program of Policy Studies in Science and Technology.

Wood, G. (1972). *The creation of the American republic, 1776–1787.* New York: W. W. Norton.

Zussman, R., & Castleman, N. (1973). *Electronic town hall meetings: A preliminary exploration.* Columbia University, Center for Policy Research. (mimeo)

Zworykin, V. K. (1959). The human aspects of the engineering progress. *Journal of the British Institute of Radio Engineers, 19,* 529–544.

NAME INDEX

SUBJECT INDEX

ABOUT THE AUTHOR

F. Christopher Arterton is the Dean of The Graduate School of Political Management in New York City. He is a former professor of Political Science and Management at Yale University, and is also a Research Associate at the Institute of Politics at Harvard University. During the course of this research he served as a Visiting Fellow at the Roosevelt Center for American Policy Studies, where he now serves as a consultant. He also serves as an advisor and polling consultant to the *Newsweek Poll*.

His research and writing focus on American institutions and the behavior of political elites in those institutions. In addition to his work on communication technologies and political participation, Dr. Arterton has written on the importance of news reporting to presidential campaigns, on the functioning of political parties and national nominating conventions, on the management of cardidate organizations, and on campaign finance. He is the author of *Media Politics: The News Strategies of Presidential Campaigns* (Lexington Books, 1984) and coauthor of *Explorations in Convention Decision Making* (W. H. Freeman, 1976). His more recent writing concerns the implications of changes in the communications industry for democratic values.